D1288447

Authors & Artists for Young Adults

ISSN 1040-5682

Authors & Artists for Young Adults

VOLUME 81

Detroit • New York • San Francisco • New Haven, Conn • Waterville, Maine • London

GALE
CENGAGE Learning

Authors and Artists for Young Adults, Volume 81

Project Editor: Dana Ferguson

Editorial: Amy Elisabeth Fuller, Michelle Kazensky, Lisa Kumar, Mary Ruby

Permissions: Savannah Gignac, Kelly Quin, Tracie Richardson, Robyn Young

Imaging and Multimedia: John Watkins

Composition and Electronic Capture: Amy Darga

Manufacturing: Rita Wimberley

Product Manager: Meggin Condino

For product information and technology assistance, contact us at
Gale Customer Support, 1-800-877-4253.
For permission to use material from this text or product,
submit all requests online at **www.cengage.com/permissions.**
Further permissions questions can be emailed to
permissionrequest@cengage.com

Gale
27500 Drake Rd.
Farmington Hills, MI, 48331-3535

LIBRARY OF CONGRESS CATALOG CARD NUMBER 89-641100

ISBN-13: 978-0-7876-7800-5
ISBN-10: 0-7876-7800-7

ISSN 1040-5682

Printed in the United States of America
1 2 3 4 5 6 7 13 12 11 10 09

Contents

Introduction

Authors and Artists for Young Adults is a reference series designed to serve the needs of middle school, junior high, and high school students interested in creative artists. Originally inspired by the need to bridge the gap between Gale's *Something about the Author,* created for children, and *Contemporary Authors,* intended for older students and adults, *Authors and Artists for Young Adults* has been expanded to cover not only an international scope of authors, but also a wide variety of other artists.

Although the emphasis of the series remains on the writer for young adults, we recognize that these readers have diverse interests covering a wide range of reading levels. The series therefore contains not only those creative artists who are of high interest to young adults, including cartoonists, graphic naovelists, photographers, music composers, bestselling authors of adult novels, media directors, producers, and performers, but also literary and artistic figures studied in academic curricula, such as influential novelists, playwrights, poets, and painters. The goal of *Authors and Artists for Young Adults* is to present this great diversity of creative artists in a format that is entertaining, informative, and understandable to the young adult reader.

Entry Format

Each volume of *Authors and Artists for Young Adults* will furnish in-depth coverage of approximately twenty-five authors and artists. The typical entry consists of:

—A detailed biographical section that includes date of birth, marriage, children, education, and addresses.

—A comprehensive bibliography or filmography including publishers, producers, and years.

—Adaptations into other media forms.

—Works in progress.

—A distinctive essay featuring comments on an artist's life, career, artistic intentions, world views, and controversies.

—References for further reading.

—Extensive illustrations, photographs, movie stills, cartoons, book covers, and other relevant visual material.

A cumulative index to featured authors and artists appears in each volume.

Compilation Methods

The editors of *Authors and Artists for Young Adults* make every effort to secure information directly from the authors and artists through personal correspondence and interviews. Sketches on living authors and artists are sent to the biographee for review prior to publication. Any sketches not personally reviewed by biographees or their representatives are marked with an asterisk (*).

Highlights of Forthcoming Volumes

Among the authors and artists planned for future volumes are:

Elizabeth Alexander
Kage Baker
Holly Black
Danny Boyle
Horton Foote
Bob Fosse
Neil Gaiman
K.L. Going
John Green
Martha Grimes
Ursula Hegi
A.M. Jenkins
Stephen King
Seth MacFarlane
Alice Munro
Christopher Nolan
Claes Oldenburg
Renzo Piano
J.K. Rowling
Gene Luen Yang

Contact the Editor

We encourage our readers to examine the entire *AAYA* series. Please write and tell us if we can make *AAYA* even more helpful to you. Give your comments and suggestions to the editor:

BY MAIL: The Editor, *Authors and Artists for Young Adults,* 27500 Drake Rd., Farmington Hills, MI 48331-3535.

BY TELEPHONE: (800) 347-GALE

Authors and Artists for Young Adults Product Advisory Board

The editors of *Authors and Artists for Young Adults* are dedicated to maintaining a high standard of excellence by publishing comprehensive, accurate, and highly readable entries on writers, artists, and filmmakers of interest to middle and high school students. In addition to the quality of the entries, the editors take pride in the graphic design of the series, which is intended to be orderly yet appealing, allowing readers to utilize the pages of *AAYA* easily, enjoyably, and with efficiency. Despite the success of the *AAYA* print series, we are mindful that the vitality of a literary reference product is dependent on its ability to serve its readers over time. As critical attitudes about literature, art, and media constantly evolve, so do the reference needs of students and teachers. To be certain that we continue to keep pace with the expectations of our readers, the editors of *AAYA* listen carefully to their comments regarding the value, utility, and quality of the series. Librarians, who have firsthand knowledge of the needs of library users, are a valuable resource for us. The *Authors and Artists for Young Adults* Product Advisory Board, made up of school, public, and academic librarians, is a forum to promote focused feedback about *AAYA* on a regular basis, as well as to help steer our coverage of new authors and artists. The advisory board includes the following individuals, whom the editors wish to thank for sharing their expertise:

- **Eva M. Davis,** Youth Department Manager, Ann Arbor District Library, Ann Arbor, Michigan

- **Joan B. Eisenberg,** Lower School Librarian, Milton Academy, Milton, Massachusetts

- **Susan Dove Lempke,** Children's Services Supervisor, Niles Public Library District, Niles, Illinois

- **Robyn Lupa,** Head of Children's Services, Jefferson County Public Library, Lakewood, Colorado

- **Caryn Sipos,** Community Librarian, Three Creeks Community Library, Vancouver, Washington

- **Stephen Weiner,** Director, Maynard Public Library, Maynard, Massachusetts

Alvar Aalto

(Photograph © Bettmann/Corbis.)

■ Personal

Born Hugo Alvar Henrik Aalto, February 3, 1898, in Kuortane, Finland; died May 11, 1976, in Helsinki, Finland; son of Johan Henrik (a surveyor) and Selma Mathilda Aalto; married Aino Marsio, 1924 (died, 1949); married Elissa Mäkiniemi (an architect), 1952; children: (first marriage) two. *Education:* Helsinki Polytechnic, Dip. Arch., 1921.

■ Career

Architect and furniture designer. Exhibition designer in Goteborg, Sweden, and with firm of Tampere and Turku, Finland, 1923-27; private practice, Jyväskylä, Finland, 1923-27, then in Turku, 1927-33, and Helsinki, Finland, 1933-76; Artek Furniture Co., co-founder, with Mairea Gallichson and wife, Aino Aalto, 1935; Massachusetts Institute of Technology, Cambridge, professor of experimental architecture, 1946-47. Senior fellow, Royal College of Arts, London, England, 1950; fellow, World Academy of Arts and Sciences, Israel, 1963. *Exhibitions:* Works exhibited at Museum of Modern Art, New York, NY, 1938; Kunstgewerbemuseum, Zurich, Switzerland, 1948 (with Aino Aalto); Gewerbemuseum,

Basel, Switzerland, 1957 (with Mies van der Rohe); Keski-Suomen Museum, Jyväskylä, Finland, 1962; Akademie der Künste, Berlin, Germany, 1963; Kunsthaus, Zurich, 1964; Palazzo Strozzi, Florence, Italy, 1965; Ateneum, Helsinki, Finland, 1967; Moderna Museet, Stockholm, Sweden, 1969; Finlandia Hall, Helsinki, 1978 (toured); Museum Folkwang, Essen, Germany, 1979; Museum of Modern Art, New York, 1984 (toured); and Barbican Art Gallery, London, England, 2007. *Military service:* Served in Finnish Army, 1939.

■ Member

Academy of Finland (president, 1963-68).

■ Awards, Honors

Honorary Royal Designer for Industry, Royal Society of Arts, London; first prize, Finland competition, 1923, for Jyväskylä Workers' Club; first prize, Finland competition, 1927, for Paimio Sanatorium and Viipuri Municipal Library, 1936, for Finnish Pavilion, Paris World's Fair, 1938, for Finnish Pavilion, New York World's Fair, 1948, for Forum Redivivum: Cultural and Administrative Centre, Helsinki; honorary doctorate, Technical University of Helsinki, 1949; first prize, Finland competition, 1950, for Lahti Church, Saynatsalo Town Hall, and

Pedagogical University, Jyväskylä, 1951, for Ruatatalo Office Building, Helsinki, and Kuopio Regional Theatre, 1952, for Church, Seinajoki, 1955, for Goteborg, Sweden, Town Hall, and 1959, for Seinajoki Town Hall; honorary member, Royal Institute of British Architects, 1937; named chevalier, French Legion of Honor, 1939; honorary doctorate, Princeton University, 1947; Gold Medal for Architecture, Royal Institute of British Architects, 1957; honorary member, Sodra Sveriges Byggnadsteniska Samfund, Sweden, 1957; honorary member, American Academy of Arts and Sciences, 1957; Kommendors Korset av Dannebrogen (Denmark), 1957; First Prize, competition project, 1958, for Town Hall, Kiruna, Sweden; honorary member, Aceademia di Belle Arti, Venice, 1958; honorary member, Association of Finnish Architects, 1958; honorary fellow, American Institute of Architects, 1958; honorary member, Norske Arkitekterns Landsforbund, 1959; honorary doctorate, Norges Tekniske Hojskole, Trondheim, Norway, 1960; first prize, 1961, for Opera House, Essen, West Germany; Sonningpriset (Denmark), 1962; honorary doctorate, Eidgenossische Technische Hochschule (Zurich, Switzerland), 1963; Gold Medal, American Institute of Architects, 1963; Gold Cube, Svenska Arkitekters Riksforbund (Sweden), 1963; Cordon del Calli de Oro, Sociedad de Arquitetos (Mexico), 1963; honorary doctorate, Columbia University, 1964; honorary doctorate, Politecnico, Milan, 1964; honorary member, Vastmanlands-Dala Nation (Uppsala, Sweden), 1965; honorary member, Colegio de Arquitetos (Perú), 1965; honorary doctorate, Technische Hochschule (Vienna, Austria), 1965; Grand Cross of the Lion of Finland, 1965; Bronzeplakette, Freie Akademie der Kunste (Hamburg, West Germany), 1965; Medaglia d'Oro, (Florence, Italy), 1965; Diplome des Palmes d'or du Merite de l'Europe, 1966; Helsingin Yliopsiton Ylioppilaskunnan Puheenjohtajiston merkki purppuranauhassa, 1966; honorary member, Engineering Society of Finland, 1966; honorary member, Bund Deutscher Architekten, 1966; Grande Ufficiale al Merito (Italy), 1966; first prize, competition project, 1967, for Protestant Parish Centre, Zurich-Altstetten, Switzerland; Thomas Jefferson Medal, University of Virginia, 1967; honorary member, American Academy of Arts and Letters, 1968; honorary member, National Institute of Arts and Letters (United States), 1968; honorary doctorate, University of Jyväskylä, 1969; Litteris et Artibus Medal (Sweden), 1969; Medaille d'or, Academie d'Architecture (Paris, France), 1972; Grand Croix, Ordre du Faucon (Iceland), 1972; first prize (with J.J. Baruel), 1958, for Art Museum, Aalborg, Denmark; Tapiola Medal, 1975; Outstanding Architect Award, National Arts Foundation (Liechtenstein), 1975; honorary member, Akademie der Bildenden Kunste (Vienna), 1975; honorary member, Royal Scottish Academy, 1975. Alvar Aalto Medal established by Museum of Finnish Architecture/Finnish Association of Architects, 1967.

■ Writings

An Experimental Town, [Cambridge, MA], 1940.
Post-war Reconstruction: Rehousing Research in Finland, [New York, NY], 1941.
Synopsis, [Stuttgart, Germany], 1970.
Alvar Aalto in His Own Words, edited by Göran Schildt, Rizzoli (New York, NY), 1998.

Contributor to periodicals, including *Technology Review*, *Architectural Forum*, and *Arkkitehti*.

■ Sidelights

Alvar Aalto was a Finnish architect and designer and one of the most important figures of twentieth-century architecture. With a career that spanned half a century, Aalto is considered to be one of the masters of modernism, was a leading member of the International Modern school of architecture, and remains known for his skillful balance of formal abstraction, individual expression, and thoughtful humanism. He is also noted for his careful attention to architectural and applied art details and his consideration of textural elements. As Pamela Buxton stated in *Building Design,* "Aalto believed design was a fundamentally human task rooted in the functionalist principle of suiting spaces and objects specifically to people's physical and psychological needs. He worked intuitively to 'harmonise the innumerable contradictory components,' and his works exhibit a balance of opposites rather than formal purity. His buildings are beautifully made, lovely to touch and incredibly humane."

Aalto's style is distinguished by certain variations from the precepts of International Style, among which include a strong interest in Finland's cultural tradition, its woodland and water landscape, and a commitment to the individual human experience. Early works that exemplify these characteristics include the Muurame Parish Church (1927-29) and the Farmers' Cooperative in Turku (1927-28). His later architectural masterworks include Villa Mairea in Noormarkku, Finland (1938-39), the Baker House Dormitory at the Massachusetts Institute of Technology in Cambridge, (1947-48), and the Saynatsalo Town Hall, Finland (1950-52). According to *Financial*

Alvar Aalto's Community Center Holy Ghost, located in Wolfsburg, Germany. (Photograph © Adam Woolfitt/Corbis.)

Times contributor Edwin Heathcote, Aalto "suggested alternatives to slabs and sculptures, to concrete and steel—undulating brick and timber walls, complex and sheltering timber roofs, sensuously solid and considered detailing. This was an architecture that considered the individual as a human being, not as an anonymous, abstract user."

Aalto was also a master of wooden furniture design, and he invented the basic bent-plywood process in 1932. Stanley Abercrombie, in *Contemporary Architects,* contended that "throughout the whole scope of this work—from stools, vases, and lighting fixtures to the planning of entire urban areas—it is possible to see not only those personal inclinations and poetic 'complexities' that separate Aalto from the mainstream of the modern movement, but also those touches of thoughtfulness and grace that raise his work above the mainstream of the architecture of any period." William C. Miller, in the *International Dictionary of Architects and Architecture,* found that "through responsive and responsible design, Aalto was able to create an architecture that was extremely humane, yet profoundly tangible." Edgar J. Kaufmann Jr., in *Interior Design* magazine, wrote that

"Aalto had a remarkably sure touch, a sense of lyrical enjoyment, and repertory of witty details. This allowed his work to maintain an appealing human scale as well as human warmth. He enlarged the horizon of modern architectural design." Almost ninety percent of Aalto's buildings are located in Finland.

Scandanavian Influences

Aalto was born Hugo Alvar Henrik Aalto on February 3, 1898, in Kuortane, near Jyväskylä, Finland. In 1916, he enrolled at Helsinki Polytechnic, where he studied architecture and became the protégé of Armas Lindgren. Polytechnic teachers Carolus Lindberg and Usko Nystrom also influenced the young architect. He graduated in 1921 and found a position as an exhibition designer with Arvid Bjerke in Goteborg, Sweden. He found subsequent work in the Finnish cities of Tampere and Turku. In 1923 he began a private architectural practice in Jyväskylä. The following year, he married the architect Aino Marsio (1894-1949), who became an equal partner in Aalto's work until her death in 1949. Miller noted that Aino Aalto "informed building design as well as the creation of furniture and applied art object, and together husband and wife formed a symbiotic unit, complementing and contrasting one another." Lloyd C. Engelbrecht, in *Contemporary Designers*, maintained that "they worked so closely together that it is impossible to identify their separate roles in their joint projects, or even to be certain which were joint projects and which were not."

Neoclassicism and Northern romanticism were the reigning forces in Scandinavian architecture during the early twentieth century. In the beginning of his career, Aalto subscribed to these forms and executed them with skill and grace. Simplicity of form, the use of classical components, a strong application of native Finnish lumbers, and the existence of well-proportioned spaces mark Aalto's early buildings, which include the Workers Club in Jyväskylä (1924-25), the Seinajoki Civil Guards Complex (1925), the Jyväskylä Civil Guards Building (1927), and the

Muurame Church (1927-29). These designs exhibit his mastery of the classical revival that was taking place in Scandinavia at the time. However, even in these early works, Miller asserted, there are hints of Aalto's mature designs: courtyards that were central to the organizational plan of the building and "a sense of whimsy and playfulness in his details." Aalto never gave up completely on traditional forms; rather he pared them down to their basic, elemental structures and re-worked them in a way that made sense to the world at the time. In the periodical *American Craft*, Paul Mattick remarked that Aalto possessed a "genius for being lucidly romantic about modern experience."

The Aaltos gained prominence in 1927 with their winning design for the Southwestern Agricultural Cooperative Building in Turku. They moved their office to the cosmopolitan city, which provided a connection to the European continent and the avant-garde thinkers who lived there. Soon, they made key associations with various important figures,

Aalto (left) in 1961, speaking with Helsinki Burgomaster Lauri Aho about his plan for the city's new design. (Paul Popper/Popperfoto/Getty Images.)

including Gunnar Asplund, Le Corbusier, Sven Markelius and Laszlo Moholy-Nagy. Aalto was a quick learner, absorbing the principles of contemporary and avant-garde architecture as well as "functionalism" (the Finnish term for modernism). In 1928, he joined the Congres Internationaux d'Architecture Moderne (CIAM), an association that exposed him to new techniques and styles. His work at this time demonstrated his rapid ideological growth, and his connection to CIAM influenced the stylistic changes in his vision. As Miller observed, Aalto's 1927 Southwestern Agricultural Cooperative was a rigid work of classicism, while his 1929 Turun Sanomat Newspaper Building became the first structure in Finland to incorporate Le Corbusier's "five points of new architecture," and his Paimio Tuberculosis Sanatorium Housing of 1933 showed the influence of Russian constructivism and the Dutch De Stijl. Engelbrecht maintained that "nowhere were the humanistic intentions of the CIAM group more readily apparent than in Aalto's work and in the high regard its members had for his work."

Aalto developed a style in furniture-making as well, creating a stackable chair for the Agricultural Cooperative and the famous curvy, bent plywood chair for the Paimio Sanatorium. Engelbrecht contended that after his union with CIAM, Aalto's furniture design became "more daring and original." In the 1930s, the Aaltos founded the Artek furniture company with Mairea Gullichson. Artek designed, manufactured, and distributed Aalto's outstanding furniture, including the famous three-legged stacking stool. His early furniture shows the influence of eighteenth-and early nineteenth-century styles, but he had a desire to refine and purify these essential forms. Engelbrecht contended that, "while there was some direct influence on Aalto from CIAM designers, such as Marcel Breuer, who developed a cantilevered chair, the ability of Breuer and others in the group to create a sense of excitement about experimental furniture was more important." Aalto's plywood stacking chair, patented in 1929, was fitted with legs outside the seat area, a design that ingeniously allowed for stacking. In the same year, he designed a bent-plywood chair that consisted of one piece of wood mounted on a cantilevered steel base. Some of his furniture was designed for use in his buildings, such as the Paimio Sanatorium and the Viipuri Municipal Library in Russia. As Mattick wrote, "There is no modern furniture more warmly elegant that Aalto's chairs and tables." Kurt Andersen, writing in *Time* magazine, maintained that "the best pieces are bareboned but sensuous, simultaneously playful and serene."

Aalto's design for the Paimio Sanatorium was the winning entry of a competition in 1929, and he was contracted to construct the building as well as all of its furnishings and equipment. In this building, Aalto demonstrates his humanistic approach to architecture by displaying a keen understanding of people's needs and how they relate to their interior environment. Abercrombie stated that "Aalto was more than a master of artistic form and of intelligent planning; he was the master as well of the details that relate a building successfully to its users. He cared for the proper shape of a handrail, for the convenience of storage elements, for the texture of a wall, and for the delights of natural light." It is clear from a study of the Paimio Sanatorium that Aalto was thoughtful down to the smallest details, considerately addressing the psychological relationship people have with their immediate environment. The lighting fixtures were placed outside the field of vision of someone lying down, while the water taps were designed to flow silently. The plywood scroll chair was made without metal parts to prevent noise, and its lack of upholstery and open structure allowed it to remain as sanitary as possible. It remains one of his finest designs, a perfect balance of form and function. According to Andersen, "an extreme, almost quixotic regard for the human factor was what separated Aalto from his more renowned contemporaries."

International Acclaim

In 1933, the Aaltos' reputation grew to international prominence, with a furniture exhibition in London organized by the *Architectural Review* and another exhibition at Milan's Triennale. In the same year, they again moved their offices, this time to Helsinki. Aalto's work underwent a transitional phase in the mid-1930s, when the twisting curvatures and free-form energy of his furniture design appeared in his architecture. Miller observed that, during this period, "Aalto's work assumed a more tactile and picturesque posture, becoming less machine-like in imagery. Coupled with a rekindled interest in Finnish vernacular building traditions and a concern for the alienated individual within modern mass society, these changes signaled Aalto's movement away from the technical functionalism of the early 1930s to a more personal style." Aalto's position as an important architect was also bolstered by his magnificent constructions in cities on the European continent and in the United States. These include the Finnish pavilions for the Paris World's Fair (1937) and the New York World's Fair (1939), which were joint commissions with Aino. The Finnish Pavilion in Paris showcased a conical skylight for the introduction of natural light into the space, an idea Aalto later revisited in various forms. It also was designed with an interior court that acted as a primary organizing structure for the rest of the

Aalto's Memorial to the Battle of Suomussalmi, Finland, commemorating those who died during the Russo-Finnish War, was erected in 1960. (Photograph © Adam Woolfitt/Corbis.)

building. This courtyard focus became a fundamental theme throughout Aalto's career. The Finnish Pavilion in New York featured a three-storey display wall that was rendered in a flowing, undulating form. This sinuosity is a significant compositional element that is somewhat of a signature in Aalto's style. Miller stated that, "exploring the tectonic possibilities of the undulating surface, he demonstrated a unique sensitivity to the dynamics of the sinuous element in architecture . . . the sinuous element is not merely a building element or spatial construct, but assumes another presence as furniture, glassware, light fixture, and door handle and handrail." Andersen commented that "an Aalto building is apt to swell or zigzag confoundingly, to have lines and textures that seem more botanical and geological than geometrical."

Aalto's remarkable ability to fuse seemingly disparate themes in his work is well illustrated in his 1935 library in Viipuri, Finland (now Vyborg, Russia). Although much of the library showcases the reductivist abstraction central to modernist ideology, there are elements that highlight themes opposed to modernism, such as non-linear, organic forms, sensual and tactile considerations, and additive fabrications. Here, Aalto's sinuous lines are manifested in the surging billows of the ceiling of the library's lecture hall, which was fitted with strips of wood to achieve a powerful acoustical environment. Miller found that the staircases, landings, and handrails of the Viipuri reading room are "dynamic elements celebrating human action and movement." The organic lines are echoed on other, smaller levels, in lighting fixtures, door handles, and even glassware. However, the exterior of the building is rendered in a strict rectilinear form that is well within the functionalistic tenets of International Style. The result is a rigid exterior formalism that provides the shell for a warm, relaxing interior, an unusual and highly effective architectural amalgam that Franz Schultze, in *Art in America*, called "a highly personal union of intention and effect." "The total effect of the building is a mixture of cool external form with an almost seductively warm and soothing interior space," Schultze added. A 1938 exhibition at the Museum of Modern Art in New York, organized by John McAndrew, solidified Aalto's international preeminence.

After World War II, Artek was revived and Aalto continued his experiments in furniture design. In 1947, he developed the "Y" leg. In the same year, he started work on his first permanent design in the United States, the Baker House dormitory at the Massachusetts Institute of Technology. Baker House was built of rough brick, and used Aalto's signature sinuous lines to provide variant views of the adjacent river. Abercrombie remarked that this work "was a clear break with modern purity, unity, and planarity," while Mattick enjoyed the "eccentric floor plans and . . . idiosyncratically meandering halls."

In 1949 Aino Aalto passed away. In the same year, Aalto won another competition, this time for the design of the village center of Saynatsalo. From 1950 to 1952, the construction of Saynatsalo Town Hall took place, under the supervision of a young architect named Elissa Mäkiniemi. Aalto and Mäkiniemi married in 1952, and, like Aalto's previous marriage, the two forged a close collaboration. Mäkiniemi managed Artek's production, which was bolstered by Aalto's development of a five-part upright frame in the shape of a fan in the mid-1950s.

The important buildings of Aalto's mature style include Villa Mairea in Noormarkku (1939), the Town Hall in Saynatsalo (1950-52), the Public Pensions Institute in Helsinki (1952-56), the Ruatatalo Office Building in Helsinki (1953-55), Jyväskylä Teachers College (1953-56), the Helsinki House of Culture (1955-58), the Church of Three Crosses in Vuoksenniska (1956-58), the Technical Institute in Otaniemi (1956-64), and the Cultural Centre in Wolfsburg, Germany (1960-63). According to Gavin Stamp, writing in *Apollo*, "Aalto's buildings of the 1940s and 1950s used red brick, copper, timber and ceramic finishes . . .; they had pitched roofs and exploited a much more free and expressive approach to form." Miller remarked that the architect's later works "seem to fuse both classical restraint and romantic exuberance."

A Style of His Own

Though Aalto eschewed some key elements of modernism to create a highly personal style, Abercrombie argued that "in Aalto's differences from other modernists, we should find not a repudiation of modernism, but a demonstration of the breadth

If you enjoy the works of Alvar Aalto, you may also want to check out the following:

The art of Pablo Picasso and Georges Braque, whose Cubist paintings influenced Aalto.
The works of Swedish architects Gunnar Asplund and Sigurd Lewerentz, who exemplify Nordic classicism.
The deconstructivist designs of American architect Frank Gehry and Dutch architect Rem Koolhaas.

and strength of that movement." Mattick believed that Aalto is "the most mysterious of all the major architects." "During his life," observed *New York Times* critic Herbert Muschamp, "Aalto's nationality gave him an aura of otherness; people regarded him as a special case whose work derived from exotic conditions: those lakes, that birch, that Finland, a country where even the factory smokestacks look to be pumping out fresh air. The young nation was not yet independent when Aalto was born. Its people spoke a peculiar language, seemingly related to no other. In retrospect, it should be clearer that nationality was only part of what set him apart. His true distinction is that his architecture was ahead of its time.

Aalto was an enigmatic creator, and a study of his work reveals some seeming contradictions that only add to the complexity by which he organized his aesthetic principles. On one hand, he was a staunch supporter of the Finnish cultural tradition; on the other, he was a global stylist, finding inspiration from international modernists. On one hand, he was a technical virtuoso, creating new methods to execute formal architectural expressions; on the other, he was extremely sensitive to the human element. He loved conventional forms, yet he was aggressively experimental. Schultze believed that "duality is the leitmotif of Aalto's architecture." However, in the final analysis of Aalto's work, it is "an honorable and simple humanism," Abercrombie concluded, "that prevails over any stylistic character."

Aalto was an intuitive creator who took cues from all sides and created hybrids that seamlessly synthesized form and function, designs that held as their motivating factor the human individual. Utilitarian, comfortable, and pure expressions of personal style, his works show the hand of an ultimately modern master. As Nicholas Ray stated in *Alvar Aalto*, "Not only were his buildings compositionally adept and formally elegant, they also gathered to themselves the meaning of the society they served, and appear to be capable of reinterpretation in succeeding decades as symbols of the highest human aspirations."

■ **Biographical and Critical Sources**

BOOKS

Alvar Aalto in Seven Buildings: Interpretations of an Architect's Work, Museum of Finnish Architecture (Helsinki, Finland), 1998.

Asensio, Paco, editor, *Alvar Aalto*, translated by William Bain, te Neues (Kempen, Germany), 2002.

Contemporary Architects, St. James Press (London, England), 1994.

Contemporary Designers, 3rd edition, St. James Press (Detroit, MI), 1997.

Dunster, David, editor, *Alvar Aalto*, St. Martin's Press (London, England), 1978.

International Dictionary of Architects and Architecture, Volume 1: *Architects*, St. James Press (Detroit, MI), 1993.

Menin, Sarah, and Flora Samuel, *Nature and Space: Aalto and Le Corbusier*, Routledge (New York, NY), 2003.

Nerdinger, Winifried, editor, *Alvar Aalto: Toward a Human Modernism*, Prestel (New York, NY), 1999.

Among Aalto's designs is the Riola Parish Church, which was constructed in Riola, Italy, in the late 1970s. (De Agostini/ Getty Images.)

The interior of the Finlandia Concert Hall in Helsinki, Finland, which Aalto saw completed in 1971. (Photograph © Adam Woolfitt/Corbis.)

Pelkonen, Eeva-Liisa, *Alvar Aalto: Architecture, Modernity, and Geopolitics,* Yale University Press (New Haven, CT), 2009.

Quantrill, Malcolm, *Alvar Aalto: A Critical Study,* Otava (Helsinki, Finland), 1983.

Ray, Nicholas, *Alvar Aalto,* Yale University Press (New Haven, CT), 2005.

Reed, Peter, editor, *Alvar Aalto: Between Humanism and Materialism,* Abrams (New York, NY), 1998.

Schildt, Göran, *Alvar Aalto: The Early Years,* Rizzoli (New York, NY), 1984.

Schildt, Göran, *Alvar Aalto: The Decisive Years,* Rizzoli (New York, NY), 1986.

Schildt, Göran, *Alvar Aalto: The Mature Years,* Rizzoli (New York, NY), 1991.

Schildt, Göran, *Alvar Aalto: The Complete Catalogue of Architecture, Design, and Art,* Wiley & Sons (New York, NY), 1996.

Schildt, Göran, editor, *Alvar Aalto: Master Works,* translated by Timothy Bingham, Otava (Helsinki, Finland), 1998.

Weston, Richard, *Alvar Aalto,* Phaidon Press (London, England), 1995.

PERIODICALS

American Craft, June-July, 1998, Paul Mattick, profile of Aalto, p. 50.

Apollo, May, 2007, Gavin Stamp, "A Is for Aalto," p. 82.

Architecture, October, 1998, Eric Adams, "Wintry Discontent," p. 166.

Architectural Review, June, 1998, Peter Davey, review of *Alvar Aalto in His Own Words,* p. 13; April, 2007, Peter Davey, "East Meets North," p. 96.

Arkkitehti, numbers 7-8, 1976, "Alvar Aalto: The Man and His Work."

Art in America, May, 1998, Franz Schultze, "Architecture as Humanism," p. 110.

Building Design, January 27, 2006, Elaine Knutt, 2006, "Humanity Restored," p. 24; February 16, 2007, Pamela Buxton, "Walking Back to Happiness," p. 26.

Canadian Architect, May, 1977, George Baird, "Reflections on the Influence of Alvar Aalto."

Financial Times, February 28, 2007, Edwin Heathcote, "Modernism's Human Side," p. 13.

Interior Design, June, 1984, Peter Blake, "The Aalto Alternative," p. 272; September, 1984, Edgar J. Kaufmann, Jr., "Aalto on First Avenue," p. 270; August, 1993, Judith Nasatir, "Alvar Aalto," p. 84; July, 1998, Stanley Abercrombie, review of *Alvar Aalto in His Own Words,* p. 105.

Interiors, April, 1996, Michael Webb, "The Aalto (Almost) Nobody Knows," p. 92.

Investor's Business Daily, December 19, 2001, Nancy Gondo, "Architect Alvar Aalto Excelled by Design Focus on Form," p. A4.

New York Times, February 26, 1998, Herbert Muschamp, "Aalto, a Modernist Ahead of His Time."

Progressive Architecture, April, 1977, "Alvar Aalto," pp. 53-77; April, 1988, William C. Miller, "Alvar Aalto: The Decisive Years," p. 173.

Space Design, January-February, 1977, "Alvar Aalto."

Time, November 19, 1984, Kurt Andersen, "Still Fresh after 50 Years," p. 138.

ONLINE

Great Buildings Web site, http://www.greatbuildings. com/ (July 1, 2009), "Alvar Aalto."*

Nancy Atherton

■ Personal

Born in Chicago, IL. *Education:* University of Chicago, B.A. (English literature), 1989. *Hobbies and other interests:* Traveling.

■ Addresses

Home—Colorado Springs, CO. *E-mail*—nancy@auntdimity.com.

■ Career

Author. Has worked as a freelance proofreader, copyeditor, and librarian, and has worked at a ski lodge, dude ranch, and day care center.

■ Awards, Honors

100 Favorite Mysteries of the Century inclusion, Independent Mystery Booksellers Association, for *Aunt Dimity's Death.*

■ Writings

MYSTERY NOVELS

Aunt Dimity's Death, Viking (New York, NY), 1992.

Aunt Dimity and the Duke, Viking (New York, NY), 1994.

Aunt Dimity's Good Deed, Viking (New York, NY), 1996.

Aunt Dimity Digs In, Viking (New York, NY), 1998.

Aunt Dimity's Christmas, Viking (New York, NY), 1999.

Aunt Dimity Beats the Devil, Viking (New York, NY), 2000.

Aunt Dimity: Detective, Viking (New York, NY), 2001.

Aunt Dimity Takes a Holiday, Viking (New York, NY), 2003.

Aunt Dimity: Snowbound, Viking (New York, NY), 2004.

Aunt Dimity and the Next of Kin, Viking (New York, NY), 2005.

Aunt Dimity and the Deep Blue Sea, Viking (New York, NY), 2006.

Aunt Dimity Goes West, Viking (New York, NY), 2007.

Aunt Dimity: Vampire Hunter, Viking (New York, NY), 2008.

Aunt Dimity Slays the Dragon, Viking (New York, NY), 2009.

Introducing Aunt Dimity, Paranormal Detective (contains *Aunt Dimity's Death* and *Aunt Dimity and the Duke*), Viking (New York, NY), 2009.

■ Sidelights

Nancy Atherton is the author of the "Aunt Dimity" series of cozy mysteries set in the quiet village of Finch in the Cotswolds region of England. The

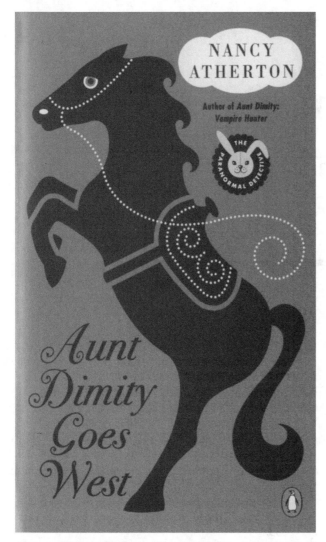

Cover of Nancy Atherton's entertaining mystery *Aunt Dimity Goes West*, **which features the author's popular paranormal detective.** (Copyright © 2007 by Nancy T. Atherton. All rights reserved. Used by permission of Penguin Group (USA) Inc.)

books feature mother, homemaker, and amateur sleuth Lori Shepherd, who channels the advice of one Aunt Dimity, a deceased friend of Lori's mother. The series resulting from this odd collaboration is both "popular and enchanting," according to *Library Journal* contributor Rex E. Klett, and Margaret Flanagan, writing in *Booklist,* described Atherton's novels as "delightfully quirky." "I don't write murder mysteries," Atherton explained to Colorado Springs *Gazette* contributor Bill Reed. "I write mysteries with no murder, no crime and no detective."

Although her books have a distinctly British flavor, Atherton is American through and through. Born and raised in Chicago, Illinois, she worked at a number of low-paying jobs after graduating from high school before spending five years abroad, including travels to the United Kingdom. She later earned a degree in English literature from the University of Chicago, married and divorced, and was living in Brooklyn when the idea for the "Aunt Dimity" series hit her. In an interview for *MysteryGuide.com*, Atherton explained its enigmatic origins: "I sat up in bed about 3:00 one morning, and the first line of the book was in my head: 'When I learned of Aunt Dimity's death, I was stunned; not because she was dead, but because she had never been alive.' I sat up in bed and I turned the light on and I wrote it down and I said, 'I wonder what that means?'"

Her interest piqued, Atherton started writing, hoping to discover the answer to her question. As she told Reed, "I remember sitting back at the keyboard and thinking, 'Oh, this is what I was born to do. This is why I'm here. All that other stuff was gathering material.'" Despite this revelation, the idea of becoming an author seemed a foreign notion to Atherton. As she recalled in the *CrimeCritics.com* interview, "I didn't spend much time dreaming about getting my first book published because I didn't think a peculiar little book that was sort of a mystery and sort of a romance, with a fantasy element, some history, a bit of gardening, and a recipe thrown in for good measure stood a snowball's chance of being published." She added, "I wrote *Aunt Dimity's Death* because I was intensely curious to find out what the first line meant and because I'd discovered the inestimable joy of writing—not because I wanted to see my name in print. That it was published came as a huge, and hugely pleasant, surprise to me."

Makes Literary Debut

Lori Shepherd, Atherton's energetic and endearing protagonist, is first introduced in 1992 in *Aunt Dimity's Death*. Lori, who is newly divorced and has recently lost her mother, is struggling as a temp when she receives a letter from the Boston law firm of Willis & Willis. Dimity Westwood, who had been corresponding with Lori's mother since they met during World War I, has left Lori an inheritance. Dimity's letters contained stories Lori's mother had read to her, yet Lori had not realized that there was a real woman behind the tales. Attorney Bill Willis accompanies Lori to Dimity's cottage in England to carry out Dimity's wishes that her stories be collected and published. The cottage, however, is haunted by the woman's ghost, and a curious and undaunted Lori attempts to uncover the facts surrounding Dimity's romance with a World War II flier. Reviewing *Aunt Dimity's Death*, a *Publishers Weekly* critic observed that Atherton "creates a potentially appealing heroine," and a *Kirkus Reviews* writer described the author's debut as "amiable, stylishly written—often with a touch of wry humor."

A *Publishers Weekly* reviewer described Atherton's second novel, *Aunt Dimity and the Duke,* as "more amusing than the first." The work centers on computer analyst Emma Porter of Boston. Emma is nearly forty years old and has recently been dumped by her lover in favor of a younger woman. She is traveling in Cornwall, England, where she meets Grayson Alexander, the duke of Penford Hall, who solicits Emma's help in finding a lantern Aunt Dimity had asked him to recover. Grayson, who was

With its touch of romance, *Aunt Dimity's Death* is the debut of Atherton's popular "Aunt Dimity" mystery series. (Copyright © 1992 by Nancy T. Atherton. All rights reserved. Used by permission of Penguin Group (USA) Inc.)

connected to the death of a rock star five years earlier, is attempting to have his garden restored before the centennial of a local supernatural event. Emma meets and falls in love with widower Derek Harris, an historian whose current interest is the stained-glass chapel window central to the upcoming celebration. *Booklist* reviewer Ilene Cooper wrote that in *Aunt Dimity and the Duke* Atherton gives her story "breadth and depth with terrific characters and an intriguing plot involving psychic phenomenon."

Lori returns in *Aunt Dimity's Good Deed* in which she is now married to attorney Bill Willis. She tries to lure away him from his heavy workload with a trip to the cottage she inherited from Aunt Dimity. However, when Bill is unable to make the trip due to his commitment to a case, his father offers to go in his stead, seeing it as a chance to make peace with family members in England. When the senior Willis disappears, Nell, the young daughter of Emma and Derek, and the ghostly Aunt Dimity lead Lori on the path to locating her father-in-law. Lori meets the English cousins, whose law firm is beset with problems, and learns the truth about the family feud. At book's end, Bill and the now-pregnant Lori have moved to England. "Heartwarming and charming, Atherton's latest bit of eccentric whimsy is sure to delight," *Booklist* reviewer Emily Melton commented, and the series was described as "pointedly cute" by a *Publishers Weekly* reviewer. A writer for *Kirkus Reviews* said of *Aunt Dimity's Good Deed* that "fans could adore it; others might like to see the author's graceful writing skills brought a bit more down to earth."

Aunt Dimity Digs In finds Lori and Bill living happily in the village of Finch as the doting parents of twin boys. Aunt Dimity keeps in touch through the blue notebooks she has left to Lori, notebooks in which her handwriting offers advice and counsel. A rare book expert, Lori is asked to help when a document concerning an archaeological find is stolen. The case involves such colorful characters as Peggy Kitchen, who is trying to evict archaeologist Adrian Culver from a schoolhouse so that she can complete plans for the Harvest Festival, and Francesca Sciaparelli, the nanny who appears just in time to pitch in so that Lori can pursue the facts behind the mystery, which include witch sightings in a local meadow. A *Publishers Weekly* reviewer wrote of *Aunt Dimity Digs In* that Atherton "delivers pure cozy entertainment," while Melton called the series "cozy as a warm fire and soothing as a hot cup of tea."

In *Aunt Dimity's Christmas* holiday festivities are interrupted when Lori finds an unconscious man laying in the snow outside their home. Dimity relays a message to Lori that she should seek the identity of the man, now comatose at the local hospital. Lori investigates with the assistance of Father Julian, a Roman Catholic priest, and together they uncover the truth about a man who has been instrumental in the lives of many. "In this most unusual mystery," wrote a *Publishers Weekly* reviewer, "Atherton offers a glimpse of the finer side of human nature."

Popular Series Garners Praise

Lori, once again aided by Aunt Dimity's writings, is on the trail of a tragic love story in *Aunt Dimity Beats the Devil*. In Scotland to examine the

Wyrdhurst clan, she investigates mysterious noises coming from an old house, only to come upon a collection of love letters dating from World War I. GraceAnne A. DeCandido, writing in *Booklist*, complimented the "romantic tale" Atherton tells in *Aunt Dimity Beats the Devil*, adding that there is "enough dreamy and ghostly wish-fulfillment to satisfy readers across several genres." Similar praise came from a *Publishers Weekly* critic who applauded the "irresistible flair and charm" of Atherton's writing. Lori more directly plays the sleuth in the next installment, *Aunt Dimity: Detective*. Returning to the village of Finch after several months in the United States, she finds that her small village is stirred by the apparent murder of one of its residents, Prunella "Pruneface" Hooper. Aided by the vicar's nephew and by Aunt Dimity's ghostly advice, Lori gets to the bottom of things in this "lightweight, easy-flowing entertainment," as a *Kirkus Reviews* critic described the work.

Lori uncovers numerous skeletons in the closet of the earl of Elstyn in *Aunt Dimity Takes a Holiday*, a "charming trifle," according to *Booklist* contributor Flanagan. Anonymous threatening letters and seeming pranks at the earl's estate lead Lori to the source of the unrest. While a *Kirkus Reviews* critic was less impressed with this eighth installment, calling it a "weightless mystery with precious few clues," a *Library Journal* writer was more positive, calling *Aunt Dimity Takes a Holiday* "delightful." Lori gets lost on a hike and finds refuge from a snow storm in a seemingly deserted mansion in *Aunt Dimity: Snowbound*. While snowbound, and with the aid of Aunt Dimity's magic writing, she solves a mystery involving missing pearls. Alan Paul Curtis, writing for *WhoDunnit.com*, concluded of the book that "all those who like a mystery without the gruesome details of a murder . . . will certainly thrive on this story."

With *Aunt Dimity and the Next of Kin*, Lori finds herself solving a missing-person's case for a woman who has just died. In *Aunt Dimity and the Deep Blue Sea*, danger strikes closer to home as Lori's lawyer husband, Bill, receives death threats, which send Lori and the twins off to the safety of a Scottish isle for a time. Once there, however, Lori becomes involved in discovering the secret of the islanders' seeming wealth. *Booklist* reviewer Jenny McLarin noted of *Aunt Dimity and the Next of Kin* that those who like cozy mysteries "will purr quietly," and called *Aunt Dimity and the Deep Blue Sea* a "testament to the staying power of Atherton's cozier-than-cozy premise."

In *Aunt Dimity Goes West*, Lori, her twin boys, and their nanny head to Colorado for a much-needed vacation. Staying at the Aerie, a wondrous cabin owned by a family friend, they learn that the

Atherton's ghostly sleuth aids her niece in solving yet another mystery in *Aunt Dimity: Detective*.

If you enjoy the works of Nancy Atherton, you may also want to check out the following books:

Agatha Christie's "Miss Marple" series, including *The Mirror Crack'd*, 1962.
The works in Jeanne M. Dams' "Dorothy Martin" series, including *The Body in the Transept*, 1995.
Donna Andrews' "Meg Langslow" series, including *Murder with Puffins*, 2000.

Lori Shepherd and her late great Aunt Dimity are set on the trail of a new mystery when a close friend dies in *Aunt Dimity and the Next of Kin.*

caretaker has mysteriously disappeared and that the home may be cursed by the spirit of an individual who died in a mining accident years earlier. Sue O'Brien, reviewing *Aunt Dimity Goes West* for *Booklist*, called the work "a humorous, satisfying cozy with exceptionally likable characters." Back in England, Lori once again turns to Aunt Dimity for help in *Aunt Dimity: Vampire Hunter.* After her twins insist they have spotted a vampire during their riding lessons, Lori teams up with stable master Kit Smith to uncover the identity of the intruder, resulting in "one of Aunt Dimity's most suspenseful mysteries," according to a *Kirkus Reviews* contributor.

A series of strange accidents plague a Renaissance faire in *Aunt Dimity Slays the Dragon.* When the life of Calvin Malvern is threatened while he performs the role of King Wilfred the Good, Lori seeks the wisdom of Aunt Dimity and her mystical writings. According to Judy Coon in *Booklist*, "one of the most charming entries in an enduringly popular series" is served up by Atherton in *Aunt Dimity Slays the Dragon.*

With more than a dozen "Aunt Dimity" novels to her credit, Atherton shows no signs of slowing down. "Since I had no idea that I would write a series in the first place, I'm probably the wrong person to ask about how long the series might run," she remarked in her *CrimeCritics.com* interview. The author concluded, "I know only that I love my characters beyond all reason and that I would consider it a privilege to be at their beck and call for many years to come."

■ **Biographical and Critical Sources**

BOOKS

Heising, Willetta L., *Detecting Women 2*, Purple Moon Press (Dearborn, MI), 1996.

PERIODICALS

Armchair Detective, summer, 1993, review of *Aunt Dimity's Death*, p. 48.
Booklist, October 15, 1992, Ilene Cooper, review of *Aunt Dimity's Death*, p. 404; October 1, 1994, Ilene Cooper, review of *Aunt Dimity and the Duke*, p. 241; September 15, 1996, Emily Melton, review of *Aunt Dimity's Good Deed*, p. 223; March 1, 1998, Emily Melton, review of *Aunt Dimity Digs In*, p. 1097; September 15, 2000, GraceAnne A. DeCandido, review of *Aunt Dimity: Detective*, p. 55; September 1, 2001, GraceAnne A. DeCandido, review of *Aunt Dimity Beats the Devil*, p. 221; February 15, 2003, Margaret Flanagan, review of

Aunt Dimity Takes a Holiday, p. 1052; January 1, 2005, Jenny McLarin, review of *Aunt Dimity and the Next of Kin*, p. 825; February 1, 2006, Jenny McLarin, review of *Aunt Dimity and the Deep Blue Sea*, p. 35; December 15, 2006, Sue O'Brien, review of *Aunt Dimity Goes West*, p. 24; January 1, 2009, Judy Coon, review of *Aunt Dimity Slays the Dragon*, p. 51.

Gazette (Colorado Springs, CO), February 12, 2005, Bill Reed, "No Murders Allowed: *Aunt Dimity* Author Prefers to Focus on Goodness."

Kirkus Reviews, September 15, 1992, review of *Aunt Dimity's Death*, p. 1152; September 1, 1994, review of *Aunt Dimity and the Duke*, p. 1165; August 15, 1996, review of *Aunt Dimity's Good Deed*, p. 1187; August 15, 2001, review of *Aunt Dimity: Detective*, p. 1163; February 1, 2003, review of *Aunt Dimity Takes a Holiday*, p. 184; December 15, 2005, review of *Aunt Dimity and the Deep Blue Sea*, p. 1300; December 1, 2006, review of *Aunt Dimity Goes West*, p. 1198; December 15, 2007, review of *Aunt Dimity: Vampire Hunter*; November 1, 2008, review of *Aunt Dimity Slays the Dragon*.

Kliatt, January, 1994, review of *Aunt Dimity's Death*, p. 4.

Library Journal, October 1, 1992, Rex E. Klett, review of *Aunt Dimity's Death*, p. 122; November 1, 1994, Rex E. Klett, review of *Aunt Dimity and the Duke*, p. 115; September 1, 1996, Rex E. Klett, review of *Aunt Dimity's Good Deed*, p. 214; October 1, 1999, Rex E. Klett, review of *Aunt Dimity's Christmas*, p. 138; September 1, 2001, Rex E. Klett, review of

Aunt Dimity: Detective, p. 238; February 1, 2003, review of *Aunt Dimity Takes a Holiday*, p. 122.

Locus, November, 1992, review of *Aunt Dimity's Death*, p. 33; December, 1993, review of *Aunt Dimity's Death*, p. 47; December, 1994, review of *Aunt Dimity and the Duke*, p. 54.

Publishers Weekly, September 14, 1992, review of *Aunt Dimity's Death*, p. 110; October 25, 1993, review of *Aunt Dimity's Death*, p. 58; October 17, 1994, review of *Aunt Dimity and the Duke*, p. 65; August 19, 1996, review of *Aunt Dimity's Good Deed*, p. 55; January 19, 1998, review of *Aunt Dimity Digs In*, p. 375; September 20, 1999, review of *Aunt Dimity's Christmas*, p. 77; August 14, 2000, review of *Aunt Dimity Beats the Devil*, p. 332; November 26, 2007, review of *Aunt Dimity: Vampire Hunter*, p. 32; December 1, 2008, review of *Aunt Dimity Slays the Dragon*, p. 32.

ONLINE

CrimeCritics.com, http://www.crimecritics.com/ (February 3, 2009), "Interrogating Nancy Atherton."

MysteryGuide.com, http://www.mysteryguide.com/ (March 4, 1998), "Nancy Atherton Interview."

Nancy Atherton Home Page, http://www.aunt-dimity.com (May 1, 2009).

WhoDunnit.com, http://www.who-dunnit.com/ (December 18, 2006), "Nancy Atherton," and Alan Paul Curtis, reviews of *Aunt Dimity, Snowbound* and *Aunt Dimity Digs In*.*

Hart Crane

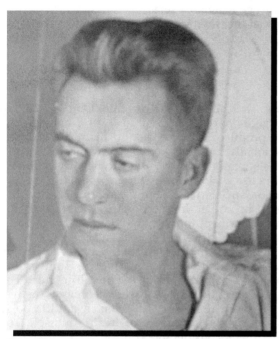

(Photograph by Walker Evans. Courtesy of the Library of Congress.)

■ Personal

Born July 21, 1899, in Garrettsville, OH; committed suicide, April 27 (some sources say April 26), 1932, in the Gulf of Mexico; son of Clarance A. (a store-owner and manufacturer) and Grace Edna (Hart) Crane. *Education:* Attended public schools in Cleveland, OH.

■ Career

Writer. Worked as mechanic bench hand and shipyard laborer in Ohio, c. mid-1910s; *Cleveland Plain Dealer,* Cleveland, OH, newspaper reporter, 1919; *Little Review,* New York, NY, advertising manager, 1919; Rheinthal & Newman, New York, NY, shipping manager, 1919; advertising copywriter in Cleveland and New York, NY, c. 1920s; in sales in New York, NY, c. mid-1920s.

■ Awards, Honors

Helen Waire Levinson Prize, 1930; Guggenheim fellow, 1931-32.

■ Writings

White Buildings (poetry), foreword by Allen Tate, Boni & Liveright (New York, NY), 1926, reprinted, Liveright (New York, NY), 1972.

The Bridge (poetry), Liveright (New York, NY), 1930, reprinted, 1970.

The Collected Poems of Hart Crane, edited by Waldo Frank, Liveright (New York, NY), 1933.

Voyages: Six Poems from White Buildings, illustrated by Leonard Baskin, Museum of Modern Art (New York, NY), 1957.

The Complete Poems and Selected Letters and Prose of Hart Crane, edited by Brom Weber, Doubleday/Anchor (New York, NY), 1966, Liveright (New York, NY), 2000.

Twenty-one Letters from Hart Crane to George Bryan, edited by Joseph Katz, Hugh C. Atkinson, and Richard A. Ploch, Ohio State University Press (Columbus, OH), 1968.

Robber Rocks: Letters and Memories of Hart Crane, 1923-1932, edited by Susan Jenkins Brown, Wesleyan University Press (Middletown, CT), 1969.

Ten Unpublished Poems, Gotham Book Mart (New York, NY), 1972.

(With others) *The Letters of Hart Crane and His Family,* edited by Thomas S.W. Lewis, Columbia University Press (New York, NY), 1974.

(With Yvor Winters) *Hart Crane and Yvor Winters: Their Literary Correspondence,* edited by Thomas Parkinson, University of California Press (Berkeley, CA), 1978.

The Poems of Hart Crane, edited by Marc Simon, Liveright (New York, NY), 1986.

O My Land, My Friends: The Selected Letters of Hart Crane, Four Walls Eight Windows (New York, NY), 1997.

The Correspondence between Hart Crane and Waldo Frank, edited by Steve H. Cook, Whitston Publishing (Troy, NY), 1998.

The Complete Poems of Hart Crane, edited by Marc Simon, Liveright (New York, NY), 2000.

Clive Fisher's Hart Crane: A Life, Yale University Press (New Haven, CT), 2002.

Complete Poems and Selected Letters, Penguin (New York, NY), 2006.

Work represented in numerous anthologies, including *The New Pocket Anthology of American Verse* and *The Norton Anthology of Modern Poetry.* Contributor to periodicals, including *Bruno's Weekly, Modern School, Modernist, Pagan,* and *S4N.*

■ Sidelights

Hart Crane is a legendary figure among American poets. In his personal life he showed little self-esteem, indulging in great and frequent bouts of alcohol abuse and homosexual promiscuity. In his art, however, he showed surprising optimism. Critics have contended that, for Crane, misery and despair were redeemed through the apprehension of beauty, and in some of his greatest verses he articulated his own quest for redemption. As Joseph Miller stated in the *Dictionary of Literary Biography,* "Both the strengths and weaknesses of Hart Crane as a poet are evidenced in his character as a man, which is inexplicable apart from the atmosphere of emotional turmoil in which he lived his life." Miller continued, "Although from an early age he was a dedicated and hard-working poet, he wrote with bursts of inspiration and suffered, when there was no inspiration, from fears that his gift had evaporated. He never achieved a calm detachment from his poetry any more than he did from his family."

Crane believed strongly in the peculiarly naïve American Romanticism extending back through Walt Whitman to Ralph Waldo Emerson. In his most ambitious work, *The Bridge,* he sought nothing less than an expression of the American experience in its entirety. Despite what some critics have viewed as a failure in this attempt, Crane not only impressed many of those same critics but also prompted a few of them to see him as a pivotal figure in American literature. Crane has since come to be regarded as both the quintessential Romantic artist and the embodiment of those extreme characteristics—hope and despair, redemption and literary damnation—

that seemed to preoccupy many of his contemporaries. As Allen Tate wrote in *Essays of Four Decades,* "Crane was one of those men whom every age seems to select as the spokesman of its spiritual life; they give the age away."

A Troubled Childhood

Crane was born in Garrettsville, Ohio, in 1899 of bourgeois parents. His father was a businessman who produced chocolates, and his mother was an emotionally unstable woman known for her beauty. Crane's relationship with his mother was stifling in its intensity. His parents fought regularly, and his mother succeeded in engaging his sympathies against his father. In addition, his mother used him as an often-inappropriate confidante in complaining about the sex act and her real and imagined health problems. During the woman's bouts of hypochondria, Crane spent a great deal of time in her company, comforting and consoling her. This unusual intimacy proved overwhelmingly distressful to the future poet, but even in adulthood he often remained incapable of freeing himself from his mother's considerable control.

As a result of real and imagined problems, Crane's mother suffered a nervous collapse in 1908. While she recuperated, the boy moved to his grandmother's home in Cleveland. There he spent most of his formative years and showed his first enthusiasm for poetry. His grandmother's library was extensive, featuring editions of complete works by poets such as Victorian Robert Browning and the Americans Ralph Waldo Emerson and Walt Whitman, the last two which became major influences on his own poetry. During his mid-teens Crane continued to read extensively, broadening his interests to include such writers as philosopher Plato, novelist Honoré de Balzac, and Romantic poet Percy Bysshe Shelley. Crane's formal education, however, was continually undermined by family problems necessitating prolonged absences from school. Finally, in 1916, he left Cleveland without graduating and moved to New York City to attend Columbia University, which he hoped to enter upon passing an entrance examination.

Once in New York City, however, Crane abandoned any pretence of acquiring a college education and began vigorously pursuing a literary career. Through a painter he knew earlier from Cleveland, Crane met other writers and gained exposure to various art movements and ideas. Reading the works of French symbolists Charles Baudelaire and Arthur Rimbaud and contemporary Irishmen William Butler Yeats and James Joyce, writing, and socializing with other artists—and aspiring artists—

left Crane little time or energy for work. Instead of seeking regular employment, he relied on his parents to provide financial support. Because their continual squabbling sometimes resulted in unfortunate delays of his funds, Crane occasionally sold advertising for the *Little Review,* a publication that promoted the work of modernists such as Joyce and T.S. Eliot.

Crane also associated with a far different periodical, *Seven Arts,* which devoted itself to traditional American literature extending from Nathaniel Hawthorne and Walt Whitman to Sherwood Anderson and Robert Frost. Both *Seven Arts* and *Little Review* exerted considerable influence on the impressionable Crane, and in his own poetry he would seek to reconcile the two magazines' disparate philosophies. At this time—around 1917—Crane was already producing publishable verse. Some of these works appeared in the local journal *Pagan.* Relatively short, Crane's poems from this period reveal his interests in both tradition and experimentation, merging a rhyming structure with jarringly contemporary imagery. These early poems, though admired by some critics, were never held highly by Crane, and he never reprinted them in his lifetime.

Initially, Crane found New York City invigorating and even inspiring. Although he abused alcohol and consistently indulged his sexual proclivity for sailors, he still managed to work diligently on his poetry. In 1917 his parents divorced, and subsequently his mother arrived—with her mother—to stay in his one-bedroom apartment. Bedridden from emotional exhaustion, Crane's mother demanded near-constant attention. His problems mounted when his father, increasingly prosperous in the chocolate business, nonetheless threatened to withhold further funds until Crane found a job. To escape the pressures of family life, the young man attempted to enlist in the U.S. Army, only to be rejected as a minor. He then left New York City for Cleveland and found work in a munitions plant for the duration of World War I.

After the war, Crane stayed in Cleveland and found work as a reporter for the *Cleveland Plain Dealer.* He held that job only briefly, however, before returning to New York City to work once again for the *Little Review.* In mid-1919 his father used his influence in obtaining a position for his son as a shipping clerk. However, Crane stayed at that job for only a few months before moving back to Ohio to work for his father's own company. Their relationship, though, was hardly congenial, for Crane's father professed little understanding of his son's lifestyle, and Crane, in turn, accorded little compassion for his father, despite the latter's trying marriage and divorce. Complicating matters further was the presence of Crane's mother, with whom Crane had begun liv-

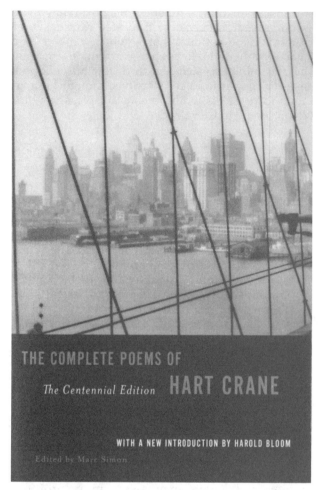

Cover of *The Complete Poems of Hart Crane,* a collection edited by Marc Simon and featuring a cover photograph by Walker Evans. (Photograph by Walker Evans. Courtesy of Metropolitan Museum of Art, New York. Used by permission of Liveright Publishing Corporation.)

ing after she returned to Cleveland. Tensions finally exploded in the spring of 1921 when Crane's father criticized the son's maternal ties, whereupon Crane apparently announced that he would no longer associate with his father. As biographer John Unterecker noted in *Voyager: A Life of Hart Crane:* "[Crane's father] . . . turned white with rage, shouting that if Hart didn't apologize he would be disinherited. Hart climaxed the scene by screaming curses on his father and his father's money." The two men did not speak to each for the next two years.

Upon leaving his father's company, Crane stayed briefly in Cleveland, working for advertising companies. He then found similar work in New York City, but moving there hardly solved his ongoing personal problems. His mother continued to ply his sympathies by mail, regaling him with accounts of her emotional and physical troubles. Crane sought solace in sex but inevitably found heartbreak, for his infatuations with other men, including many sailors, went largely unreciprocated. Curiously, his fluctuating emotional state—which ranged from manic euphoria to dire depression, both exacerbated by alcohol abuse—led him to distort his childhood memories into fond recollections, though he managed to resist his mother's constant pleas to return to her home in Cleveland.

Poetry Earns Notice

By 1922 Crane had already written many of the poems that would comprise his first collection, *White Buildings.* Among the most important of these verses is "Chaplinesque," which he produced after viewing comic actor Charlie Chaplin's film *The Kid.* In this poem Chaplin's signature character—a fun-loving, mischievous tramp—represents the poet, whose own pursuit may be perceived as trivial but is nonetheless profound. For Crane, the tramp's optimism and sensitivity bear similarities to the poet's outlook on adversity, and his apparent disregard for his own persecution is an indication of his innocence: "We will sidestep, and to the final smirk / Dally the doom of that inevitable thumb / That slowly chafes its puckered index toward us, / Facing the dull squint with what innocence / And what surprise!"

In "Lachrymae Christi," another major poem from this period, Crane expresses a more profound sympathy for the poet, whose suffering inevitably leads to redemption. Here, through mysterious imagery and symbolism, Crane portrays Nature, specifically as it is renewed in springtime, as a reflection of the poet's own rejuvenation: "Lean long from sable, slender boughs, / Unstanched and luminous. And as the nights / Strike from Thee perfect spheres, / Lift up in lilac-emerald breath the grail / Of earth again—/ Thy face / From charred and riven stakes, O / Dionysus, Thy / Unmangled smile." In his volume *Hart Crane,* Vincent G. Quinn noted of this work that "the birthpangs of spring, and the anguish of the poet are presented as analogous instances of torment" and added: "From this gathering of pain, a chorus of triumph emerges."

Aside from "Chaplinesque" and "Lachrymae Christi," the most impressive poem Crane produced before 1924 was probably "For the Marriage of Faustus and Helen," a relatively expansive work reveling in the optimism that the poet believed was prevalent throughout America at the time. With this poem, he reinforces his own optimism by setting the marriage in contemporary times: Faustus rides a streetcar and Helen appears at a jazz club. Here Faustus represents the poet seeking ideal beauty, and Helen embodies that beauty. In the poem's concluding section, Helen's beauty encompasses the triumph of the times too, and Crane calls for recognition of the age as one in which the poetic imagination surpasses the despair of recent events, notably World War I: "Distinctly praise the years, whose volatile / Blamed bleeding hands extend and thresh the height / The imagination spans beyond despair, / Outpacing bargain, vocable and prayer."

Unfortunately, the optimism expressed in such poems as "For the Marriage of Faustus and Helen" was hardly indicative of Crane's emotional state at the time. Soon after completing the aforementioned poem in the spring of 1923, he moved back to New York City and found work at another advertising agency. Not surprisingly, he once again found the job tedious and unrewarding. Adding to his displeasure was the unwelcome tumult and cacophony of city occurrences. Automobile traffic, street vendors, and endless waves of marching pedestrians corrupted his concentration and stifled his imagination. By autumn Crane feared that his anxiety would soon lead to a nervous breakdown and so he fled the city for nearby Woodstock, New York. There he reveled in the relative tranquility of the rural environment and enjoyed the company of a few close friends.

Once revived, Crane returned to New York City. Soon afterwards he fell in love with a sailor, Emil Opffer, and their relationship—one of intense sexual passion and occasional turbulence—inspired "Voyages," a poetic sequence in praise of love. In *Hart Crane,* Quinn described this poem as "a celebration of the transforming power of love" and added that the work's "metaphor is the sea, and its movement is from the lover's dedication to a human and therefore changeable lover to a beloved beyond time and change." Here the sea represents love in all its shifting complexity from calm to storm, and love, in turn, serves as the salvation of us all: "Bind us in time, O Season clear, and awe. / O minstrel galleons of Carib fire, / Bequeath us to no earthly shore until / Is answered in the vortex of our grave / The seal's wide spindrift gaze toward paradise." With its dazzling poeticism and mysteriously inspiring perspective, this poem is often hailed as Crane's greatest achievement. R.W.B. Lewis, for instance, wrote in *The Poetry of Hart Crane* that the poem was Crane's "lyrical masterpiece."

The Bridge

By the time he finished "Voyages" in 1924, Crane had already commenced the first drafts of his ambitious poem *The Bridge,* which he intended, at least in part, as an uplifting alternative to T.S. Eliot's bleak masterwork *The Waste Land.* In this work, according to *New Criterion* reviewer Eric Ormsby, "Crane worked to articulate a voice that was radiantly affirmative while remaining unmistakably modern." In the poem's fifteen sections and sixty pages, Crane sought to provide a panorama of what he called "the American experience." Adopting the Brooklyn Bridge as the poem's sustaining symbol, he celebrates, in often hopelessly obscure imagery, various peoples and places—from explorer Christopher Columbus and the legendary Rip Van Winkle to the contemporary New England landscape and the East River tunnel. The bridge, in turn, serves as the structure uniting, and representing, all that is America. In addition, it functions as the embodiment of an uniquely American optimism and serves as a source of inspiration and patriotic devotion: "O Sleepless as the river under thee, / Vaulting the sea, the prairies' dreaming sod, / Unto us lowliest sometime sweep, descend / And of the curveship lend a myth to God."

In 1926, while Crane worked on *The Bridge,* his verse collection *White Buildings* was published. This work earned him substantial respect as an imposing stylist whose lyricism and imagery recalled the French Romantics Baudelaire and Rimbaud. It also prompted speculation that Crane was an imprecise and confused artist, one who sometimes settled for sound instead of sense. Edmund Wilson, for instance, wrote in *New Republic* that "though [Crane] can sometimes move us, the emotion is oddly vague." For Wilson, whose essay was later reprinted in *The Shores of Light,* Crane possesses "a style that is strikingly original—almost something like a great style, if there could be such a thing as a great style which was . . . not . . . applied to any subject at all."

Crane, for his part, responded to similar charges from *Poetry* editor Harriet Monroe by claiming, in an appropriately confused manner, that his poetry is consistent with the *illogicality* of the genre. "It all comes to the recognition," he declared, "that emotional dynamics are not to be confused with any absolute order of rationalized definitions; ergo, in poetry the *rationale* of metaphor belongs to another order of experience than science, and is not to be limited by a scientific and arbitrary code or relationships either in verbal inflections or concepts."

By the time *White Buildings* appeared in print, Crane's intense romantic relationship with Opffer had run its course. He returned to his former ways, enjoying promiscuity, abusing alcohol, and alternating between obnoxious euphoria and disturbing

depression. Constant conflicts with his mother further aggravated his already unstable demeanor, as did the death of his grandmother in 1928. More positively, Crane realized a reconciliation with his father around that time, but the parent's death soon afterward only served to plunge the poet once more into depression.

With his inheritance, Crane fled his manipulative mother and traveled to Europe. There he associated with prominent figures in Paris's American expatriate community, notably publisher and poet Harry Crosby, who murdered his mistress and killed himself the following year. Crane wrote little in Europe, indulging instead in drinking and carousing. When he returned to the United States he wallowed further in excessive alcohol consumption and sexual relations. Furthermore, his self-confidence was shaken by the disappointing reception accorded *The Bridge* by critics, many of whom expressed respect for his effort but dissatisfaction with his achievement. Even critics who deemed Crane's work a failure readily expressed respect for his creative undertaking, however. William Rose Benet, for instance, declared in the *Saturday Review of Literature* that Crane "failed in creating what might have been a truly great poem," but deemed *The Bridge* a "fascinating" work that "reveals potencies in the author that may make his next work even more remarkable." "Apart from questions of its ultimate success or failure," Miller stated in the *Dictionary of Literary Biography,* "*The Bridge* retains its character as a monumental experiment, and as such stands as a landmark in twentieth-century American poetry."

A Tragic End

Despite the continued respect accorded him by critics, Crane entered a creative slump from which he would not recover. Perhaps sensing a decline in his literary skills, he applied for a Guggenheim fellowship with the intention of studying European culture and the American poetic sensibility. After obtaining the fellowship, however, Crane traveled to Mexico and continued his self-destructive behavior. At this time he also experienced a heterosexual romance—presumably his only one—with Peggy Baird, who was then married to prominent literary figure Malcolm Cowley. During this time Crane wrote only infrequently, producing largely inferior work that confirmed his fear that his talent had declined significantly. Finally, in 1932, his despair turned all-consuming, and on April 27, while traveling by ship with Baird, Crane killed himself by leaping into the Gulf of Mexico.

In the years since his death, Crane has earned recognition as an ambitious and accomplished—if not entirely successful—poet, one whose goals vastly exceeded his capabilities (and, probably, anyone else's) but whose talent nonetheless enabled him to explore the limits of self-expression both provocatively and profoundly. Allen Tate, writing in his *Essays of Four Decades,* assessed Crane's artistic achievement as an admirable, but unavoidable, failure. Tate noted that Crane, like the earlier Romantics, attempted the overwhelming imposition of his own will in his poetry, and in so doing reached the point at which his will, and thus his art, became self-reflexive, and thus self-destructive. "By attempting an extreme solution to the romantic problem," Tate contended, "Crane proved that it cannot be solved." Writing in *Poetry,* William Logan stated: "In the case of Hart Crane, there can be no last word. His star has been up and down so often . . . since his death, it seems unlikely that critic or reader will settle the matter soon. Crane was the great might-have-been of American verse—superbly talented, ambitious as a hammer blow, full of plans and postures and persuasions galore."

If you enjoy the works of Hart Crane, you may also want to check out the following books:

Walt Whitman, *Leaves of Grass,* an epic poem published in nine editions, 1855-92.
Waldo Frank, *Our America,* 1919.
William Carlos Williams, *Paterson,* a five-volume poem, 1946-58.

Other critics have tended to share Tate's general assessment of Crane as a flawed but nonetheless invaluable poet. R.P. Blackmur, in his essay collection *The Double Agent,* acknowledged the poet's shortcomings and accepted that in reading Crane one "must make allowances for him." "Merely because Crane is imperfect in his kind is no reason to give him up," Blackmur added; "there is no plethora of perfection, and the imperfect beauty, like life, retains its fascination. And there is about him, too—such were his gifts for the hearts of words, such the vitality of his intelligence—the distraught but exciting splendour of a great failure." Likewise laudatory was poet Brother Antonius, who wrote in *Commonweal* that Crane, despite his failings, achieved much as an artist. "Woefully deficient in the stabilizing apprehension of the concrete," An-

tonius conceded. Crane nonetheless "purchased a kind of heroic redemption, in that he was enabled to register most vividly reality as he did apprehend it . . . , and hence make of his death that sacrifice by which an age enables those whom it destroys to accomplish what we others need to know."

■ Biographical and Critical Sources

BOOKS

Blackmur, R.P., *The Double Agent: Essays in Craft and Elucidation,* Arrow Editions (New York, NY), 1935.

Bloom, Harold, editor, *Hart Crane,* Chelsea House (Philadelphia, PA), 2003.

Butterfield, R.W., *The Broken Arch: A Study of Hart Crane,* Oliver & Boyd (Edinburgh, Scotland), 1969.

Clark, David R., editor, *The Merrill Studies in "The Bridge,"* Merrill (Columbus, OH), 1970.

Clark, David R., editor, *Critical Essays on Hart Crane,* G.K. Hall (Boston, MA), 1982.

Combs, Robert, *Vision of the Voyage: Hart Crane and the Psychology of Romanticism,* Memphis State University Press (Memphis, TN), 1978.

Cowley, Malcolm, *Exile's Return: A Literary Odyssey of the 1920s,* Viking (New York, NY), 1951.

Crane, Hart, *The Collected Poems of Hart Crane,* edited by Waldo Frank, Liveright (New York, NY), 1933.

Dembo, L.S., *Hart Crane's Sanskrit Charge: A Study of The Bridge,* Cornell University Press (Ithaca, NY), 1960.

Dictionary of Literary Biography, Gale (Detroit, MI), Volume 4: *American Writers in Paris, 1920-1939,* 1980, Volume 48: *American Poets, 1880-1945, Second Series,* 1986, Volume 288: *The House of Boni & Liveright, 1917-1933, A Documentary Volume,* 2004.

Fisher, Clive, *Hart Crane,* Yale University Press (New Haven, CT), 2002.

Frank, Waldo, *In the American Jungle: 1925-1936,* Farrar & Rinehart (New York, NY), 1937.

Hanley, Alfred, *Hart Crane's Holy Vision: "White Buildings,"* Duquesne University Press (Pittsburgh, PA), 1981.

Hazo, Samuel, *Hart Crane: An Introduction and Interpretation,* Barnes & Noble (New York, NY), 1963.

Horton, Philip, *Hart Crane: The Life of an American Poet,* Norton (New York, NY), 1937.

Leibowitz, Herbert A., *Hart Crane: An Introduction to the Poetry,* Columbia University Press (New York, NY), 1968.

Lewis, R.W.B., *The Poetry of Hart Crane: A Critical Study,* Princeton University Press (Princeton, NJ), 1967.

Mariani, Paul, *The Broken Tower: A Life of Hart Crane,* Norton (New York, NY), 1999.

Munson, Gorham B., *Destinations: A Canvass of American Literature since 1900,* J.H. Sears (New York, NY), 1928.

Nilsen, Helge Normann, *Hart Crane's Divided Vision: An Analysis of The Bridge,* Universitetssforlaget (Oslo, Norway), 1980.

Paul, Sherman, *Hart's "Bridge,"* University of Illinois Press (Urbana, IL), 1972.

Perry, Robert L., *The Shared Vision of Waldo Frank and Hart Crane,* University of Nebraska Press (Lincoln, NE), 1966.

Poetry Criticism, Volume 3, Gale (Detroit, MI), 1999.

Quinn, Vincent G., *Hart Crane,* Twayne (New York, NY), 1963.

Reed, Brian M., *Hart Crane: After His Lights,* University of Alabama Press (Tuscaloosa, AL), 2006.

Schwartz, Joseph, *Hart Crane: A Reference Guide,* G.K. Hall (Boston, MA), 1983.

Spears, Monroe K., *Hart Crane,* University of Minneapolis Press (Minneapolis, MN), 1965.

Sugg, Richard P., *Hart Crane's "The Bridge": A Description of Its Life,* University of Alabama Press (Tuscaloosa, AL), 1976.

Tate, Allen, *Essays of Four Decades,* Swallow Press (Chicago, IL), 1968.

Trachtenbert, Alan, editor, *Hart Crane: A Collection of Critical Essays,* Prentice-Hall (Englewood Cliffs, NJ), 1982.

Twentieth-Century Literary Criticism, Gale (Detroit, MI), Volume 2, 1979, Volume 5, 1981, Volume 80, 1999.

Unterecker, John, *Voyager: A Life of Hart Crane,* Farrar, Strauss (New York, NY), 1969.

Uroff, M.D., *Hart Crane: The Patterns of His Poetry,* University of Illinois Press (Urbana, IL), 1974.

Weber, Brom, *Hart Crane: A Biographical and Critical Study,* Bodley Press (New York, NY), 1948.

Wilson, Edmund, *The Shores of Light: A Literary Chronicle of the Twenties and Thirties,* Farrar, Straus (New York, NY), 1952.

PERIODICALS

American Literature, March, 1967, Joseph J. Arpad, "Hart Crane's Platonic Myth: The Brooklyn Bridge," pp. 75-86; March, 1968, L.S. Dembo, "Hart Crane's 'Verticalist' Poem," pp. 77-81.

Arizona Quarterly, spring, 1964, Deena Posy Metzger, "Hart Crane's Bridge: The Myth Active," pp. 36-46.

Commonweal, October 26, 1962, Brother Antonius, profile of Crane.

ELH, December, 1966, Joseph Riddel, "Hart Crane's Poetics of Failure," pp. 473-496.

New Criterion, February, 2001, Eric Ormsby, "The Last Elizabethan: Hart Crane at 100," p. 12.

New Leader, August 31, 1953, Allen Tate, "The Self-made Angel," pp. 17-21; April 7, 1986, Phoebe Pettingell, "The Poems of Hart Crane," p. 21.

New Republic, April 23, 1930, Malcolm Cowley, "A Preface to Hart Crane," pp. 276-277; March 16, 1927, Waldo Frank, "The Poetry of Hart Crane," pp. 116-117.

New York Times, January 28, 2007, William Logan, "Hart Crane's Bridge to Nowhere."

PMLA, March, 1951, Stanley K. Coffman, Jr., "Symbolism in *The Bridge,*" pp. 65-77; January, 1981, Donald Pease, "Blake, Crane, Whitman, and Modernism: A Poetics of Pure Possibility," pp. 64-85.

Poetry, October, 2008, William Logan, "On Reviewing Hart Crane," p. 53.

Saturday Review of Literature, July 5, 1930, William Rose Benet, review of *The Bridge.*

Sewanee Review, January-March, 1950, Barbara Herman, "The Language of Hart Crane," pp. 52-67; spring, 1981, Malcolm Cowley, "Two Views of *The Bridge,*" pp. 191-205.

Southern Review, July, 1975, Thomas Parkinson, "Hart Crane and Yvor Winters: A Meeting of Minds," pp. 491-512.

ONLINE

Poets.org, http://www.poets.org/ (July 1, 2009), "Hart Crane."*

(Photograph © by Hulton-Deutsch Collection/Corbis.)

Walter de la Mare

■ Personal

Born April 25, 1873, in Charlton, Kent, England; died June 22, 1956, in Twickenham, Middlesex, England; buried at St. Paul's Cathedral, London, England; son of James Edward (a church warden) and Lucy Sophia (Browning) de la Mare; married Constance Elfrida Ingpen, 1899 (died, 1943); children: Dick, Florence, Jenny, Colin. *Education:* Attended St. Paul's Cathedral Choir School (London, England).

■ Career

Poet, novelist, short-story writer, critic, essayist, anthologist, and dramatist. Anglo-American (Standard) Oil Company, London, England, clerk in statistics department, 1890-1908. Reviewer for London *Times, Westminster Gazette, Bookman,* and other London journals.

■ Member

Athenaeum Club.

■ Awards, Honors

Polignac Prize, Royal Society of Literature, 1911; James Tait Black Memorial Prize for fiction, 1922, for *Memoirs of a Midget;* Carnegie Medal, American Library Association, 1947, for *Collected Stories for Children;* named companion of honour, 1948; received Order of Merit, 1953; Foyle Poetry Prize, 1954; honorary degrees from universities, including Oxford, Cambridge, St. Andrews, Bristol, and London.

■ Writings

FICTION

Henry Brocken: His Travels and Adventures in the Rich, Strange, Scarce-Imaginable Regions of Romance (novel), J. Murray (London, England), 1904, Knopf (New York, NY), 1924.

The Return (novel), Arnold (London, England), 1910, Putnam (New York, NY), 1911, revised edition, Knopf (New York, NY), 1922, published with a new introduction by S.T. Joshi, Dover Publications (Mineola, NY), 1997.

Memoirs of a Midget (novel), Collins (London, England), 1921, Knopf (New York, NY), 1922, with a foreword by Alison Lurie, Paul Dry Books (Philadelphia, PA), 2004.

Lispet, Lispett, and Vaine (short stories), Morland Press (London, England), 1923.

The Riddle, Selwyn & Blount (London, England), 1923, published as *The Riddle and Other Tales*, Knopf (New York, NY), 1923.

Ding Dong Bell (short stories), Knopf (New York, NY), 1924.

Two Tales: The Green-Room, The Connoisseur, Bookman's Journal (London, England), 1925.

The Connoisseur and Other Stories, Knopf (New York, NY), 1926.

At First Sight (short stories), Crosby Gaige (New York, NY), 1928.

On the Edge: Short Stories, wood engravings by Elizabeth Rivera, Faber (London, England), 1930, Knopf (New York, NY), 1931.

Seven Short Stories, illustrated by John Nash, Faber (London, England), 1931.

A Forward Child (short stories), Faber (London, England), 1934.

The Nap and Other Stories, Nelson (London, England), 1936.

The Wind Blows Over (short stories), Macmillan (New York, NY), 1936.

Ghost Stories, illustrated by Barnett Freedman, Folio Society (London, England), 1936.

The Picnic and Other Stories, Faber (London, England), 1941.

Best Stories of Walter de la Mare, Faber (London, England), 1942.

The Collected Tales of Walter de la Mare, edited by Edward Wagenknecht, Knopf (New York, NY), 1950.

A Beginning and Other Stories, Faber (London, England), 1955.

Best Stories, Faber (London, England), 1957.

Some Stories, Faber (London, England), 1962.

Eight Tales, Arkham House (Sauk City, WI), 1971.

Short Stories, 1895-1926, edited by Giles de la Mare, Giles de la Mare Publishers (London, England), 1996.

POETRY

Poems, Murray (London, England), 1906.

The Listeners and Other Poems, Constable (London, England), 1912, Holt (New York, NY), 1916.

The Old Men, Flying Fame (London, England), 1913.

The Sunken Garden and Other Poems, Beaumont Press (London, England), 1917, published as *The Sunken Garden and Other Verses*, Birmingham School of Printing (Birmingham, England), 1931.

Motley and Other Poems, Holt (New York, NY), 1918.

Flora, illustrated by Pamela Bianco, Lippincott (Philadelphia, PA), 1919.

Poems 1901 to 1918, two volumes, Constable (London, England), 1920, published as *Collected Poems 1901 to 1918*, two volumes, Holt (New York, NY), 1920.

The Veil and Other Poems, Constable (London, England), 1921, Holt (New York, NY), 1922.

Thus Her Tale: A Poem, illustrated by William Oglivie, Porpoise Press (Edinburgh, Scotland), 1923.

A Ballad of Christmas, Selwyn & Blount (London, England), 1924.

The Hostage, Selwyn & Blount (London, England), 1925.

(With Rudyard Kipling) *St. Andrews: Two Poems*, A. & C. Black (London, England), 1926.

Walter de la Mare, edited by Edward Thompson, Benn (London, England), 1926.

Alone, wood engravings by Blair Hughes-Stanton, Faber & Gwyer (London, England), 1927.

Selected Poems, Holt (New York, NY), 1927.

The Captive and Other Poems, Bowling Green Press (New York, NY), 1928.

Self to Self, Faber (London, England), 1928.

A Snowdrop, illustrated by Claudia Guercio, Faber (London, England), 1929.

News, illustrated by Barnett Freedman, Faber (London, England), 1930.

To Lucy, illustrated by Albert Rutherston, Faber (London, England), 1931.

Two Poems, privately printed, 1931.

The Fleeting and Other Poems, Knopf (New York, NY), 1933.

Poems 1919 to 1934, Constable (London, England), 1935, Holt (New York, NY), 1936.

Poems, Corvinus Press (London, England), 1937.

Memory and Other Poems, Holt (New York, NY), 1938.

(With Arthur Rogers) *Two Poems*, privately printed, 1938.

Haunted: A Poem, Linden Press (London, England), 1939.

Collected Poems, Holt (New York, NY), 1941.

Time Passes and Other Poems, edited by Anne Ridler, Faber (London, England), 1942.

Collected Rhymes and Verse, illustrated by Berthold Wolpe, Faber (London, England), 1944, illustrated by Errol Le Cain, 1970.

The Burning-Glass, Viking Press (New York, NY), 1945, illustrated by John Piper, Faber (London, England), 1946.

The Traveller, Faber (London, England), 1946.

Two Poems: Pride, The Truth of Things, Dropmore Press (London, England), 1946.

Inward Companion, Faber (London, England), 1950.

Winged Chariot and Other Poems, Viking (New York, NY), 1951.

O Lovely England, and Other Poems, Faber (London, England), 1953, Viking (New York, NY), 1956.

Selected Poems, edited by R.N. Green-Armytage, Faber (London, England), 1954.

The Winnowing Dream, illustrated by Robin Jacques, Faber (London, England), 1954.

The Morrow, privately printed, 1955.

Collected Poems, illustrated by Berthold Wolpe, Faber (London, England), 1961.

Poems, edited by Eleanor Graham, illustrated by Margery Gill, Penguin (New York, NY), 1962.

Walter de la Mare, edited by John Hadfield, Vista Books (London, England), 1962.

A Choice of de la Mare's Verse, edited and with an introduction by W.H. Auden, Faber (London, England), 1963.

Envoi, privately printed, 1965.

The Complete Poems of Walter de la Mare, edited by Leonard Clark and others, Faber (London, England), 1969, Knopf (New York, NY), 1970.

The Collected Poems of Walter de la Mare, Faber (London, England), 1979.

FOR CHILDREN

(Under pseudonym Walter Ramal) *Songs of Childhood* (poetry), Longmans Green (London, England), 1902, revised edition (published under name Walter de la Mare), Longman (London, England), 1916, new edition published as *Songs of Childhood,* illustrated by Estella Canziani, 1923, reprinted, Granger Book Co, 1984, illustrated by Marion Rivers-Moore, Faber (London, England), 1956.

The Three Mulla-Mulgars (fiction), illustrated by J.R. Monsell, Duckworth (London, England), 1910, illustrated by Dorothy P. Lathrop, Knopf (New York, NY), 1919, illustrated by J.A. Shepherd, Selwyn & Blount (London, England), 1924, published as *The Three Royal Monkeys,* illustrated by Mildred E. Eldridge, Faber (London, England), 1969.

A Child's Day (poetry), illustrated by Carine Cadby and Will Cadby, Constable (London, England), 1912, illustrated by Winifred Bromhall, Holt (New York, NY), 1923.

Peacock Pie (poetry), Constable (London, England), 1913, illustrated by W. Heath Robinson, 1916, illustrated by Jocelyn Crow, Holt (New York, NY), 1936, illustrated by Edward Ardizzone, Faber (London, England), 1946, illustrated by Barbara Cooney, Knopf (New York, NY), 1961, revised edition, Faber (London, England), 1969, Holt (New York, NY), 1989.

Crossings: A Fairy Play, music by Cecil Armstrong Gibbs, illustrated by Randolph Schwabe (produced in Sussex, England, 1919; produced in London, England, 1925), Beaumont Press, 1921, illustrated by Dorothy P. Lathrop, Knopf (New York, NY), 1923, illustrated by Gwendolen Raverat, Faber (London, England), 1942.

Story and Rhyme (fiction), Dutton (New York, NY), 1921.

Down-Adown-Derry (poetry), illustrated by Dorothy P. Lathrop, Holt (New York, NY), 1922.

(Editor, with Alec Buckels) *Come Hither,* illustrated by Buckels, Knopf (New York, NY), 1923, revised edition, 1928.

(Editor, with Thomas Quayle) *Readings: Traditional Tales Told by the Author,* illustrated by A.H. Watson and C.T. Nightingale, six volumes, Blackwell (Oxford, England), 1925–1928, in one volume, Knopf (New York, NY), 1927.

Broomsticks and Other Tales (fiction), illustrated by Bold, Knopf (New York, NY), 1925.

Miss Jemima (fiction), illustrated by Alec Buckels, Basil Blackwell (Oxford, England), 1925, Artists and Writers Guild (Poughkeepsie, NY), 1935, published as *The Story of Miss Jemima,* illustrated by Nellie H. Farnam, Grosset & Dunlap (New York, NY), 1940.

(With others) *Number Three Joy Street,* Appleton (New York, NY), 1925.

(With others) *Number Four Joy Street,* Appleton (New York, NY), 1926.

(With others) *Number Five Joy Street,* Appleton (New York, NY), 1927.

Lucy, illustrated by Hilda T. Miller, Basil Blackwell (Oxford, England), 1927.

Old Joe (fiction), illustrated by C.T. Nightingale, Basil Blackwell (Oxford, England), 1927.

Stuff and Nonsense and So On (poetry), woodcuts by Bold, Holt (New York, NY), 1927, revised edition, Faber (London, England), 1946, illustrated by Margaret Wolpe, Faber (London, England), 1957.

Told Again: Traditional Tales, illustrated by A.H. Watson, Blackwell (Oxford, England), 1927, published as *Told Again: Old Tales Told Again,* Knopf (New York, NY), 1927, published as *Tales Told Again,* illustrated by Alan Howard, Faber/Knopf (New York, NY), 1959.

(With others) *Number Six Joy Street,* Appleton (New York, NY), 1928.

Stories from the Bible, illustrated by Theodore Nadejen, Cosmopolitan, (New York, NY), 1929, illustrated by Irene Hawkins, Faber (London, England), 1947, illustrated by Edward Ardizzone, Knopf (New York, NY), 1961, reprinted, 1977.

Poems for Children, Holt (New York, NY), 1930.

The Dutch Cheese and the Lovely Myfanwy (fiction), illustrated by Dorothy P. Lathrop, Knopf (New York, NY), 1931, illustrated by Irene Hawkins, Faber (London, England), 1946.

(Editor) *Tom Tiddler's Ground: A Book of Poetry for the Junior and Middle Schools,* illustrations from Thomas Bewick, three volumes, Collins (London, England), 1931, illustrated by Margery Gill, one volume, Knopf (New York, NY), 1962.

(Editor) *Old Rhymes and New, Chosen for Use in Schools,* two volumes, Constable (London, England), 1932.

The Lord Fish and Other Tales (fiction), illustrated by Rex Whistler, Faber (London, England), 1933, Candlewick Press (Cambridge, MA), 1997.

Letters from Mr. Walter de la Mare to Form Three, privately printed, 1936.

(With Harold Jones) *This Year: Next Year* (poetry), illustrated by Jones, Holt (New York, NY), 1937.

Animal Stories, Chosen, Arranged, and in Some Part Re-Written, Faber (London, England), 1939, Scribner (New York, NY), 1940.

Bells and Grass: A Book of Rhymes, illustrated by F. Rowland Emett, Faber (London, England), 1941, illustrated by Dorothy P. Lathrop, Viking (New York, NY), 1942.

The Old Lion and Other Stories (fiction), illustrated by Irene Hawkins, Faber (London, England), 1942.

Mr. Bumps and His Monkey (fiction), illustrated by Dorothy P. Lathrop, J.C. Winston (Philadelphia, PA), 1942.

The Magic Jacket, and Other Stories, illustrated by Irene Hawkins, Faber (London, England), 1943, illustrated by Paul Kennedy, Knopf (New York, NY), 1962.

The Scarecrow and Other Stories, illustrated by Irene Hawkins, Faber (London, England), 1945.

The Dutch Cheese and Other Stories, illustrated by Irene Hawkins, Faber (London, England), 1946.

Collected Stories for Children, illustrated by Irene Hawkins, Faber (London, England), 1947, illustrated by Robin Jacques, 1967.

Rhymes and Verses: Collected Poems for Children, illustrated by Elinore Blaisdell, Holt (New York, NY), 1947, reprinted, 2002.

Dick Whittington (adapted from a story in *Told Again*), illustrated by Ionicus, Hulton (London, England), 1951.

Jack and the Beanstalk (adapted from a story in *Told Again*), illustrated by William and Brenda Stobbs, Hulton (London, England), 1951.

Selected Stories and Verses, edited by Eleanor Graham, Penguin (New York, NY), 1952.

The Story of Joseph, illustrated by Edward Ardizzone, Faber (London, England), 1958.

The Story of Moses, illustrated by Edward Ardizzone, Knopf (New York, NY), 1960.

The Story of Samuel and Saul, illustrated by Edward Ardizzone, Faber (London, England), 1960.

A Penny a Day (fiction), illustrated by Paul Kennedy, Knopf (New York, NY), 1960.

Molly Whuppie, illustrated by Errol Le Cain, Farrar, Straus (New York, NY), 1983.

The Voice: A Sequence of Poems, edited and illustrated by Catherine Brighton, Faber (London, England), 1986, Delacorte (New York, NY), 1987.

Visitors, Creative Education (Mankato, MN), 1986.

The Three Sillies, Creative Education (Mankato, MN), 1991.

The Turnip, illustrated by Kevin Hawkes, D.R. Godine (Boston, MA), 1992.

COLLECTIONS AND SELECTIONS

Stories, Essays, and Poems, edited by M.M. Bozman, Dent (London, England), 1938.

Walter de la Mare: A Selection from His Writings, edited by Kenneth Hopkins, Faber (London, England), 1956.

Secret Laughter, illustrated by Margery Gill, Penguin (New York, NY), 1969.

(Author of poems) Richard Rodney Bennett, *Dream-Songs: For Unison Voices or Solo Voice and Piano,* Novello (London, England), 1990.

OTHER

M.E. Coleridge: An Appreciation, The Guardian (London, England), 1907.

Rupert Brooke and the Intellectual Imagination: A Lecture, Sidgwick & Jackson (London, England), 1919, Harcourt (New York, NY), 1920.

Some Thoughts on Reading (lecture), Yellowlands Press, 1923.

Some Women Novelists of the 'Seventies, Cambridge University Press (London, England), 1929.

(Editor) *Desert Islands and Robinson Crusoe* (literary quotations and discussion), illustrated by Rex Whistler, Fountain Press, 1930, revised edition, Faber (London, England), 1932.

(Editor) Christina Rossetti, *Poems,* Gregynog Press (Newton, England), 1930.

(Editor) *The Eighteen-eighties: Essays by Fellows of the Royal Society of Literature,* Macmillan (New York, NY), 1930.

The Printing of Poetry (lecture), Cambridge University Press (London, England), 1931.

The Early Novels of Wilkie Collins, Cambridge University Press (London, England), 1932.

Lewis Carroll, Faber (London, England), 1932.

Early One Morning in the Spring: Chapters on Children and on Childhood as It Is Revealed in Particular in Early Memories and in Early Writings, Macmillan (New York, NY), 1935.

Poetry in Prose (lecture), H. Milford (London, England), 1935, Oxford University Press (New York, NY), 1937.

Arthur Thompson: A Memoir, privately printed, 1938.

An Introduction to Everyman, Dent (London, England), 1938.

(Editor) *Behold, This Dreamer!* (essays), Knopf (New York, NY), 1939.

Pleasures and Speculations (essays), Faber (London, England), 1940, Books for Libraries Press (Freeport, NY), 1969.

(Editor) *Love*, Faber (London, England), 1943, Morrow (New York, NY), 1946.

Private View (essays), Faber (London, England), 1953, Hyperion (New York, NY), 1979.

■ **Adaptations**

The television program *Reading Out Loud: Archibald MacLeish*, featuring a reading of de la Mare's poems, was produced for Westinghouse Broadcasting in 1960. Some of de la Mare's poems were included in Cecil Armstrong Gibbs's musical suite, *In a Dream's Beguiling.*

■ **Sidelights**

Walter de la Mare is considered one of modern literature's chief exemplars of the romantic imagination. His complete works form a sustained treatment of romantic themes: dreams, death, rare states of mind and emotion, fantasy worlds of childhood, and the pursuit of the transcendent. Commenting on Walter de la Mare's literary diversity, *Dictionary of Literary Biography* contributor Michael Kirkham stated that the author "will be remembered chiefly as a poet and writer of children's verse, the two genres not always clearly distinguishable in his work. But until 1928 he was also a novelist and until the mid-1930s a short-story writer; he was an anthologist of great individuality, an essayist, and a reviewer." According to Eric Linn Ormsby in the *New Criterion*, "De la Mare has been called a Romantic or a Symbolist, but these designations sit uneasily on his work; in his verse, the moon is always itself, cold and alone and afloat beyond all our longing. Of course, one of the advantages of official unimportance is that it baffles our categories. To categorize de la Mare is to catch at a fog with tweezers."

De la Mare's life was outwardly uneventful. Born in 1873, he attended St. Paul's Cathedral school in London, where he became founder and editor of the *Choristers' Journal*. At age seventeen, too poor to continue his education, he began working as a clerk for the Anglo-American Oil Company and he also edited and wrote for the company's internal publication. De la Mare retained his bookkeeping position with the Anglo-American Oil Company—a cheerless work—for eighteen years, until he received a government pension that enabled him to become a full-time writer. His first published short story, "Kismet," appeared in the journal *Sketch* in 1895.

Releases Significant Volume of Poetry

In 1902 de la Mare published his first major work, the poetry collection *Songs of Childhood*, which was recognized as a significant example of children's literature for its creative imagery and variety of meters. Like his other early books and magazine stories, it was printed under the pseudonym Walter Ramal ("Ramal" being an anagram of "de la Mare"). Critics often assert that a childlike richness of imagination influenced everything de la Mare wrote, emphasizing his frequent depiction of childhood as a time of intuition, deep emotion, and closeness to spiritual truth. In 1908, following the publication of his novel *Henry Brocken: His Travels and Adventures in the Rich, Strange, Scarce-Imaginable Regions of Romance* and the poetry collection titled *Poems*, de la Mare was granted a Civil List pension, enabling him to terminate his corporate employment and focus exclusively on writing.

The appearance of *Songs of Childhood* introduced de la Mare as a talented author of children's literature, a genre in which he produced collections of fiction and verse, and several highly praised anthologies. Conrad Aiken, writing in his *Scepticisms: Notes on Contemporary Poetry* in 1919 found that de la Mare's *Peacock Pie* "contains some of the most delightful work he has done." The world of childhood, however, is only a facet of de la Mare's work, though critics have remarked that a childlike richness of imagination informs everything he wrote. According to a contributor in the *St. James Guide to Children's Writers*, "De la Mare was a profoundly platonic thinker who felt that children lived closer to primal truths, being as yet unshadowed by the miseries and burdens of adult life. He resisted the temptation to idealize, and several stories, . . ., reveal the callousness, even cruelty of the young; but despite their prevailing self-absorption, children seem to him powerfully, if only too briefly, in contact with underlying spiritual truths."

In order to entertain his own children, de la Mare wrote his best-known novel, *The Three Mulla-Mulgars* (later reprinted as *The Three Royal Monkeys*).

Illustration by Estella Canziani from Walter de la Mare's *Songs of Childhood,* **a work first published in 1902.** (Granger Book Company, Inc., 1984. Reproduced by permission.)

The world of *The Three Mulla-Mulgars* "is inhabited primarily by the various races of monkeys ('Mulgars'), among whom man is only another subspecies (or 'Oomgar-Mulgar')," noted the contributor in the *St. James Guide to Children's Writers,* who also observed that "the highest in rank are the 'Mulla-Mulgars' or royal monkeys such as the book's heroes, the brothers Thumb, Thimble, and Nod. Their quest for the paradisal land of Tishnar, their destined home, provides the main narrative thread." Some critics who enjoyed reading *The Three Mulla-Mulgars* questioned whether the writing style is sufficiently accessible to young readers. For example, *Junior Bookshelf* reviewer M.S. Crouch asserted that the work is "difficult for children to read themselves, for its strange names and its complex symbolism." However, Crouch also said that "it is, for all that, a very great children's book, a great adventure-story, superbly told." De la Mare's novel is regarded by some critics as a precursor to such modern British fantasies as J.R.R. Tolkien's *Lord of the Rings* and Richard Adams' *Watership Down.* "Today de la Mare's works are frequently overlooked in favor of more recent authors," noted *Writ-*

ers for Children contributor Ellin Greene, who added that "the loss is ours. His fantasies are every bit as good as those by Tolkien, C.S. Lewis, and Lloyd Alexander. His poems and stories are part of the canon of children's literature."

A Celebrated Writer

In general, critics have especially praised de la Mare's appreciation for the imaginative life of childhood. "Looking back over the years since *Songs of Childhood* and *Peacock Pie* first became widely known," wrote *Horn Book* contributor Margery Bianco in a 1942 issue devoted to consideration of the author, "one can only now begin to realize how great has been Walter de la Mare's influence upon the whole field of imaginative literature for children, and the full significance of his contribution. . . . When he speaks of a tree, a bird, a flower, it is as though one were seeing it—really seeing it—for the first time, through the eyes of one who is sensitive to beauty in whatever form, even under the guise of what is called ugliness."

As a poet de la Mare is often compared with Thomas Hardy and William Blake for their respective themes of mortality and visionary illumination. His greatest concern was the creation of a dreamlike tone implying a tangible but nonspecific transcendent reality. This characteristic of the poems has drawn many admirers, though also eliciting criticism that the poet indulged in an undefined sense of mystery without systematic acceptance of any specific doctrine. As Ormsby stated, "It would be going too far to call de la Mare's misty-mindedness a credo, let alone to claim it as the foundation of an aesthetic; and yet, for all his love of the nebulous, which abhors formulation, his poems create a distinctive, and powerful, impression." Some commentators also criticize the poetry for having an archness of tone more suitable for children's verse, while others value this playful quality. It is generally agreed, however, that de la Mare was a skillful manipulator of poetic structure, a skill which is particularly evident in the earlier collections. "De la Mare used the music of words as a way of extending them," Ormsby stated. "He wanted words to be suffused with a sort of penumbra; he wanted them to cast a spell. Enchantment was what he was after. Words served as contrivances of enchantment but they served deeper purposes as well; they were secret accomplices in his quest for something just beyond them, something scarcely audible, akin perhaps to the 'unheard melodies' of [John] Keats."

Writing in the *Wilson Quarterly*, Anthony Hecht noted that "de la Mare's poetry is richly, sometimes dreamily, melodic, and the subtlety and skill of his prosody probably derives in part from his familiarity with folk literature and traditional English nursery rhymes." The critic also noted, however, that "readers should immediately be warned against supposing such rifles promise a poetry that is 'twee' or sentimental. De la Mare was keenly aware that the imagination of a child is haunted by spirits, ghosts, crime, and danger, as well as by moods of deep sorrow and overpowering fear." Discussing de la Mare's poetry, Kirkham warned against seeing him as primarily a writer for children: "De la Mare's double poetic vocation, as writer of poems for adults and writer of children's verse, has confused his reputation. It is often mistakenly assumed that poetry about children and from the child's consciousness is heavily represented in his adult volumes, and such poems have received disproportionate attention from the commentators. . . . De la Mare wrote more such poems than poets commonly do, but in fact they form a very small part of his serious work."

With *The Burning Glass and Other Poems* critics perceived a falling off from the author's past artistic virtuosity, which afterward was only periodically regained. According to Henry Charles Duffin in his *Walter de la Mare: A Study of His Poetry* (1949), the "poetry of Walter de la Mare is not essentially either a criticism of life or (as some think it) an escape from life. It will fulfill both these functions for those who require them, but the primary end of de la Mare's poetry is to heighten life."

Imaginative Tales

Closely linked with his poetry in theme and mood are de la Mare's short stories. Collections like *The Riddle* are imbued with the same indefiniteness and aura of fantasy as his poetry. In a review of *The Connoisseur, and Other Stories*, a critic for the *Times Literary Supplement* asserted in 1926 that "de la Mare has the poet's imagination, and it is a poetic emotion that delights us in his stories." As a short story writer, de la Mare is frequently compared to Henry James, particularly for his elaborate prose style and his ambiguous, often obscure treatment of supernatural themes. This latter quality is particularly apparent in de la Mare's frequently discussed short story "The Riddle," in which seven children go to live with their grandmother after the death of their father. The grandmother warns the children that they may play anywhere in the house except in an old oak chest in one of the spare bedrooms. Nevertheless, the children are drawn by ones and twos to play in the trunk, where they mysteriously disappear. While the meaning of their disappearance remains enigmatic, commentators have generally interpreted the events as a symbolic presentation of aging and death. "Virtually nothing about Walter de la Mare is straightforward or clear-cut; there are no cheap and easy resolutions," remarked a contributor in the *St. James Guide to Horror, Ghost, and Gothic Writers*. "That is precisely why, as a writer, he fascinates so. He writes, as it were, not of something rushing towards us, gabbling and gobbling, but of something just glimpsed, momentarily, at the peripheries of one's vision. The kind of glimpse that, at its worst, can truly raise the hairs at the back of the neck."

The novels of de la Mare rival his poetry in importance. His early novels, such as *Henry Brocken*, are works of fantasy written in a genre traditionally reserved for realistic subjects. In his tale of supernatural possession, *The Return,* de la Mare deals with a primarily naturalistic world while maintaining a fantastic element as the thematic core. Even though it contains no fantasy in a strict sense, *Memoirs of a Midget* includes a strong ingredient of the unusual and is considered by many critics to be a masterpiece. Storm Jameson in the *English Review* called the novel "the most notable achievement in prose fiction of our generation," and J.C. Squire, in his *Books Reviewed: Critical Essays on Books and Authors*, judged *Memoirs of a Midget* "a poet's book. I can think of no prose book by an English poet which is a more substantial achievement." The definitive de la Mare novel, *Memoirs* is a study of the social and spiritual outsider, a concern central to the author's work.

If you enjoy the works of Walter de la Mare, you may also want to check out the following books:

Frances Hodgson Burnett, *The Secret Garden*, 1911.
Roald Dahl, *The BFG*, 1982.
Robert Westall, *Demons and Shadows: The Ghostly Best Stories of Robert Westall*, 1993.

For his extravagance of invention, de la Mare is sometimes labeled an escapist who retreats from accepted definitions of reality and the relationships of conventional existence. His approach to reality, however, is not escapist; rather, it profoundly explores the world he considered most significant— that of the imagination. In the *London Mercury* J.B. Priestly favorably concluded in 1924 that de la Mare is "one of that most lovable order of artists who never lose sight of their childhood, but re-live it continually in their work and contrive to find expression for their maturity in it, memories and impressions, its romantic vision of the world."

■ **Biographical and Critical Sources**

BOOKS

Aiken, Conrad, *Scepticisms: Notes on Contemporary Poetry*, Knopf (New York, NY), 1919, reprinted by Books for Libraries Press (Freeport, NY), 1967.

Atkins, John, *Walter de la Mare: An Exploration*, C. & J. Temple (London, England), 1947.

Avery, Gillian, and Julia Briggs, *Children and Their Books: A Celebration of the Work of Iona and Peter Opie*, Oxford at the Clarendon Press (Oxford, England), 1989.

Bingham, Jane M., editor, *Writers for Children: Critical Studies of Major Authors since the Seventeenth Century*, Scribner (New York, NY), 1988.

Brain, Russell, *Tea with Walter de la Mare*, Faber (London, England), 1957.

Brenner, Rica, *Ten Modern Poets*, Harcourt (New York, NY), 1930.

Briggs, Julia, *Night Visitors*, Faber (London, England), 1977.

Cecil, David, *The Fine Art of Reading and Other Literary Studies*, Bobbs-Merrill (Indianapolis, IN), 1957.

Child, Harold, *Essays and Reflections*, Cambridge University Press (London, England), 1948.

Clark, Leonard, *Walter de La Mare: A Checklist*, Cambridge University Press (London, England), 1956.

Clark, Leonard, *Walter de la Mare*, Bodley Head (London, England), 1960.

Davison, Edward, *Some Modern Poets and Other Critical Essays*, Harper (New York, NY), 1928, pp. 113-140.

Dictionary of Literary Biography, Gale (Detroit, MI), Volume 19: *British Poets, 1880-1914*, 1983, Volume 153: *Late-Victorian and Edwardian British Novelists, First Series*, 1995, Volume 162: *British Short-Fiction Writers, 1915-1945*, 1996, Volume 255: *British Fantasy and Science-Fiction Writers, 1918-1960*, 2002.

Duffin, Henry Charles, *Walter de la Mare: A Study of His Poetry*, Sidgwick & Jackson (London, England), 1949.

Ford, B., editor, *The Pelican Guide to English Literature*, Volume 7: *The Modern Age*, Penguin (New York, NY), 1961.

Freeman, John, *English Portraits and Essays*, Hodder & Stoughton (London, England), 1924.

Gosse, Edmund, *Books on the Table*, Scribner (New York, NY), 1921.

Greene, Graham, *Collected Essays*, Viking (New York, NY), 1969.

Hopkins, Kenneth, *Walter de la Mare*, Longmans, Green (London, England), 1953, revised edition, British Council, 1957.

Jarrell, Randall, *Poetry and the Age*, Knopf (New York, NY), 1953.

Leavis, F.R., *New Bearings in English Poetry*, Chatto & Windus (London, England), 1932, new edition, 1950.

McCrosson, Doris Ross, *Walter de la Mare*, Twayne (New York, NY), 1966.

Megroz, R.L., *Walter de la Mare: A Biographical and Critical Study*, Hodder & Stoughton (London, England), 1924.

Megroz, R.L., *Five Novelist Poets of To-Day*, Joiner & Steele (London, England), 1933.

Muir, Edwin, *The Present Age from 1914*, Cresset (London, England), 1939.

Murry, J. Middleton, *Countries of the Mind,* Collins (London, England), 1922.

Penzoldt, Peter, *The Supernatural in Fiction,* Peter Nevill (London, England), 1952.

Perkins, David, *A History of Modern Poetry,* Volume 1, Harvard University Press (Cambridge, MA), 1976.

Priestly, J.B., *Figures in Modern Literature,* John Lane/ Bodley Head (London, England), 1924.

Punter, David, *The Literature of Terror: A History of Gothic Fictions from 1765 to the Present Day,* Longman (London, England), 1980.

Reid, Forrest, *Walter de la Mare: A Critical Study,* Holt (New York, NY), 1929.

Richards, I.A., *Science and Poetry,* Kegan Paul, Trench & Trubner (London, England), 1926.

St. James Guide to Children's Writers, St. James Press (Detroit, MI), 1999.

St. James Guide to Horror, Ghost, and Gothic Writers, St. James Press (Detroit, MI), 1998.

Schmidt, Michael, *A Reader's Guide to Fifty Modern British Poets,* Barnes & Noble (New York, NY), 1979.

Shanks, Edward, *First Essays on Literature,* W. Collins Sons, 1923.

Squire, J.C., *Books Reviewed: Critical Essays on Books and Authors,* Doran, 1922, reprinted by Kennikat Press (Port Washington, NY), 1968.

Swinnerton, Frank, *Figures in the Foreground,* Hutchinson (London, England), 1963.

Tribute to Walter de la Mare on His Seventy-fifth Birthday, Faber (London, England), 1948.

Walsh, William, *The Use of Imagination,* Chatto & Windus (London, England), 1959.

Wagenknecht, Edward, *Cavalcade of the English Novel: From Elizabeth to George VI,* Holt (New York, NY), 1948.

Whistler, Theresa, *Imagination of the Heart: The Life of Walter de la Mare,* Duckworth (London, England), 1993.

Williams, Charles, *Poetry at Present,* Oxford at the Clarendon Press (Oxford, England), 1930.

PERIODICALS

Contemporary Review, March, 1994, Randle Manwaring, "Memories of Walter de la Mare," p. 149.

English Review, May, 1922, Storm Jameson, review of *Memoirs of a Midget,* pp. 424-430.

Horn Book, May-June, 1942, Margery Bianco, "De la Mare," pp. 141-147; June, 1957, Eleanor Farjeon, "Walter de la Mare," pp. 197-205.

London Mercury, May, 1924, J.B. Priestley, "Mr. de la Mare's Imagination," pp. 33-43.

New Criterion, April, 2008, Eric Linn Ormsby, "The Kingdom of Never-to-Be," p. 4.

Times Literary Supplement, June 17, 1926, review of *The Connoisseur, and Other Stories,* p. 412.

Wilson Quarterly, summer, 1997, Anthony Hecht, "Walter de la Mare," p. 108.

ONLINE

Walter de la Mare Society Web site, http://www. bluetree.co.uk/wdlmsociety/ (July 1, 2009).

■ **Obituaries**

PERIODICALS

Commonweal, July 6, 1956.

Illustrated London News, June 30, 1956.

Junior Bookshelf, October, 1956, M.S. Crouch, "Farewell to Walter de la Mare," pp. 187-191.

New York Times, June 23, 1956.

Newsweek, July 2, 1956.

Publishers Weekly, July 2, 1956.

Time, July 2, 1956.

Wilson Library Bulletin, September, 1956.*

Jo Dereske

(Photograph by Margaret Ziegler. Courtesy of Jo Dereske.)

■ Personal

Born October 1, 1947, in Ludington, MI; daughter of John (an electrician) and June (a homemaker) Dereske; married Kip Winsett (a salesman), September 12, 1987; children: Karen Marie, Erik Jon. *Education:* Western Michigan University, B.A., 1969, M.L.S., 1971.

■ Addresses

Home—Everson, WA. *Agent*—Susan Schulman, 454 W. 44th St., New York, NY 10036. *E-mail*—email@jodereske.com.

■ Career

Freelance writer; author of children's books and mystery novels; librarian. Western Washington University, Bellingham, WA, interlibrary loan librarian, 1978-88; Corridor Information Services, owner-operator, 1983-87. Public speaker and presenter of writing workshops.

■ Awards, Honors

William Allen White Children's Book Award, 1985, for *Glom Gloom;* Artist Trust grant, 1989; Dorothy Canfield Fisher Children's Award nomination, 1989, and South Carolina Children's Book Award, 1991-92, both for *The Lone Sentinel.*

■ Writings

CHILDREN'S BOOKS

Glom Gloom, Atheneum (New York, NY), 1985.
The Lone Sentinel, Atheneum (New York, NY), 1989.
My Cousin, the Poodle, Atheneum (New York, NY), 1991.

"RUBY CRANE" MYSTERY SERIES

Savage Cut, Dell Books (New York, NY), 1996.
Cut and Dry, Dell Books (New York, NY), 1997.
Short Cut, Dell Books (New York, NY), 1998.

"MISS ZUKAS" MYSTERY SERIES

Miss Zukas and the Library Murders, Avon (New York, NY), 1994.
Miss Zukas and the Island Murders, Avon (New York, NY), 1995.

Miss Zukas and the Stroke of Death, Avon (New York, NY), 1996.

Miss Zukas and the Raven's Dance, Avon (New York, NY), 1996.

Out of Circulation, Avon (New York, NY), 1997.

Final Notice, Avon (New York, NY), 1998.

Miss Zukas in Death's Shadow, Avon (New York, NY), 1999.

Miss Zukas Shelves the Evidence, Avon (New York, NY), 2000.

Bookmarked to Die, Avon (New York, NY), 2006.

Catalogue of Death, Avon (New York, NY), 2007.

Index to Murder, Avon (New York, NY), 2008.

OTHER

Also contributor of articles and short stories to periodicals.

■ **Sidelights**

A former librarian, Jo Dereske is the author of more than a dozen titles for adults and children, including the works in the popular "Miss Zukas" mystery series featuring a sleuthing librarian living and working in the fictional town of Bellehaven, Washington. "As a librarian, I was exposed to a gamut of personalities, who walk through my books in one form or another, from the man who accused me of stealing words from the pages of a book to the child found hiding in the adult reference section so he could feast on a set of encyclopedias," Dereske told *Bellingham Herald* interviewer Margaret Bikman. "Librarians especially will tell me tales from their own libraries. I'm always learning from readers!"

Dereske developed an interest in books and literature at an early age, but she did not have the cosmopolitan background she imagined that authors need to be successful. As she noted on her home page, "I longed to be a writer but as a child believed it was impossible since I didn't live anywhere near New York City." Dereske grew up in a rural town of some 300 residents in western Michigan within bicycling distance of the Manistee National Forest. She also attended a one-room school through the eighth grade. However, she did have siblings and parents—a family of seven in all—who loved reading, and there was the bookmobile that made regular stops at their home for all the avid readers.

Dereske's love for books carried her to Western Michigan University, where she studied library science. Thereafter, she worked for more than a decade as a corporate librarian and as an interlibrary loan librarian at Western Washington University. Dereske finally made her childhood dream come true, publishing her first book, *Glom Gloom,* in 1985. By the mid-1990s, however she had moved to mystery fiction for adults, publishing two series, the "Ruby Crane" mysteries set in rural Michigan, and the "Miss Zukas" mysteries. Though Dereske has never lived anywhere near New York City, she has followed the golden rule of fiction writing: write what you know about firsthand.

A Foray into Children's Books

The author's debut work evolved from an idea she had while living abroad with her husband and children. Dereske and her family lived in Scotland

Cover of Jo Dereske's 2006 novel *Bookmarked to Die,* which marks the return of crime-solving librarian Wilhelmina Zukas.

during one winter; while there, she began writing a short story for her two children about a forest inhabited by tall, peaceful creatures called Bulkings and small, evil ones called Weeuns. Four years later she expanded the story into her first children's book, *Glom Gloom.* The work received generally warm reviews. *Booklist* reviewer Barbara Elleman, noted that the story took a bit of time at the beginning to sort out its characters and setting, adding, "Once the plot gets under way, episodes move briskly and tension quickly builds. Characters are likable and fantasy fans will become easily involved." *School Library Journal* contributor Susan McCord found the book "enjoyable" and commented that it contained just enough Bulking vernacular to create a "sense of place." A reviewer for *Publishers Weekly* also noted that the plot was fundamentally interesting.

Dereske thought of the plot for her second book, *The Lone Sentinel,* while traveling past the looming radio towers of the Midwest during a driving tour with her family. The novel centers on a boy named Erik who helps his father oversee the construction of a sentinel on a faraway planet. When the father dies, Erik keeps the man's passing a secret in hopes of being able to stay at his post. Reviewer Lisa Lane, writing in *Voice of Youth Advocates,* praised the "fast-pace, action-packed" book as "a gripping saga." *Booklist* reviewer Stephanie Zvirin wrote that the "tightly structured plot builds nicely to a climax." *School Library Journal* contributor Pam Spencer also appreciated the "charm and warmth" of the "well-plotted" work, with its "suspenseful and exciting chase scenes."

Set in 1955, Dereske's third children's book, *My Cousin, The Poodle,* depicts the comic misadventures of a couple and their much-indulged canine. A *Kirkus Reviews* contributor called the work "determinedly wacky," praising its "effective period detail and some interestingly off-center characters." *School Library Journal* reviewer Carla Kozak was lukewarm about the rendering of the time period and found some of the characters and events overdrawn, but the critic pointed out that the book was as a whole charming.

Turns to Mysteries

After completing the three children's books, Dereske turned to another genre, the mystery novel for adults. In the 1994 novel *Miss Zukas and the Library Murders,* Dereske introduces Helma Zukas, an "always correct and always correcting" librarian, as a contributor in *Detecting Women 2* described her. In the series opener, readers also meet Zukas's artistic friend, Ruth, and the local police chief, Wayne Gallant, who is a potential love interest for the librarian.

In Dereske's *Miss Zukas and the Island Murders* a mystery casts a pall over the librarian's work to plan her high-school's twenty-year reunion. (Copyright © 1995 by Jo Dereske. All rights reserved. Reproduced by permission of HarperCollins Publishers Inc.)

More "Miss Zukas" novels followed in quick succession. In *Miss Zukas and the Island Murders,* danger lies in wait for the librarian when she organizes a class reunion. In *Miss Zukas and the Stroke of Death,* the title character is cajoled into joining the library's Snow to Surf event, a grueling thirty-eight mile race on skis, bike, and canoe. An avid canoeist as a youth, Zukas agrees to participate in the canoeing portion of the competition, but she is also preoccupied with more important matters: proving her good friend Ruth innocent of murder. Writing for *ReviewingTheEvidence.com,* Mary V. Welk felt that this series addition "can be read as a standalone due to Dereske's deft introduction of the characters and setting." Welk went on to praise

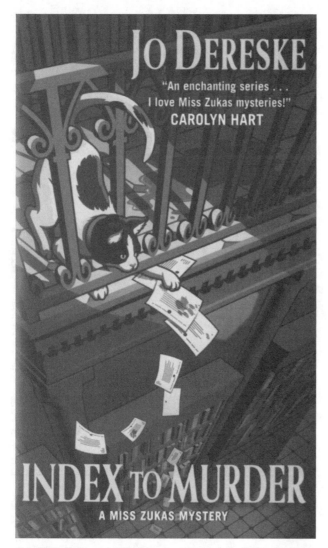

Set in Bellehaven, Washington, Dereske's *Index to Murder* finds Miss Zukas aiding an artistic friend in need.
(Copyright © 2008 by Jo Dereske. All rights reserved. Reproduced by permission of HarperCollins Publishers Inc.)

Dereske's main character: "The cool, calm, and collected Miss Zukas is a delightful protagonist with her mid-western commonsense approach to life's little trials, including murder." In the fourth series title, *Miss Zukas and the Raven's Dance,* a library cataloguer working for a wealthy eccentric is murdered. According to a *Publishers Weekly* reviewer, the presence of contrived elements in the plot would be overlooked by most readers because of Miss Zukas's attractive integrity, the high quality of the dialogue, the realistic glimpses of libraries, and the "consistently straightforward, no-nonsense prose," which was "a welcome bonus" in the novel.

Dereske opened a second mystery series in 1996 with the publication of *Savage Cut,* featuring recently widowed Ruby Crane, who is returning to her Michigan hometown after giving up her work as a graphologist for the Los Angeles police department. Ruby has decided to make these life changes to care for her daughter, who was injured in the same car accident that took Ruby's husband's life. Things are not all that peaceful in her hometown, however. The husband of her best friend, Mina, is killed in a logging accident, and then Mina herself is murdered. Ruby reluctantly plays detective to get to the bottom of things in a work that "deftly interweaves plot elements with details of the logging culture," according to a *Publishers Weekly* reviewer.

The "Ruby Crane" series also includes *Cut and Dry* and *Short Cut.* In the former title, Ruby begins to investigate the strangulation of a woman in her small town and soon becomes the target of the killer. She is aided in her investigation by a mysterious neighbor who turns out to be an ex-cop with a dark past. In *Short Cut* Ruby comes to the aid of her sister Phyllis, and she uses her expertise in handwriting analysis to try to solve a desperate crime.

Although Dereske has made no series additions to the "Ruby Crane" mysteries since 1998, she has continued with her books featuring her intrepid librarian. *Out of Circulation* finds Zukas and her friend Ruth hiking in the Cascade Mountains. Their bucolic adventure is waylaid, however, by the discovery of a body with a bullet-sized hole in its chest. Thereafter the duo helps to track down the dead person's missing companion. In *Final Notice* a visit from Helma's dotty Aunt Em brings homicide along with it, while in *Miss Zukas in Death's Shadow* the sleuthing librarian herself comes under suspicion of a murder at a shelter where she is volunteering. Writing for *Crescent Blues Book Views* online, Dawn Goldsmith noted of this series addition: "Dereske writes a rather low-key mystery with quiet twists and introspection," and peoples her "not-too-predictable mystery with multi-faceted characters whose lives enrich the read."

K.W. Becker, tracing the development of Zukas's character on the *Mystery Reader* Web site, observed that Dereske "guides her character's growth gently, bringing her along incrementally from the stereotypic old-maid librarian to become someday (one hopes) a well-rounded human being." With *Miss Zukas Shelves the Evidence* the long awaited romance between Zukas and the police chief, Gallant, seems to be about to get off the ground. Gallant has actually set up a meeting between his children and the librarian. However, police business, in the form of a dead body, intervenes. When Gallant himself becomes a target of the killer, Miss Zukas takes it personally and begins her own investigation. *Romantic Times* reviewer Toby Bromberg offered praised

If you enjoy the works of Jo Dereske, you may also want to check out the following books:

Sarah Caudwell, *Thus Was Adonis Murdered*, 1981.
Lawrence Block's "Bernie Rhodenbarr" series, including *The Burglar in the Library*, 1997.
Ian Sansom, *Mr. Dixon Disappears*, 2007.

for the novel, predicting that "cozy fans are sure to enjoy the latest entry in the charming Miss Zukas series."

Returns after Long Hiatus

Several years elapsed between the publication of *Miss Zukas Shelves the Evidence* and the next title in the series, *Bookmarked to Die.* Here the librarian is in charge of a local authors' project at the library that turns contentious because of jealousies, while a younger librarian seems to have set her eyes on Police Chief Gallant. When murder erupts as a result of her project, Zukas begins to investigate. However, her beloved cat goes missing and a sinister telephone caller threatens the animal's safety if Helma continues sleuthing. For *Romantic Times* contributor Sheri Melnick, this ninth book in the series serves as a "captivating cozy." Bridget Bolton, writing for *ReviewingtheEvidence.com,* also complimented this title, noting that the "usual fine cast of characters is back, and the plot is intriguing and peppered with enough red herrings to keep the reader guessing until the end."

In *Catalogue of Death*, which appeared one year later, Zukas investigates the death of local billionaire Franklin Harrington, who was killed while examining the site of the proposed library he planned to donate to Bellehaven. Although she initially sets out to convince the Harrington clan to honor Franklin's wishes, Zukas is soon involved in finding a murderer in the midst of the same clan. Another addition to the series, *Index to Murder*, finds Zukas and her artist friend Ruth investigating the theft of two of Ruth's paintings. This investigation soon heats up, however, as the theme of the pictures were ex-lovers who met untimely ends. And soon it seems that such an ending may come for Zukas and Ruth, as well.

Discussing the origins of her popular amateur sleuth, Dereske has noted that she drew for inspiration from her own Lithuanian heritage as well as

from the world of librarians. Jennifer Dunning, writing in the *New York Times,* called Miss Zukas a "loving sendup of the stereotype of the prim librarian." Nancy Pearl, writing in *Library Journal,* also complimented Dereske's protagonist, stating that Zukas's "logical mind, research skills, and ability to remain collected under any circumstances" make her a memorable character.

■ Biographical and Critical Sources

BOOKS

Heising, Willeta L., editor, *Detecting Women 2*, Purple Moon Press (Dearborn, MI), 1996.

As a new library goes up in Bellehaven, Miss Helma Zukas takes on a new mystery in Dereske's *Catalogue of Death.* (Copyright © 2007 by Jo Dereske. All rights reserved. Reproduced by permission of HarperCollins Publishers Inc.)

PERIODICALS

Bellingham Herald (Bellingham, WA), May 11, 2008, Margaret Bikman, "Dereske's Mystery-solving Librarian Back for More."

Booklist, October 15, 1985, Barbara Elleman, review of *Glom Gloom*, p. 335; December 15, 1989, Stephanie Zvirin, review of *The Lone Sentinel*, p. 826.

Kirkus Reviews, August 15, 1991, review of *My Cousin, the Poodle*, p. 1088.

Library Journal, September 1, 2004, Nancy Pearl, review of *Miss Zukas and the Library Murders*, p. 207.

New York Times, September 1, 2006, Jennifer Dunning, "Last Call for Summer," p. 13.

Publishers Weekly, August 30, 1985, review of *Glom Gloom*, p. 423; November 25, 1996, review of *Miss Zukas and the Raven's Dance*, pp. 70-71; October 14, 1996, review of *Savage Cut*, p. 81.

School Library Journal, October, 1985, Susan McCord, review of *Glom Gloom*, p. 171; October, 1989, Pam Spencer, review of *The Lone Sentinel*, p. 131; September, 1991, Carla Kozak, review of *My Cousin, the Poodle*, p. 252.

Voice of Youth Advocates, December, 1989, Lisa Lane, review of *The Lone Sentinel*, p. 287; April, 1998, review of *Miss Zukas and the Library Murders*, p. 41.

ONLINE

Crescent Blues Book Views Web site, http://www.crescentblues.com/ (April 8, 2009), Dawn Goldsmith, review of *Miss Zukas in Death's Shadow*.

Jo Dereske Home Page, http://www.jodereske.com (April 9, 2009).

Mystery File Web log, http://mysteryfile.com/blog/ (May 9, 2008), review of *Final Notice*.

Mystery Reader Web site, http://www.themystery reader.com/ (January 13, 2000), K.W. Becker, review of *Miss Zukas in Death's Shadow*; (May 14, 2001) Kathy Sova, review of *Miss Zukas Shelves the Evidence*.

ReviewingtheEvidence.com, http://www.reviewing theevidence.com/ (April 1, 2006), Bridget Bolton, review of *Bookmarked to Die*; (December 1, 2006) Mary V. Welk, review of *Miss Zukas and the Stroke of Death*.

Romantic Times Web site, http://www.romantictimes.com/ (April 11, 2009), Toby Bromberg, review of *Miss Zukas Shelves the Evidence*; Sheri Melnick, review of *Bookmarked to Die*.*

Tananarive Due

(Photograph courtesy of AP Images.)

■ Personal

Name is pronounced "tah-nah-nah-*reeve* doo"; born 1966; daughter of John Dorsey (an attorney) and Patricia (a civil rights activist) Due; married Steven Barnes (a science-fiction novelist and screenwriter); children: Nicki (stepdaughter); Jason. *Education:* Northwestern University, B.S., 1987; University of Leeds (England), M.A., 1988. *Religion:* African Methodist Episcopal. *Hobbies and other interests:* Playing piano and keyboard, roller blading.

■ Addresses

Home—CA. *Agent*—c/o John Hawkins & Associates, 71 W. 23rd St., Ste. 1600, New York, NY 10010. *E-mail*—tdue@tananarivedue.com; TheLivingBlood@aol.com.

■ Career

Journalist, novelist, screenwriter, and lecturer. Columnist for *Miami Herald.* Antioch University, Los Angeles, CA, instructor in creative writing.

Former instructor at Hurston-Wright Foundation's Writers' Week, Clarion Science-Fiction and Fantasy Writers' Workshop, and summer Imagination conference at Cleveland State University. Has performed with Rockbottom Remainders (rock band that includes authors Stephen King, Dave Barry, and Amy Tan) as keyboardist/vocalist/dancer.

■ Awards, Honors

Finalist, Bram Stoker Award for Outstanding Achievement in a First Novel, Horror Writers Association, 1995, for *The Between; Publishers Weekly* Best Book citation, 1997, for *My Soul to Keep,* and 2001, for *The Living Blood;* National Association for the Advancement of Colored People (NAACP) Image Award nomination for *The Black Rose;* American Book Award, 2002, for *The Living Blood;* New Voice in Literature Award, 2004; Image Award (with Steven Barnes and Blair Underwood), NAACP, 2009, for *Casanegra.*

■ Writings

The Between (novel), HarperCollins (New York, NY), 1995.

The Black Rose: The Magnificent Story of Madam C.J. Walker, America's First Black Female Millionaire, Ballantine (New York, NY), 2000.

(With mother, Patricia Stephens Due) *Freedom in the Family: A Mother-Daughter Memoir of the Fight for Civil Rights,* One World (New York, NY), 2003.

The Good House (novel), Atria (New York, NY), 2003.

Joplin's Ghost (novel), Atria Books (New York, NY), 2005.

(With L.A. Banks and Brandon Massey) *The Ancestors* (novellas), Dafina Books (New York, NY), 2006.

"AFRICAN IMMORTALS" SERIES

My Soul to Keep (novel), HarperCollins (New York, NY), 1997.

The Living Blood (novel), Pocket Books (New York, NY), 2001.

Blood Colony, Atria Books (New York, NY), 2008.

"TENNYSON HARDWICK" SERIES

(With Blair Underwood and Steven Barnes) *Casanegra,* Atria Books (New York, NY), 2007.

(With Steven Barnes) *In the Night of the Heat,* Atria Books (New York, NY), 2008.

OTHER

Contributor to *Naked Came the Manatee,* Putnam (New York, NY); *Voices from the Other Side: Dark Dreams II,* edited by Brandon Massey, Kensington Books (New York, NY), 2006; and *Whispers in the Night: Dark Dreams III,* edited by Brandon Massey, Dafina Books (New York, NY), 2007.

■ **Adaptations**

Film rights to *My Soul to Keep* were obtained by Fox Searchlight; *Joplin's Ghost* was adapted as an audiobook, Recorded Books, 2006.

■ **Sidelights**

"A house haunted by a curse and memories. African immortals with healing blood. The ghost of Scott Joplin. I often write about the supernatural, which is my favorite prism for glimpses of our shared history and humanity." So noted novelist and screenwriter Tananarive Due on her author home page. This description covers much of what Due has writ-

ten, beginning with her debut novel *The Between* and including the 2008 addition to her "African Immortals" series, *Blood Colony.*

Winner of the 2002 American Book Award for her "African Immortals" novel *The Living Blood,* Due has also teamed up with her husband, writer Steven Barnes, and actor Blair Underwood to create a novel series featuring Tennyson Hardwick, a former gigolo and Hollywood actor turned investigator. Due has been praised by critics for her accurate evocation of scene and character. "Ever since I was a kid, I used to cut out pictures from catalogs to represent characters in my stories," she told Susan McHenry in *Black Issues Book Review.* Due further elaborated on her technique: "I have to feel that I'm surrounded by a three-dimensional environment—that it's real. If there's a location, I want to see the location. If there's a person, I wanted to see the person."

From Journalist to Novelist

Due was born in 1966, the daughter of a father who was a lawyer and a mother who was a civil rights activist. She set her sights on a writing career at an early age, and as a sixth grader watching the landmark television miniseries *Roots,* Due traced her own family's history, titling her work "My Own Roots." As a young woman, she attended a summer program for young writers at Northwestern University and won numerous awards for both writing and oratory. After earning her bachelor's degree in journalism, she completed a Rotary Foundation scholarship in Leeds, England. There she completed her master's degree, concentrating her studies on Nigerian literature. Originally from Florida, Due returned to that state to begin a career in journalism, becoming a columnist at the *Miami Herald.* At the same time she began sending her short stories to publishers, although none responded in the affirmative. "No one likes rejection," Due told Alison Hibbert of the *Miami Times,* "but as long as I got rejection slips, I knew I had to keep going. I had my mind set on being a serious writer."

An interview with Anne Rice, author of such gothics as *The Vampire Lestat,* inspired Due to try her hand at horror. She drafted her first novel, *The Between,* in her spare time before and after work. This time Due caught the attention of a publisher, and *The Between* was released in 1995. That novel, along with subsequent works, helped set the author apart in the genre of mystery/horror: her books feature African-American characters.

The Between is "a skillful blend of horror and the supernatural," according to a reviewer for *Publishers Weekly.* The story centers on a forty-year-old social

"A finely honed work that always engages and frequently surprises."
—*New York Times Book Review*

THE BETWEEN

A NOVEL

TANANARIVE DUE

Cover of Tananarive Due's young-adult novel *The Between*, featuring artwork by Jody Hewgill. (Cover illustration © 1995 by Jody Hewgill. Reproduced by permission of HarperCollins Publishers Inc.)

worker in Miami's inner city who is plagued by nightmares that seem to indicate either his insanity or his status as a person "in between" life and death. As a child, Hilton James barely escaped death by drowning when he was involved in the same accident that killed his grandmother. Now, as the husband of the only African-American woman judge in Miami, he receives subconscious messages that indicate his survival all those years ago was a mistake that must be rectified. Due's portrait of Hilton's crumbling personality is "sympathetic and credible," according to a *Publishers Weekly* reviewer, although the critic maintained that the rest of the cast fails to achieve the same verisimilitude. M.J. Simmons, reviewing *The Between* for *Library Journal*, noted that, rather than a tale of supernatural horror, Due's first novel is "a chilling and sympathetic portrait of a man whose madness needs explanation in the psychic realm." Although Simmons found Due's ending a disappointment, *Booklist* critic Lil-

lian Lewis praised the "intriguing and suspenseful plot" of *The Between* concluding that "Due may very well develop a loyal following with her first novel."

The "African Immortals"

Due followed *The Between* with *My Soul to Keep,* another tale of supernatural horror in which reporter Jessica discovers that her otherwise-perfect husband David has a secret: he is actually a five-hundred-year-old member of an Ethiopian band of immortals willing to kill to keep its members' existence a secret. When David reveals the truth to Jessica, he endangers himself and the family he has come to love when the brotherhood sends a member to make sure their secret does not get out. In *Booklist* Lewis found Due's second novel "more compelling than her first," and compared *My Soul to Keep* with Octavia Butler's *Kindred* for its grounding in "African and African-American heritage and culture." Several critics lauded Due's realistic details and strong sense of family life, which provide a convincing foundation for a somewhat melodramatic plot. *My Soul to Keep* is "a novel populated with vivid, emotional characters that is also a chilling journey to another world," concluded a reviewer for *Publishers Weekly*.

The second volume of Due's "African Immortals" series, *The Living Blood*, reintroduces Jessica and David, as Jessica joins her husband among the immortals after a ceremonial infusion of magical blood. Now a part of the ancient Life Brothers society, she finds herself alone and pregnant after David, accused of murder, disappears. She raises her daughter, Fana, to age two and when she discovers that her child possesses the Life Brothers' psychic powers, Jessica embarks on a desperate mission to find David in Africa. Larger in scope than *My Soul to Keep, The Living Blood* drew mixed reaction from some reviewers. Patricia Altner commented in *Library Journal* that the sequel suffers from a "poorly executed" plot and "flaccid" writing. On the other hand, Lewis welcomed the novel, saying that even newcomers to the Jessica-and-David saga will likely enjoy the story. While noting that the author "does not fully develop the fascinating theological implications of her story," *Black Issues Book Review* contributor Paulette Richards still praised *The Living Blood* as "an engrossing, well-paced narrative." The work won an American Book Award in 2002.

The third "African Immortals" novel, *Blood Colony,* is set in 2015 and features David and Jessica's daughter, Fana, who is believed to be a deity by the Life Brothers. When Fana's best friend is imprisoned by the immortals, she helps to set the young woman free, and together they run away to join a new Underground Railway: a distribution system for the drug Glow, which is supposedly made from immortal blood and can cure all disease, including AIDS. There are dangers ahead, however, as an ancient Italian sect with connections to the Vatican, the Sanctus Cruor, are also after Fana. A *Publishers Weekly* contributor termed *Blood Colony* "profoundly moving," noting that "Due brings Fana's complex and passionate story to life with her trademark flair."

Tales of the Supernatural and the Natural

Also in the supernatural vein, *The Good House* finds divorcee Angela Toussaint moving with her teenaged son Corey to her family's summer home. The house was built in 1907 and was once occupied by Angela's Creole "mambo" grandmother Marie, a suspected witch. When an ancient evil is brought back to life, voodoo, family ties, murder, and suicide all figure in the story. "Due keeps richly packed and layered description alive with suspense," maintained a *Kirkus Reviews* contributor, the critic concluding that in *The Good House* the author "weaves a stronger net than ever." Praising the novel's "themes of family ties, racial identity and moral responsibility," a *Publishers Weekly* reviewer added that Due traverses the intricate plot deftly, "interjecting powerfully orchestrated moments of supernatural horror that sustain the tale's momentum." Although of the opinion that the novel would have been better served by a stronger ending, Jennifer Baker praised *The Good House* in *Library Journal* as "a cleverly plotted tale of possession and magic gone awry."

By the late 1990s Due had gained a sufficient reputation as a novelist and journalist for the estate of the late author Alex Haley to offer her the opportunity to complete a biographical novel begun by Haley and based on the life of pioneering African-American executive Madam C.J. Walker. In the early twentieth century Walker—born Sarah Breedlove and the daughter of former slaves—rose from laundress to millionaire on the strength of her business savvy and her line of hair-care products. At the time of his death in 1992, Haley left behind an outline for the Walker novel, along with reams of archival clippings, letters, and photographs.

The resulting book, *The Black Rose: The Magnificent Story of Madam C.J. Walker, America's First Black Female Millionaire,* traces Walker from childhood to her death at age fifty-two. Combining fiction and fact, *The Black Rose* uses Walker's point of view to explore the challenges of life in the segregated South of the early twentieth century. Recognizing a need for beauty products aimed at underserved black women, Walker not only created her own cosmetics, but recruited as many as 20,000 women to sell them door to door—"empowering them, in many cases, to transform themselves from cooks or maids to entrepreneurs," according to Valerie Boyd in an *Atlanta Journal-Constitution* article. Boyd labeled Due's account "compelling," adding that, "with the patience of a born storyteller, [the author] slowly allows Walker's stirring story to unfold." The reviewer also cited Due for presenting a well-rounded, flaws-and-all picture of her subject.

In 2003 Due once again turned to nonfiction with *Freedom in the Family: A Mother-Daughter Memoir of the Fight for Civil Rights.* Written with her mother, Patricia Stephens Due, the volume relates a personal history of the struggle for equality, from the lunch counter sit-ins of the 1950s to a racially motivated police raid on the Due family's Miami home decades later. The book, noted a *Publishers Weekly* contributor, is "cathartic in its recounting of past obstacles, and optimistic of its hopes for the future."

Talking to *Publishers Weekly* contributor Stefan Dziemianowicz about her supernatural novels, Due remarked that she "really never set out to write a trilogy or create a franchise." Still, she did not rule out the idea of another book in the gothic series about Jessica and David, noting that, with the completion of *Freedom in the Family,* "it may be time to revisit the immortals."

A Ghost of Ragtime and a Gigolo Turned Sleuth

Meanwhile, with *Joplin's Ghost,* Due bypassed the horror genre to tell the story of R&B singer Phoenix Smalls, a woman literally haunted by the ghost of African-American pianist and composer Scott Joplin, the King of Ragtime. Smalls visits the Joplin home while on tour in St. Louis, Missouri, and as she leaves the house, the specter of Joplin follows her. Due thereafter juxtaposes Joplin's difficult life in the nineteenth century against that of the twenty-four-year-old Smalls, who is attempting to break into the modern-day music business. A *Publishers Weekly* reviewer had praise for *Joplin's Ghost,* observing that here "Due shows herself true to her own powerful gift." A contributor to *Ebony* was also enthusiastic about the novel, terming it "spellbinding," while *Essence* reviewer Margaret Williams called it a "you-won't-sleep-tonight thriller." Writing in the *Washington Post,* Thrity Umrigar added to these positive assessments, commenting: "Even while she brings to life Scott Joplin the man, Due makes us appreciate Scott Joplin the icon, the symbol. This understanding gives *Joplin's Ghost* its haunting power."

Due again teamed up with Barnes and Underwood on *Casanegra*, the first novel in a series featuring former gigolo and current actor Tennyson Hardwick. Hardwick is forced by circumstances to play amateur detective when one of his former clients from his sex-for-sale days, rapper Afrodite, is found brutally murdered and Hardwick becomes the central suspect. With a father who was a former cop, and with some interesting skills of his own, such as martial arts abilities, Hardwick decides to investigate this murder in order to clear his name. A *Publishers Weekly* reviewer called *Casanegra* "seamlessly entertaining," and *Entertainment Weekly* contributor Adrienne Day further commended the work, writing that "the pace is taut . . . [and] the dialogue is snappy."

In Hardwick's second outing, *In the Night of the Heat*, the reluctant detective is approached by T.D. Jackson, a former football star, after T.D. has been found innocent of murdering his wife. Now the man wants to hire Hardwick to protect him, but Hardwick is currently involved in a new series that is becoming popular. However, when Jackson is later found dead, an apparent suicide victim, Hardwick once again puts on his sleuthing cap and uncovers secrets in high places. A *Washington Post* reviewer found this series addition "a fun, fast read."

If you enjoy the works of Tananarive Due, you may also want to check out the following books:

Stephen King, *The Dead Zone*, 1979.
John Saul, *Darkness*, 1991.
Mark Z. Danielewski, *House of Leaves*, 2000.

In an interview for the *League of Reluctant Adults* Web log, Due elaborated on the inspiration for much of her fiction: "When I went to the University of Leeds, I had my very first exposure to Nigerian literature. Rather than looking at if from a folkloric point of view, I chose to write my thesis on the role of authors in conveying the pain and national trauma of the Nigerian civil war." She continued, "I

was left with a very strong imprint that a writer can have a relevant voice in cultural dialogue. So my use of black history in my novels is a way of conveying to all readers that while the past is behind us, it isn't quite gone. That past doesn't always have to be a source of pain or shame—it can also serve as a source of strength and resolve to do better."

■ Biographical and Critical Sources

BOOKS

Contemporary Black Biography, Gale (Detroit, MI), 2001.

PERIODICALS

Atlanta Journal-Constitution, July 16, 2000, Valerie Boyd, "Black Female Entrepreneur Finally Gets Her Due," p. L8.

Black Issues Book Review, July, 2000, Natasha Tarpley, review of *The Black Rose: The Magnificent Story of Madam C.J. Walker, America's First Black Female Millionaire*, p. 19; May, 2001, Paulette Richards, review of *The Living Blood*, p. 18; January-February, 2004, Susan McHenry, "Blair Underwood Goes for the Greenlight," p. 24; January-February, 2006, Denise Simon, review of *Joplin's Ghost*, p. 58.

Booklist, May 15, 1995, Lillian Lewis, review of *The Between*, p. 1631; July 19, 1997, Lillian Lewis, review of *My Soul to Keep*; April 15, 2000, Brad Hooper, review of *The Black Rose*, p. 1500; April 1, 2001, Lillian Lewis, review of *The Living Blood*, p. 1447.

Ebony, July, 2000, review of *The Black Rose*, p. 14; June, 2001, review of *The Living Blood*, p. 23; January, 2006, review of *Joplin's Ghost*, P. 31.

Entertainment Weekly, June 22, 2007, Adrienne Day, review of *Casanegra*, p. 75.

Essence, November, 2005, Margaret Williams, review of *Joplin's Ghost*, p. 96; January, 2009, Karen Holt, review of *The Ancestors*, p. 56.

Houston Chronicle, May 27, 2001, Mark Johnson, review of *The Living Blood*, p. 21.

Kirkus Reviews, November 1, 2002, review of *Freedom in the Family: A Mother-Daughter Memoir of the Fight for Civil Rights*, p. 1585; August 15, 2003, review of *The Good House*, p. 1033.

Library Journal, June 1, 1995, M.J. Simmons, review of *The Between*, p. 158; February 15, 2001, Patricia Altner, review of *The Living Blood*, p. 200; November 1, 2002, Ann Burns, review of *Freedom in the Family*, p. 115; August, 2003, Jennifer Baker, review of *The Good House*, p. 129.

Miami Times, May 18, 1995, Alison Hibbert, review of *The Between*, p. 18.

Publishers Weekly, April 24, 1995, review of *The Between*, p. 60; June 2, 1997, review of *My Soul to Keep*, p. 55; November 8, 1999, John Baker, "First Black Millionaire," p. 14; March 15, 2000, review of *The Black Rose*, p. 87; March 19, 2001, Stefan Dziemianowicz, "PW Talks to Tananarive Due" and review of *The Living Blood*, p. 81; December 23, 2002, review of *Freedom in the Family*, p. 56; July 14, 2003, review of *The Good House*, p. 61; July 25, 2005, review of *Joplin's Ghost*, p. 44; May 14, 2007, review of *Casanegra*, p. 34; April 28, 2008, review of *Blood Colony*, p. 116; October 13, 2008, review of *The Ancestors*, p. 40.

St. Louis Post-Dispatch, July 16, 2000, Naima Watts, "Novel Tells Fact-based Story of First Black Female Millionaire," p. F10.

School Library Journal, December, 2000, review of *The Black Rose*, p. 168.

Science Fiction Chronicle, August, 2001, review of *The Living Blood*, p. 34.

Washington Post, October 9, 2005, Thrity Umrigar, review of *Joplin's Ghost*, p. T6; Dec 21, 2008, review of *In the Night of the Heat*, p. B4.

Washington Post Book World, February 4, 2001, review of *The Black Rose*, p. 10; May 6, 2001, review of *The Living Blood*, p. 8.

ONLINE

African American Literature Book Club Web site, http://aalbc.com/ (April 10, 2009), "Tananarive Due."

League of Reluctant Adults Web log, http://www.leagueofreluctantadults.com/ (February 16, 2008), "Interview: Tananarive Due, American Book Award-Winning Author."

Tananarive Due Home Page, http://www.tananrivedue.com (April 11, 2009).

Tananarive Due's Reading Circle, http://www.tananarivedue.blogspot.com/ (April 11, 2009).*

(Photograph by Duane Nelson. Reproduced by permission of the photographer.)

Gail Giles

■ Personal

Born September 24, in Galveston, TX; daughter of Isabel Human; married Jim Giles; children: Josh. *Education:* Attended Stephen F. Austin State University. *Hobbies and other interests:* Watercolor painting, reading, computer solitaire, playing guitar.

■ Addresses

Home—Woodland, TX. *Agent*—Scott Treimel, 434 Lafayette St., New York, NY 10003. *E-mail*—gail@gailgiles.com.

■ Career

Writer. Taught high school in Angleton, TX.

■ Awards, Honors

Best Books for Young Adults selection and Quick Pick for Reluctant Readers selection, American Library Association (ALA), both 2003, both for *Shattering Glass;* ALA Teens Top Ten selection, 2003, for *Dead Girls Don't Write Letters.*

■ Writings

Breath of the Dragon, illustrated by June Otani, Clarion Books (New York, NY), 1997.

Shattering Glass, Roaring Brook Press (Brookfield, CT), 2002.

Dead Girls Don't Write Letters, Roaring Brook Press (Brookfield, CT), 2003.

Playing in Traffic, Roaring Brook Press (Brookfield, CT), 2004.

What Happened to Cass McBride? (novel), Little, Brown (New York, NY), 2006.

Right behind You (novel), Little, Brown (New York, NY), 2007.

Contributor of stories to anthologies, including *What a Song Can Do* and *What Are You Afraid Of?* Contributor of articles to Alaskan outdoor magazine, *Dandelion.*

■ Adaptations

Shattering Glass was adapted as an audiobook, Listening Library, 2003, and for audible.com, 2005; *Playing in Traffic, Dead Girls Don't Write Letters, What Happened to Cass McBride?,* and *Right behind You* were all adapted for audiobook, audible.com, 2008.

■ **Sidelights**

Gail Giles is the author of a well-received novel for middle graders titled *Breath of the Dragon,* as well as critically acclaimed and edgy young-adult novels such as *Shattering Glass, Playing in Traffic,* and *Right behind You.* "Giles is leading the field in innovation in teen literature," Beverly Rowe stated on *MyShelf. com.* Rowe noted that Giles "writes psychological thrillers for kids that lay bare the emotions and fears that kids harbor in this difficult and troubled world we live in," adding, "Her kids aren't the wealthy, have-everything, spoiled youngsters that you encounter in those books, but average kids that seem real and that teen readers can relate to. Gail's novels don't always have a pat happily-ever-after ending, but neither does life."

Reckless in Texas

Born in Galveston, Texas, Giles was a "rebellious, fractious child," as she later admitted to Rowe. She was also intelligent and displayed a talent for story-telling at a young age. On her home page, Giles described the genesis of her writing career, which began during elementary school: "I wasn't the best behaved kid in the fourth grade. I tended to do my class work at the speed of light and then, well, cause trouble." Giles recalled that one day her teacher, a nun, needed cheering up and asked her to write a humorous tale. "Okay, I'm game," Giles stated. "The nun told me to write a story about a family having a holiday dinner. Okay, bored now. But, she said, write it from an ant's point of view. Back in the game and swinging for the bleachers. So, I wrote. And erased and wrote some more. And I handed it in. The nun took the paper and began reading. And she chuckled. Then she blushed. I guess because she had chuckled. Then she laughed right out loud. I was a star!"

That episode helped propel Giles to further academic success. After graduating from high school, she attended Stephen F. Austin State University and later taught remedial reading to high school students. That experience made her look at children's literature more seriously, as she told Rowe: "When I taught the remedial readers I learned that one reason they didn't like to read was that the books didn't connect with their lives. And frankly I thought having all the books out there being so—soft—and always offering hope—was doing a disservice to teens. . . . So, I wanted to write some stories that shows that sometimes it can't be fixed. That reality is harsh."

Giles' first tale, *Breath of the Dragon,* appeared in 1997. In the work, a young Thai girl named Malila is left in the care of her grandmother after Malila's father is killed by police and her mother emigrates from Thailand to the United States. Malila's grandmother teaches the girl about the traditions of her country, which Malila translates into beautiful drawings. A teacher recognizes Malila's artistic talents, and she eventually makes plans to reunite with her mother. *Breath of the Dragon,* "is simply written," remarked Susan DeRonne in *Booklist,* "and the beauty of the Thai culture emerges on every page." In *School Library Journal,* Susan Hepler wrote that Giles' "gentle story portrays the prior experiences and emotions of many immigrants—hardship, vivid memories, and hope."

Takes Edgier Path with Young-Adult Novels

"Simon Glass was easy to hate. I never knew exactly why, there was too much to pick from. I guess, re

Cover of Gail Giles' hard-hitting YA novel *Shattering Glass.* (Jacket design and photo montage copyright © 2002 by Jaye Zimet. Reprinted by permission of Henry Holt & Company, LLC.)

ally, we each hated him for a different reason, but we didn't realize it until the day we killed him." Thus begins Giles's novel *Shattering Glass*, "an intriguing and at times painfully real story of high school life," according to Sarah Applegate in *Kliatt*. This young-adult novel describes the efforts of a powerful clique, headed by charismatic Rob Haynes, to flaunt its power by elevating the status of class geek Simon Glass. The plan works but has unexpected consequences: a newly confident Simon challenges Rob's authority and even discovers a terrible secret about Rob's past. Simon's actions only serve to anger Rob and his cronies, among them Thaddeus R. "Young" Steward, the book's narrator. The clique enacts its revenge on Simon in a "shockingly violent climax," according to *Kliatt* reviewer Paula Rohrlick.

On her home page, Giles stated that two famous works influenced her novel: William Golding's *Lord of the Flies* and F. Scott Fitzgerald's *The Great Gatsby*. "*Lord of the Flies* . . . made me think about the ability of power to corrupt. I even named my nerd character Simon as an homage to the book," Giles explained. She patterned "Young" Steward after the character of Nick Carraway in *The Great Gatsby*. "I liked the narrator, Nick, how he was enamored of the main character, so that his voice was not quite reliable. Now, Nick, in Fitzgerald's novel, is also the moral center of the book and I needed Young not quite that honorable." Giles also addressed her decision to reveal Simon's death so early in her work: "Why did I choose to give away the ending? The ending is violent and the book is not about the violence but what caused it. How things spin out of control. About little wrongs leading to big ones. If I gave the violence away at the beginning, I felt like I defused the shock—and shock wasn't the reason for this book to exist."

Critics found much to praise in *Shattering Glass*. Vicki Reutter, writing in *School Library Journal,* stated that the "plot is fast-paced and compelling and there is power in the brewing violence and shocking end." Ilene Cooper, reviewing the work in *Booklist,* noted some holes in the plot but added that Giles' "pacing is superb, and the story's twists are unexpected and disquieting." A critic in *Kirkus Reviews* remarked that "most intriguing are the quotes heading each chapter, revealing the perspectives of the characters five years later, and which raise questions of justice, mercy, and individual responsibility."

In *Dead Girls Don't Write Letters* strange events are set in motion after Sunny Reynolds receives a letter from her older sister, Jazz, who was presumed killed

Cover of *Dead Girls Don't Write Letters*, Giles' haunting novel about a sister who returns home after being thought dead. (Illustration copyright © 2003 by BTDNYC. Reproduced by permission of Henry Holt & Company, LLC.)

in a fire months earlier. Jazz then returns home and is immediately welcomed by Sunny's mother and father. Although Jazz seems to know much about the family's history, Sunny believes that the woman is an impostor and she sets about discovering her true identity. *Dead Girls Don't Write Letters* "is a page-turner with sharp dialogue and psychologically intriguing viewpoints," remarked Ilene Cooper in *Booklist,* and a critic in *Kirkus Reviews* stated that "teen readers will love having their preconceptions continually turned topsy-turvy, and will endlessly debate the tale's maddeningly ambiguous conclusion." Some reviewers found the conclusion of *Dead Girls Don't Write Letters* unconvincing, however a *Publishers Weekly* critic wrote that "the swift wrap-up . . . undercuts the carefully crafted nuances of complicated familial relationships," and Lynn Evarts maintained in *School Library Journal* that while "the plot is intriguing, . . . the ending is just too unclear." In *Kliatt,* Claire Rosser wrote: "There are plot twists here, which the author manages to pull off if the reader isn't too questioning."

Exploring Difficult Themes

Giles's novel *Playing in Traffic* concerns two students, shy Matt Lathrop and rebellious Skye Colby, and their odd, unlikely relationship. When Skye takes an interest in Matt, he is intrigued, despite the danger Skye represents. He becomes sexually involved with the mysterious girl who favors the Goth look, and their affair is kept secret, even though other friends subtly warn Matt about Skye's instability and controlling ways. Things come to a head when Skye demands that Matt do her a favor and threatens to harm Matt's beloved little sister if he does not comply. A *Publishers Weekly* reviewer found this a "suspenseful, psychologically gripping novel," and further noted: "Giles's narrative pace

If you can't forgive yourself . . . will anyone else?

RIGHT BEHIND YOU
GAIL GILES

A teen haunted by a horrific secret from his childhood takes center stage in Giles' 2007 novel *Right behind You*.
(Cover design and photography by Ben Mautner. Boy image © Image Source Photography/Veer. Reproduced by permission.)

If you enjoy the works of Gail Giles, you may also want to check out the following books:

Joan Lowery Nixon, *Don't Scream,* 1996.
Sonya Sones, *Stop Pretending: What Happened When My Big Sister Went Crazy,* 1999.
Alex Flinn, *Breaking Point,* 2002.

never slackens, and readers will find themselves racing to the finish." Similarly, a *Kirkus Reviews* contributor felt that by letting the plot unfold without sensational revelations, the author "makes her final shock all the more effective." In *School Library Journal* Karen Hoth was less impressed with *Playing in Traffic,* however, finding "too many loose ends," and observing that "Skye's sinister over-the-top demands detract from the character study of a quiet young man and a deeply disturbed girl." Ilene Cooper, writing in *Booklist,* had a higher assessment, however, noting that the "pacing is impeccable, and the story races along." Cooper further praised Giles' "sharp and strong" characterizations and her authentic-sounding dialogue.

In *What Happened to Cass McBride?* Giles narrates the story through three contrasting perspectives: high schooler Cass McBride, college student Kyle Kirby, and Detective Ben Gray. Through interviews with the teens' family and friends, the detective learns of Kyle's terrible desire for revenge: He blames Cass single-handedly for his younger brother's suicide, which he attributes to Cass's nasty rejection letter after his brother asked her out. To enact his revenge, Kyle drugs and kidnaps Cass, then buries her alive in a wooden box equipped with an air supply and a walkie-talkie, so he can inflict psychological pain. Reviews for *What Happened to Cass McBride?* were mostly positive, even though many critics were startled by the plot. Norah Piehl, writing in *TeenReads.com,* concluded that Giles' "complex, sophisticated suspense novel . . . will challenge readers' expectations while still keeping them up late at night." In *Kliatt* Janis Flint-Ferguson noted that "the setting is claustrophobic, the characters are complex, and the story will keep readers on the edge of their seats." In *School Library Journal,* Sherry Quinones described the novel as "a thrilling, one-sitting read that [readers] won't be able to put down." A critic for *Kirkus Reviews* summed up the work by calling *What Happened to Cass McBride?* "a damn scary read."

In *Right behind You* Giles focuses on a seventeen-year-old high-school student with a dark past. Kip is a smart, good-looking teen, and no one would guess that after his mother died of cancer when he was nine, he brutally murdered a younger boy. After spending several years in a mental institution, Kip was given a different name—Wade—and pronounced sane and safe to be in society again. He knows he must keep his past a secret, for students at other schools have ostracized him once they discovered his true identity. Now, however, he is in love with a young girl who seems to have her own ghosts to hide and he must decide whether to share information about his former life with her or not. Like other young adult novels from Giles, *Right behind You* earned praise from reviewers. Writing in *School Library Journal*, Lynn Rashid predicted that "reluctant readers will be drawn to the story's accessibility, and many teens will be pulled in by the larger questions the novel poses about innocence and acceptance." Similarly, a *Kirkus Reviews* contributor found the novel "thought-provoking and heart-wrenching." Noting the less-dramatic aspects of *Right behind You*, *Booklist* contributor Stephanie Zvirin concluded that "Giles' fans won't find outright thrills, but they'll come away with a greater understanding of redemption and forgiveness." Likewise, a *Publishers Weekly* reviewer wrote that *Right behind You* "explores, with sympathy and compassion, the nature of guilt, atonement and forgiveness." For *Kliatt* contributor Myrna Marler, *Right behind You* is "crisply written without sentimentality," and Kip, "in spite of his horrific past, is an honest and likable character."

Giles' frightening and thrilling novels reflect her sometimes pessimistic outlook on life. As she remarked during an online interview for the Cynthia Leitich Smith Web site, "I'm more cynical than most people. I know how very often people lie and I like to understand why they do. I think I'm a searcher. I love to find out new things. I kind of like to poke things with sticks and look in the dark places." Asked by Smith to describe the themes of her works, Giles stated, "Masks. People not being who they think they are or project themselves to be. Refusing to be a victim. Darkness runs in everyone—how one handles that darkness is what makes them good or evil." She further explained on her home page, "Why do I write such dark and edgy stuff? I want the reader to come up and sneak a peak at violence and darkness, check out the edge of the abyss and decide it is a trip not to be taken. Read about the road that leads to oblivion, but take another."

■ Biographical and Critical Sources

BOOKS

Giles, Gail, *Shattering Glass*, Roaring Brook Press (Brookfield, CT), 2002.

PERIODICALS

Booklist, April 1, 1997, Susan DeRonne, review of *Breath of the Dragon*, p. 1334; March 1, 2002, Ilene Cooper, review of *Shattering Glass*, p. 1133; March 15, 2003, Ilene Cooper, review of *Dead Girls Don't Write Letters*, p. 1317; September 1, 2004, Ilene Cooper, review of *Playing in Traffic*, p. 107; January 1, 2007, Ilene Cooper, review of *What Happened to Cass McBride?*, p. 80; October 15, 2007, Stephanie Zvirin, review of *Right behind You*, p. 45

Bookseller, January 16, 2004, Claudia Mody, "Teenage Reads," pp. 37-42.

Kirkus Reviews, February 1, 2002, review of *Shattering Glass*, p. 181; February 15, 2003, review of *Dead Girls Don't Write Letters*, p. 305; August 15, 2004, review of *Playing in Traffic*, p. 86; October 15, 2006, review of *What Happened to Cass McBride?*, p. 1071; August 1, 2007, review of *Right behind You*.

Kliatt, July, 2002, Paula Rohrlick, review of *Shattering Glass*, p. 10; May, 2003, Claire Rosser, review of *Dead Girls Don't Write Letters*, p. 8; September, 2003, Sarah Applegate, review of *Shattering Glass*, pp. 16-17; September 1, 2006, Janis Flint-Ferguson, review of *What Happened to Cass McBride?*, p. 12; September, 2007, Myrna Marler, review of *Right behind You*, p. 12.

Publishers Weekly, February 11, 2002, review of *Shattering Glass*, p. 188; January 13, 2003, review of *Dead Girls Don't Write Letters*, p. 61; October 13, 2003, review of *Shattering Glass*, p. 82; October 4, 2004, review of *Playing in Traffic*, p. 89; November 13, 2006, review of *What Happened to Cass McBride?*, p. 59; June 18, 2007, review of *Right behind You*, p. 56.

St. Petersburg Times (St. Petersburg, FL), March 15, 2004, Holly Atkins, interview with Giles, p. 4E.

School Library Journal, June, 1997, Susan Hepler, review of *Breath of the Dragon*, p. 117; April, 2002, Vicki Reutter, review of *Shattering Glass*, pp. 148-149; May, 2003, Lynn Evarts, review of *Dead Girls Don't Write Letters*, p. 152; December, 2004, Karen Hoth, review of *Playing in Traffic*, p. 146; February 1, 2007, Sherry Quinones, review of *What Happened to Cass McBride?*, p. 116; September, 2007, Lynn Rashid, review of *Right behind You*, p. 196.

Teacher Librarian, February, 2004, Ruth Cox, "Tough Guys," pp. 10-11.

Voice of Youth Advocates, April, 2003, Bonnie Kunzel, "Shattered by *Shattering Glass*: A Teen Book Group Forsakes Fantasy for Realism," pp. 19-21.

ONLINE

Cynsations Web log, http://cynthialeitichsmith. blogspot.com/ (March 6, 2006), "Gail Giles."

Cynthia Leitich Smith Web site, http://www. cynthialeitichsmith.com/ (May, 2002), interview with Giles.

Dear Author Web site, http://www.dearauthor.com/ (January 23, 2009), review of *Right behind You.*

Gail Giles Home Page, http://www.galegiles.com (April 13, 2009).

MyShelf.com, http://www.myshelf.com/ (January 1, 2007), Beverly Rowe, "Author of the Month: Gail Giles."

TeenReads.com, http://www.teenreads.com/ (July 11, 2007), Norah Piehl, review of *What Happened to Cass McBride?*

TeensReadToo.com, http://www.teensreadtoo.com/(-April 13, 2009), interview with Giles.

Young Adult Books Central Web site, http://www. yabookscentral.com/ (April 13, 2009), "Gail Giles Biography."*

(Courtesy of Alan Gratz.)

Alan Gratz

Library Association (ALA), 2007, for *Samurai Short-stop;* Quick Pick for Young Adult Readers, ALA, 2008, for *Something Rotten.*

■ Personal

Born January 27, 1972, in Knoxville, TN; married; wife's name Wendi; children: Jo. *Education:* University of Tennessee, Knoxville, B.A., M.A. *Hobbies and other interests:* Baseball, reading, writing, collecting comics and action figures, playing fantasy sports and computer games.

■ Addresses

Home—Penland, NC. *E-mail*—bigcheese@alangratz. com.

■ Career

Writer. Has also worked as a bookseller, librarian, eighth-grade English teacher, and TV and radio freelance writer.

■ Awards, Honors

Kimberly Colen memorial grant, Society of Children's Book Writers and Illustrators, cowinner, 2003; Top Ten Best Books for Young Adults, American

■ Writings

NOVELS FOR YOUNG ADULTS

Samurai Shortstop, Dial Books (New York, NY), 2006.
Something Rotten ("Horatio Wilkes" series), Dial Books (New York, NY), 2007.
Something Wicked ("Horatio Wilkes" series), Dial Books (New York, NY), 2008.
The Brooklyn Nine: A Novel in Nine Innings, Dial Books (New York, NY), 2009.

PLAYS

Sweet Sixteen, produced at Knoxville Actors Co-op, TN, 1998.
Indian Myths and Legends, produced at Knoxville Actors Co-op, TN, 1998.
Young Hickory, produced at Knoxville Actors Co-op, TN, 1999.
The Gift of the Magi (adapted from a story by O. Henry), produced at Knoxville Actors Co-op, TN, 1999.
Measured in Labor: The Coal Creek Project, produced at Knoxville Actors Co-op, TN, 2004.

The Legend of Sleepy Hollow (adapted from the story by Washington Irving), produced at Knoxville Actors Co-op, TN, 2004.

OTHER

Also contributor of articles to periodicals. Writer of several episodes of *City Confidential*, Arts and Entertainment (A&E) network.

■ **Adaptations**

Samurai Shortstop was adapted for audiobook, Listening Library, 2006; *Something Rotten* was adapted for audiobook, Listening Library, 2007.

■ **Sidelights**

Alan Gratz did not always want to be an author for young adults. "First I wanted to be a train engineer," he told an interviewer for *Powells.com*. "Then . . . I decided I was going to be a Jedi Master. . . . When that failed, I turned to my grandfather's old Underwood typewriter in the garage and started banging out a weekly newspaper for my street. I was pretty much going to be a writer of some kind from that point on." With the publication of his 2006 debut novel, *Samurai Shortstop*, Gratz made that early promise come true, crafting an historical tale of baseball in Japan that has earned widespread critical acclaim. He followed this success with a pair of novels featuring a spirited teenage detective: *Something Rotten* and *Something Wicked,* both of which feature plots rewritten from Shakespeare's plays. With *The Brooklyn Nine: A Novel in Nine Innings*, Gratz again focuses on the great American pastime of baseball. Gratz has also written a number of plays, produced in his hometown of Knoxville, Tennessee, and additionally has written for television.

The *Bushido* of Writing

Gratz was born in 1972, in Knoxville, into a family "uniformly mad for American football," as he later told his *Powells.com* interviewer. He had players, referees, cheerleaders, and coaches on both sides of the family, so when he developed a passion for baseball, it was seen as something of a betrayal. "My brother and I were aliens in the football country of my father's family, but it never mattered

to my dad," Gratz explained. Despite his love for the game, Gratz was not an accomplished baseball player, however. As he remarked in an *ALAN Online* interview, "My greatest Little League moment: I misplayed a long drive to left field, then absolutely launched the ball, trying to throw a runner out at the plate. The ball sailed up the first base line, over the fence, and into the bleachers, where it hit my little brother in the arm. All the runners scored. After the inning was over, the coach told me I had a good arm. He also told me not to come back."

Besides baseball, Gratz loved writing as a youth. By his fifth-grade year he had written a novel about the evils of spinach. As he noted on his home page, "I kept writing stories and newspaper articles all through middle school and high school, and studied writing in college." By 1998, he had decided to join

Cover of Alan Gratz's novel *Samurai Shortstop*, which finds a Japanese-American baseball fan learning the ancient discipline honored by his family. (Cover image © 2006 by Tony Sahara. Reproduced by permission of Speak, a division of Penguin Putnam Books for Young Readers.)

in the renaissance that young-adult books were then experiencing. While working for a bookstore, he found time to write two novels: one about a group of teenage superheroes, and the other a romantic comedy about a high school boy who invents long-distance girlfriends so that the girls in his school might find him more attractive. Neither of these books sold. This changed, though, when Gratz became interested in Japan and Japanese history.

Gratz's first publication, *Samurai Shortstop*, "is the story of a sixteen-year-old boy in 1890s Tokyo who learns to blend baseball with *bushido*—the samurai way of the warrior—to prove to his father there is still room for ancient samurai traditions in a new and changing Japan," the author explained to Cynthia Leitich Smith in a *Cynsations* online interview. As Gratz told Smith, his path to publication was "definitely not a sprint. . . . It took me six years of writing and submitting to finally make a sale." Speaking with Aline Pereira of *PaperTigers.org*, Gratz remarked on his inspiration for *Samurai Shortstop*: "I was wistfully reading a travel guide to Japan when I discovered a photo of a kimono-clad man throwing out the first pitch at a Japanese high school baseball tournament in 1915." Before seeing that photo, Gratz had assumed that American soldiers most likely introduced the game to Japan after World War II. While researching the topic, however, Gratz discovered that American sailors actually brought baseball to Japan in the mid-nineteenth century. He began to see a similarity between the baseball bat and the sword of a samurai, or warrior. "One thing led to another," Gratz told Pereira, "baseball, bushido, the Meiji Restoration [the series of modernizing and Westernizing changes in Japan's social and political structure in the late nineteenth century], the historical tension between East and West—and *Samurai Shortstop* was born."

The novel centers on Toyo, a teen growing up in Tokyo during the 1890s, as Emperor Meiji forbids many of the old customs, including the samurai way, a tradition that has held Toyo's family together for generations. The young man is a witness to his beloved uncle's ritual suicide; Toyo's father Sotaro also feels bereft at the loss of the old ways. Toyo attends a prominent high school in Tokyo, where he is subjected to savage hazing rituals. He finds solace in the game of baseball, using his father's samurai code to help him become more proficient in the sport. In doing so, Toyo shows his father that there is still room for *bushido* in the modern world. All of this leads up to the climax of a big game. Reviewing the novel in *Booklist,* Carolyn Phelan found it "a memorable chronicle of boys' inhumanity to boys, and a testament to enduring values in a time of social change." Further praise came from *School Library Journal* contributor Marilyn Taniguchi, who

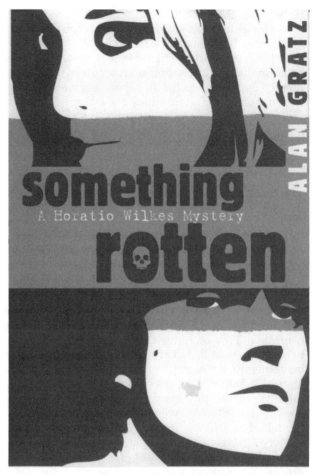

Gratz takes readers to Denmark, Tennessee, in his novel *Something Rotten*, which introduces teen sleuth Horatio Wilkes. (Jacket art © 2007 by Emilian Gregory. Reproduced by permission of Dial Books, a division of Penguin Putnam Books for Young Readers.)

termed *Samurai Shortstop* a "well-written tale [that] offers plenty of fascinating detail, a fast-paced story, and a flesh perspective on 'American's pastime.'" Similarly, a *Publishers Weekly* reviewer found the same work "an intense read about a fascinating time and place in world history."

Shakespeare's Detective

Gratz's second novel moved away from the historical aspect of *Samurai Warrior*. With *Something Rotten,* he uses William Shakespeare's *Hamlet* as a template and springboard for a contemporary mystery set in Denmark, Tennessee, and featuring Horatio Wilkes, "recast as a wry, sarcastic, seventeen-year-old detective," as Gratz explained to Smith. Horatio actually had his genesis, however, during Gratz's own undergraduate days at the University of Tennessee.

He created the young detective for a mystery and detective fiction class, basing him on the character of Horatio from Shakespeare's *Hamlet*. "I like that Horatio is grounded where Hamlet always has his head in lofty philosophical inner debate," Gratz further explained to Smith. Gratz enjoyed writing the character and giving him a skeptical character. Originally, Horatio was an adult forensic anthropologist, but after Gratz began writing for young adults, he transformed the character into a teenager with an attitude.

The result was the novel *Something Rotten*. Attending the exclusive Wittenburg Academy in Tennessee, Horatio Wilkes becomes friends with Hamilton (Hamlet) Prince, whose wealthy family owns the Elsinore Paper Company in Denmark, Tennessee. Hamilton's father has recently died and his mother has remarried. Just as with Shakespeare's play, *Hamlet*, this new husband is Hamilton's uncle. Horatio accompanies Hamilton to his home for the summer and finds a great deal rotten in the town of Denmark. This includes the polluting of the river by the paper mill and the belief by Hamilton that his father, Rex, was murdered. Horatio comes to the rescue on both of these fronts in this "witty, modern retelling of the old story from Horatio's point of view," as *Kliatt* reviewer Myrna Marler described the tale. For a *Kirkus Reviews* contributor, *Something Rotten* is a "well-crafted mystery [that] has appeal for readers familiar with both Raymond Chandler's novels and Shakespeare's masterpiece"

The author admitted that transforming the Bard's play into a novel for teens was no easy task. He told Smith that "turning Shakespeare's six-hour philosophical opus into a young adult page turner was a challenge, but I overcame that by focusing on the really pulpy parts of the story—some of which, like Ophelia's drowning—originally happen off stage. I also had to be fairly intimate with the play as a whole, which meant multiple re-readings and deconstructions, all of which was fun for me because I really do enjoy Shakespeare."

In *Something Wicked,* a follow-up, Gratz takes Shakespeare's *Macbeth* as his inspiration. Here Horatio is attending a Scottish festival at a Tennessee mountain and discovers the body of Duncan MacRae, the owner of said mountain. MacRae has obviously been murdered, and Horatio tries to sort out the clues, especially after suspicion falls on his friend Mac, the son of the murdered man. Mac and his girlfriend, Beth, are also in attendance at the festival and appear to have a motive, as they have become involved in a hostile takeover of the mountain so they can open a ski resort. *Kliatt* contributor Paula Rohrlick felt that "this suspenseful mystery will

Cover of Gratz's teen novel *Something Wicked*, which marks the return of sleuth Horatio Wilkes. (Jacket art © 2008 by Greg Stadnyk. Reproduced by permission of Dial Books, a division of Penguin Putnam Books for Young Readers.)

work even for those unfamiliar with the Shakespeare play." Likewise, a *Kirkus Reviews* contributor called *Something Wicked* "a satisfying remake of one of the Bard's most familiar works."

Baseball Dreams

With *The Brooklyn Nine* Gratz returns to baseball and historical fiction. Speaking with Pereira, he noted that this work "will chronicle nine 'innings' or generations, of an immigrant American family from the 1830s to the present through their ongoing connections to baseball." The nine interlocking tales that comprise the book each feature a different generation of the Schneider (later Snider) family of Brooklyn. Young Felix Schneider is a recent immigrant from Germany when he watches the Knickerbockers play an early version of the game in 1845, then helps Alexander Cartwright, who invented the modern game of baseball, battle a fire. Walter Snider plays the game at the turn of the twentieth century and battles discrimination against both Jews and African Americans. The story later focuses on a female offspring, Kat Flint, who plays in the first professional women's league during World War II. Further tales take the family history up to the twenty-first century in this "wonderful baseball book that is more than the sum of its parts," as *Horn Book* reviewer Jonathan Hunt noted. A *Kirkus Reviews* contributor also had praise for *The Brooklyn Nine*, terming it "an entertaining and compelling look at the deep roots of our national pastime." Similarly, *Booklist* reviewer Ian Chipman lauded Gratz's book as a "sweeping diaspora of Americana."

If you enjoy the works of Alan Gratz, you may also want to check out the following books:

David Klass, *The Atami Dragons*, 1984.
Virginia Euwer Wolff, *Bat 6*, 1998.
Anthony Horowitz's "Diamond Brothers" series, including *The Falcon's Malteser*, 2004.

Speaking with Smith, Gratz expounded on the pleasures of writing for young adults. "I love that everything for teenagers is so immediate and monumental," he remarked, adding: "It's a bizarre time in our lives, when the future is wide open and unwritten and yet the present feels so consuming and indelible. It's a fun time to write about and to write for because the emotions and passions run so high. . . . We need books that give teenagers something to read in that ever-shrinking period between childhood and adulthood, something that is intelligent and mature enough to appeal to the 'adult' in young adults, and yet still entertaining and riveting enough to keep the 'young' part of them engaged as well."

■ Biographical and Critical Sources

PERIODICALS

Booklist, April 15, 2006, Carolyn Phelan, review of *Samurai Shortstop*, p. 58; November 1, 2008, Carolyn Phelan, review of *Something Wicked*, p. 36; February 1, 2009, Ian Chipman, review of *The Brooklyn Nine: A Novel in Nine Innings*, p. 40.

Horn Book, March-April, 2009, Jonathan Hunt, review of *The Brooklyn Nine*, p. 194.

Kirkus Reviews, April 15, 2006, review of *Samurai Shortstop*, p. 406; September 1, 2007, review of *Something Rotten*; October 1, 2008, review of *Something Wicked*; January 15, 2009, review of *The Brooklyn Nine*.

Kliatt, September, 2007, Myrna Marler, review of *Something Rotten*, p. 13; September, 2008, Paula Rohrlick, review of *Something Wicked*, p. 11.

Publishers Weekly, May 22, 2006, review of *Samurai Shortstop*, p. 53.

School Library Journal, May, 2006, Marilyn Taniguchi, review of *Samurai Shortstop*, p. 62; July, 2006, Marilyn Taniguchi, review of *Samurai Shortstop*, p. 102; January, 2008, John Leighton, review of *Something Rotten* p. 118; January, 2009, Jake Pettit, review of *Something Wicked*, p. 102.

Voice of Youth Advocates, December, 2007, Angelica Delgado, review of *Something Rotten*, p. 427.

Washington Post, December 10, 2006, Elizabeth Ward, review of *Samurai Shortstop*, p. T7.

ONLINE

Alan Gratz Home Page, http://www.alangratz.com (March 31, 2009).

Alan Gratz Web log, http://gratzindustries.blogspot.com/ (March 31, 2009).

ALAN Online, http://www.alan-ya.org/ (January 4, 2007, interview with Gratz.

Cynsations Web log, http://cynthialeitichsmith.blogspot.com/ (March 31, 2009), "Author Interview: Alan Gratz on *Something Rotten*."

PaperTigers.org, http://www.papertigers.org/ (March 31, 2009), Aline Pereira, interview with Gratz.

Powells.com, http://www.powells.com/ (March 31, 2009), "Kids' Q&A: Alan Gratz."*

H. Rider Haggard

(Photograph, Library of Congress.)

■ Personal

Born Henry Rider Haggard, June 22, 1856, in Bradenham, Norfolk, England; died May 14, 1925, in London, England; son of William Meybohm (a barrister) and Ella (Doveton) Haggard; married Louisa Mariana Margiston, August 11, 1880; children: Arthur John, Angela, Dorothy, Lilias. *Education:* Attended Lincoln's Inn, 1881-85.

■ Career

Writer and attorney. Lawyer; called to the Bar, 1885; secretary to Lieutenant-Governor Henry Bulwer in Natal, South Africa, 1875-77; member of the staff of Sir Theophilus Shepstone (special commissioner in the Transvaal, South Africa), 1877; master and registrar of High Court of Transvaal, 1877-79; returned to England, 1879; managed wife's estate in Norfolk, England, beginning 1880; assistant to Henry Bargave Deane, 1885-87; Unionist and Agricultural candidate for East Norfolk, 1895; researched agricultural conditions and rural populations in England, 1901-02; British Government Special Commissioner to report on Salvation Army settlements in the United States, 1905; chair of Reclamation and Unemployed Labour Committee of Royal Commission on Coast Erosion and Afforestation, 1906-11; member of Dominions Royal Commission, 1912-17.

■ Member

Society of Authors (chair of committee, 1896-98), Royal Colonial Institute (vice president, 1917), Athenaeum Club, National Club, Cecil Club.

■ Awards, Honors

Knighted, 1912; made knight commander, Order of the British Empire, 1919.

■ Writings

NOVELS

Dawn, three volumes, Hurst & Blackett (London, England), 1884, one-volume edition, Appleton (New York, NY), 1887.

The Witch's Head, three volumes, Hurst & Blackett (London, England), 1884, one-volume edition, Appleton (New York, NY), 1885.

King Solomon's Mines, Cassell (New York, NY), 1885.

She: A History of Adventure, Harper (New York, NY), 1886, annotated edition published as *The Annotated She: A Critical Edition of H. Rider Haggard's Victorian Romance,* edited by Norman Etherington, Indiana University Press (Bloomington, IN), 1991.

Allan Quatermain, Being an Account of His Further Adventures and Discoveries in Company with Sir Henry Curtis, Bart., Commander John Good, R.N., and One Umslopogaas, Harper (New York, NY), 1887.

Jess, Harper (New York, NY), 1887.

A Tale of Three Lions, and On Going Back, Munro (New York, NY), 1887, published as *Allan the Hunter,* Lothrop (Boston, MA), 1898.

Mr. Meeson's Will, Harper (New York, NY), 1888.

Maiwa's Revenge: or, The War of the Little Hand, Harper (New York, NY), 1888.

My Fellow Laborer (includes "The Wreck of the Copeland"), Munro (New York, NY), 1888.

Colonel Quatrich, V.C.: A Tale of Country Life, Lovell (New York, NY), 1888.

Cleopatra, Being an Account of the Fall and Vengeance of Harmachis, the Royal Egyptian, as Set Forth by His Own Hand, Harper (New York, NY), 1889.

Beatrice, Harper (New York, NY), 1890.

(With Andrew Lang) *The World's Desire,* Harper (New York, NY), 1890.

Eric Brighteyes, U.S. Book Company (New York, NY), 1891.

Nada the Lily, Longman (New York, NY), 1892.

An Heroic Effort, Butler & Tanner, 1893.

Montezuma's Daughter, Longman (New York, NY), 1893.

The People of the Mist, Longman (New York, NY), 1894.

Heart of the World, Longman (New York, NY), 1895.

Joan Haste, Longman (New York, NY), 1895.

The Wizard, Longman (New York, NY), 1896.

Doctor Therne, Longman (New York, NY), 1898.

Swallow: A Tale of the Great Trek, Longman (New York, NY), 1899.

The Spring of a Lion, Neeley (New York, NY), 1899.

Lysbeth, Longman (New York, NY), 1901.

Pearl-Maiden, Longman (New York, NY), 1903.

The Brethren, Doubleday (New York, NY), 1904.

Stella Fregelius: A Tale of Three Destinies, Longman (New York, NY), 1904.

Ayesha: The Return of She, Doubleday (New York, NY), 1905.

The Spirit of Bambatse, Longman (New York, NY), 1906, published as *Benita: An African Romance,* Longman (London, England), 1906.

The Way of the Spirit, Hutchinson (London, England), 1906.

Fair Margaret, Hutchinson (London, England), 1907, published as *Margaret,* Longman (New York, NY), 1907.

The Yellow God, Cupples & Leon (New York, NY), 1908.

The Ghost Kings, Cassell (London, England), 1908, published as *The Lady of the Heavens,* Authors & Newspapers Association (New York, NY), 1908.

The Lady of Blossholme, Hodder & Stoughton (London, England), 1909.

Morning Star, Longman (New York, NY), 1910.

Queen Sheba's Ring, Doubleday (New York, NY), 1910.

Red Eve, Doubleday (New York, NY), 1911.

The Mahatma and the Hare: A Dream Story, Holt (New York, NY), 1911.

Marie, Longman (New York, NY), 1912.

Child of Storm, Longman (New York, NY), 1913.

The Wanderer's Necklace, Longman (New York, NY), 1914.

The Holy Flower, Ward, Lock (London, England), 1915, published as *Allan and the Holy Flower,* Longman (New York, NY), 1915.

The Ivory Child, Longman (New York, NY), 1916.

Finished, Longman (New York, NY), 1917.

Moon of Israel, Longman (New York, NY), 1918.

Love Eternal, Longman (New York, NY), 1918.

When the World Shook, Longman (New York, NY), 1919.

The Ancient Allan, Longman (New York, NY), 1920.

She and Allan, Longman (New York, NY), 1921.

The Virgin of the Sun, Doubleday (New York, NY), 1922.

Wisdom's Daughter: The Life and Love Story of She-Who-Must-Be-Obeyed, Doubleday (New York, NY), 1923.

Heu-Heu: or, The Monster, Doubleday (New York, NY), 1924.

Queen of the Dawn: A Love Tale of Old Egypt, Doubleday (New York, NY), 1925.

The Treasure of the Lake, Doubleday (New York, NY), 1926.

Allan and the Ice-Gods: A Tale of Beginnings, Doubleday (New York, NY), 1927.

Mary of Marion Isle, Hutchinson (London, England), 1929, published as *Marion Isle,* Doubleday (New York, NY), 1929.

Belshazzar, Doubleday (New York, NY), 1930.

Novels also published in omnibus and multi-title editions.

SHORT STORIES

Allan's Wife, and Other Tales, Harper (New York, NY), 1889.

Black Heart and White Heart, and Other Stories, Longman (London, England), 1900, published as *Elissa: The Doom of Zimbabwe; Black Heart and White Heart: A Zulu Idyll*, Longman (New York, NY), 1900.

Smith and the Pharaohs, and Other Tales, Arrowsmith (Bristol, England), 1920, Longman (New York, NY), 1921.

The Best Short Stories of Rider Haggard, edited by Peter Haining, Joseph (London, England), 1981.

Hunter Quatermain's Story: The Uncollected Adventures of Alan Quatermain, edited by Peter Haining, Peter Owen (London, England), 2003.

OTHER

Cetywayo and His White Neighbors; or, Remarks on Recent Events in Zululand, Natal, and the Transvaal, Truebner (London, England), 1882, revised edition, 1888, abridged edition published as *A History of the Transvaal*, New Amsterdam (New York, NY), 1899, published as *The Last Boer War*, Kegan Paul (London, England), 1899.

Church and the State: An Appeal to the Laity, privately printed, 1895.

A Farmer's Year, Being His Commonplace Book for 1898, Longman (New York, NY), 1899.

The New South Africa, Pearson (London, England), 1900.

A Winter Pilgrimage, Being an Account of Travels through Palestine, Italy, and the Island of Cyprus, Accomplished in the Year 1900, Longman (New York, NY), 1901.

Rural England, Being an Account of Agricultural and Social Researches Carried out in the Years 1901 and 1902, two volumes, Longman (New York, NY), 1902.

A Gardener's Year, Longman (New York, NY), 1905.

The Poor and the Land, Longman (New York, NY), 1905, published as *Report on the Salvation Army Colonies*, His Majesty's Stationery Office (London, England), 1905.

Regeneration, Being an Account of the Social Work of the Salvation Army in Great Britain, Longman (New York, NY), 1910.

Rural Denmark and Its Lessons, Longman (New York, NY), 1911.

A Call to Arm to the Men of East Anglia, privately printed, 1914.

The After-War Settlement and the Employment of Ex-Service Men in the Overseas Dominions, St. Catherine Press (London, England), 1916.

The Days of My Life: An Autobiography, two volumes, edited by C.J. Longman, Longman (New York, NY), 1926.

The Private Diaries of Sir H. Rider Haggard, 1914-1925, edited by D.S. Higgins, Stein & Day (New York, NY), 1980.

Diary of an African Journey: The Return of Rider Haggard, edited with an introduction and notes by Stephen Coan, New York University Press (New York, NY), 2000.

Contributor to periodicals. Coeditor of *African Review*, 1898.

■ Adaptations

She was filmed in 1916, 1917, 1935, and—with Ursula Andress—1965; *Mr. Meeson's Will* was filmed as *The Grasp of Greed*, 1916; *Jess* was filmed as *Heart and Soul*, 1917; *Moon of Israel* was filmed in 1927; *King Solomon's Mines* was filmed with Stewart Granger and Deborah Kerr in 1950, as *Watusi* in 1959, and with Richard Chamberlain and Sharon Stone in 1985; *Allan Quatermain* was filmed as *Allan Quatermain and the Lost City of Gold* with Richard Chamberlain and Sharon Stone in 1986. *Allan Quatermain* and *She* have also been adapted as audiobooks.

■ Sidelights

H. Rider Haggard, a prolific Victorian-era British writer, remains best known for his adventure novels, notably *King Solomon's Mines* and *She: A History of Adventure*. According to Richard C. Carpenter, writing in the *Dictionary of Literary Biography*, Haggard's "great talent lay not only in his ability to imagine exotic situations but also to create one adventure after another, so that the reader is swept breathlessly along on a current of suspense. His plots carry extraordinary vividness and conviction, partly through the empathy he creates by the sheer peril of the situations but also . . . though the wealth of circumstantial detail that embeds his exotic locales and events in a matrix of reality."

Although the author's works may be unfamiliar to contemporary audiences, *Dictionary of Literary Biography* contributor P.T. Whelan noted that "in his day Haggard was the most popular writer in England and among the highest earning, commanding large sums from publishers' advances, magazine serializations, and the sheer volume of sales of his romances." Haggard's works were informed by his extensive travels, especially his time in Africa,

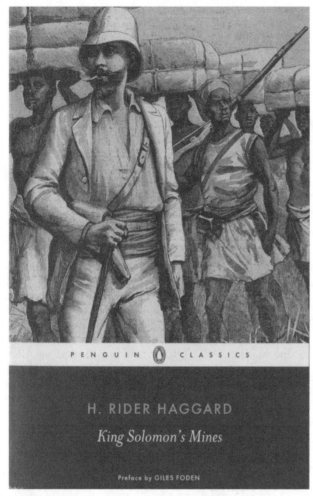

PENGUIN CLASSICS

H. RIDER HAGGARD

King Solomon's Mines

Preface by GILES FODEN

Cover of H. Rider Haggard's classic adventure novel *King Solomon's Mines,* **featuring an engraving by Dortune Louis Meaulle and Henri Meyer.** (Cover photograph © 2007 by Bridgeman Art Library. Reproduced by permission of Penguin Books, Ltd.)

where he served as a government official. According to another *Dictionary of Literary Biography* contributor, John M.W. Hallock, the author's "sympathies were global. While colonists were busy exporting British culture, Haggard became a medium by which a great knowledge of other realms from Peru to Denmark was imported into the collective English imagination."

Haggard came slowly to a career in literature. He was born Henry Rider Haggard in 1856 into what Carpenter described as an "old and respected Norfolk family." In his childhood he was considered slow witted and inclined to daydreaming. His parents consequently decided to end his education when he was seventeen. Two years later, he was placed by his father into the service of Henry Bulwer, who worked in South Africa as lieutenant-governor of Natal. South Africa would prove

inspirational to Haggard, who remained there for most of the next six years and developed a keen appreciation for the indigenous population, jungles, and wildlife.

Travels Influence Adventure Tales

After returning to England, Haggard saw publication of his *Cetywayo and His White Neighbors; or, Remarks on Recent Events in Zululand, Natal, and the Transvaal,* an account of his African experiences and observations. He followed that volume with *Dawn,* an unsatisfactory novel, according to critics, that nonetheless manages to convey a sense of suspense despite unfolding a convoluted narrative. Haggard later issued another novel, *The Witch's Head,* which likewise failed to intrigue an English readership, although George Saintsbury, writing in *Academy,* proclaimed the novel "well written" and added that "it has considerable interest of plot."

While writing both *Dawn* and *The Witch's Head,* Haggard was studying for a career in law. Upon completion of his studies, as legend has it, he wagered that he could produce a tale equal to Robert Louis Stevenson's *Treasure Island,* which was enormously popular at that time. The result was *King Solomon's Mines,* which is an account of adventurer Allan Quatermain's search for lost treasure in Africa. During his quest, Quatermain nearly freezes to death in the mountains, becomes a captive of barbaric natives, and narrowly avoids a dangerous trap while recovering a cache of lost diamonds. This exciting tale, although described as somewhat slapdash in style by some reviewers, found considerable favor with English readers. As Andrew Lang noted in an 1885 edition of *Saturday Review,* "Since *Treasure Island* we have seen no such healthily exciting volume." A century later, *Armchair Detective* contributor Robert Sandels would comment that *King Solomon's Mines* "has an appeal and durability which leads one to wonder if it isn't more than just a well-told tale."

Buoyed by the immense success of *King Solomon's Mines,* Haggard produced *Allan Quatermain,* wherein the adventurer and his loyal cohorts uncover a lost civilization in Africa. In the ensuing years, Haggard added further to the "Quatermain" series, although none of the succeeding volumes would quite match the status of *King Solomon's Mines.* Still, as Gerald Monsman commented in *H. Rider Haggard on the Imperial Frontier: The Political and Literary Contexts of His African Romances,* Haggard "fused the heterogeneous fields of comparative literature, religion, and anthropology to perfect the imperial adventure novel. This deliberate blending of motifs and themes from other disciplines . . . gave his novels more character than those of his predecessors and represented the ultimate step in the development of this genre."

Issued in 1887, Haggard's novel *She: A History of Adventure* does rank with *King Solomon's Mines* as an enduring adventure tale, according to many critics. In *She,* a young man discovers that he is the lone descendant of an ancient Egyptian priest who had been executed for having loved a princess. The priest's executioner, a beautiful and jealous queen, still reigns in the faraway city of Kor, and so the hero, Leo Vincey, endeavors to find her. Together with an old friend and a servant, Leo undertakes the dangerous journey to Kor. Once there, Leo meets the immortal queen, Ayesha—also known as She-Who-Must-Be-Obeyed. While she believes him to be the reincarnation of the priest she loved—and killed—centuries earlier, Leo is hypnotized by her extraordinary beauty and believes himself in love with her even though he senses her evil nature. *She* builds to a climax replete with a pillar of fire and a harrowing escape across a dangerous chasm. "Where pulp exotica tends to offer images of buried treasure found or ancient powers restored, generic resolutions for artificial problems, *She* raises real dilemmas and leaves them gapingly unresolved, on a note of unattainable desire and irretrievable loss," observed Geoffrey O'Brien in the *Voice Literary Supplement.*

She brought Haggard considerable fame and wealth, and through that novel, as well as *King Solomon's Mines,* his reputation as a masterful adventure

The 1937 film version of *King Solomon's Mines* starred John Loder in the role of Haggard's heroic adventurer Alan Quatermain. (Gaumont-British/The Kobal Collection/The Picture Desk, Inc.)

Richard Chamberlain starred as Alan Quatermain in the 1985 film version of Haggard's *King Solomon's Mines*. (Cannon/ The Kobal Collection/The Picture Desk, Inc.)

writer has been sustained. Although he continued to write many more tales in the ensuing decades, however, he failed to duplicate the success of *She*. As Carpenter observed in his *Dictionary of Literary Biography* profile, "[*She*] is Haggard's masterpiece; he did not write another work to match it in the long career that followed." Still, the lucrative success of his early tales gave Haggard sufficient funds to maintain the country estate inherited by his wife. There, at Ditchingham, he produced many more novels, including further "Quatermain" adventures and a *She* sequel, *Ayesha: The Return of She*, in which the cruel, beautiful queen is reincarnated and again sought by Leo. In 1921 Haggard released *She and Allan*, in which he unites his two most popular characters.

In the years after his greatest success, Haggard pursued other interests in addition to writing. He became increasingly active in agricultural reform and produced several volumes on gardening, English farming, and rural life. Notable here are such works as the two-volume *Rural England, Being an Account of Agricultural and Social Researches Car-*

ried out in the Years 1901 and 1902 and *A Gardener's Year*. Haggard also served on government commissions concerning land maintenance, and it is for these endeavors, as much as for his literary achievements, that he was knighted in 1912.

Haggard's Legacy

Haggard died in 1925, and in the years since much of his literary work has been forgotten or ignored. However, with *King Solomon's Mines*—and the heroic Quatermain—as well as *She*, he remains a prominent figure in the adventure genre. The film industry has regularly turned to Haggard's greatest creations for inspiration. *She* alone has been made into at least four films, while *King Solomon's Mines* has inspired two adaptations, including a film featuring Richard Chamberlain and Sharon Stone. "Haggard's influence is still discernible in popular fiction, particularly science fiction and fantasy," Whelan stated. "In film, not only have Haggard's own works appealed to directors, but every chil-

If you enjoy the works of H. Rider Haggard, you may also want to check out the following books:

Edgar Rice Burroughs, *Tarzan of the Apes*, 1914.
Iris Johansen, *The Tiger Prince*, 1993.
The mystery novels of Elizabeth Peters, including *Tomb of the Golden Bird*, 2006.

dren's animated film or television serial about lost cities or Egyptian curses owes something to him directly or indirectly."

Contemporary criticism of Haggard has focused on what some view as racist, sexist, and imperialistic themes in his works. "He believed straightforwardly in Britain's civilizing mission; that a race higher (albeit temporarily) on the ladder of evolution had a duty to rule and help those on the lower rungs," Anthony Lejeune reported in the *National Review*. "He believed what, until recently, would have been generally accepted as quite obviously true—that different races have different characteristics, some of which are more admirable than others." Similarly, Whelan noted, "The racism and sexism that were such a powerful part of the ethos of his time are undeniably present in his works, more egregiously in some than in others. Yet the theosophical wisdom and love that are Haggard's highest values transcend boundaries of race and gender."

In 1997 one of Haggard's diaries was found among his papers. Published three years later as *Diary of an African Journey: The Return of Rider Haggard*, the diary is an account of Haggard's journeys throughout southern Africa as a member of the Dominions Royal Commission. The commission was sent on a government fact-finding mission to determine what role England's dominions could play in strengthening the British Empire through trade and other means. The diary provides a look into Haggard's thoughts about his old African home, which he had not seen in nearly three decades, and contains an early and insightful assessment of South Africa circa 1914. The book also features Haggard's meetings with political leaders and old friends, including his former servant, Mazooku. "Anyone who is interested in South African history or the British Empire at its zenith will be intrigued by Haggard's descriptions of the country and its leaders shortly after the establishment of the Union of South Africa and only thirteen years after the end of the Anglo-Boer War," wrote F.W. de Klerk in an article for the London *Times*. "His observations regarding Rhodesia and Kenya—which he also visited—paint a vivid picture of the times." Considering the age in which he wrote *Diary of an African Journey*, Haggard shows himself to be sympathetic to the native Africans' plight. He spent the last three weeks of his trip in Zululand and was especially sympathetic toward the Zulus, who, like most native Africans, had their lands seized by the whites. As he reported back to his superiors, the "white man has a very heavy bill to pay to the native."

Ultimately, Haggard's reputation rests on the publication of *King Solomon's Mines* and *She*, "and even those two titles are no longer well known to the casual reader," Elizabeth S. Davidson wrote in the *Dictionary of Literary Biography*. "Yet lovers of fantasy and science fiction can still feel the force of Haggard's discovery of places for adventures of the body, mind, and spirit. In Allan Quatermain and Ayesha he created two characters who, once encountered, are not easily forgotten."

■ **Biographical and Critical Sources**

BOOKS

Barclay, Glen St. John, *Anatomy of Horror: The Masters of Occult Fiction*, St. Martin's Press (New York, NY), 1979.

Haggard's novel *She* was adapted for film in 1965 and featured well-known actress Ursula Andress. (Hulton Archive/Getty Images.)

Chrisman, Laura, *Rereading the Imperial Romance: British Imperialism and South African Resistance in Haggard, Schreiner, and Plaatje,* Oxford University Press (New York, NY), 2000.

Cohen, Morton, *Rider Haggard: His Life and Works,* Hutchinson (London, England), 1960.

Dictionary of Literary Biography, Gale (Detroit, MI), Volume 70: *British Mystery Writers, 1860-1919,* 1988, Volume 156: *British Short-Fiction Writers, 1880-1914: The Romantic Tradition,* 1995, Volume 174: *British Travel Writers, 1876-1909,* 1997, Volume 178: *British Fantasy and Science-Fiction Writers before World War I,* 1997.

Ellis, Peter Beresford, *H. Rider Haggard: A Voice from the Infinite,* Routledge & Kegan Paul (London, England), 1978.

Etherington, Norman, *Rider Haggard,* Twayne (Boston, MA), 1984.

Fraser, Robert, *Victorian Quest Romance: Stevenson, Haggard, Kipling, and Conan Doyle,* Northcote House (Plymouth, England), 1998.

Haggard, H. Rider, *The Days of My Life: An Autobiography,* Longman (New York, NY), 1926.

Haggard, Lilian Rider, *The Cloak That I Left: A Biography of the Author Henry Rider Haggard, K.B.E.,* Hodder & Stoughton (London, England), 1951.

Higgins, D.S., *Rider Haggard: The Great Storyteller,* Cassell (London, England, 1981.

In and Out of Africa: The Adventures of H. Rider Haggard: An Exhibition, text by Kriston Sites, Lilly Library (Bloomington, IN), 1995.

Katz, Wendy R., *Rider Haggard and the Fiction of Empire: A Critical Study of British Imperial Fiction,* Cambridge University Press (Cambridge, England), 1988.

Lewis, C.S., *On Stories, and Other Essays on Literature,* edited by Walter Hooper, Harcourt Brace Jovanovich (New York, NY), 1982.

Monsman, Gerald, *H. Rider Haggard on the Imperial Frontier: The Political and Literary Contexts of His African Romances,* ELT Press (Greensboro, NC), 2006.

Pocock, Tom, *Rider Haggard and the Lost Empire,* Weidenfeld & Nicolson (London, England), 1993.

Pritchett, V.S., *The Tale Bearers: Literary Essays,* Random House (New York, NY), 1980.

St. James Guide to Science-Fiction Writers, 4th edition, St. James Press (Detroit, MI), 1996.

St. James Guide to Fantasy Writers, St. James Press (Detroit, MI), 1996.

Twentieth-Century Literary Criticism, Volume 11, Gale (Detroit, MI), 1983.

Twentieth-Century Romance and Historical Writers, 3rd edition, St. James Press (Detroit, MI), 1994.

PERIODICALS

Academy, March 22, 1884, George Saintsbury, review of *The Witch's Head,* p. 200.

Armchair Detective, winter, 1987, Robert Sandels, review of *King Solomon's Mines,* p. 90.

Atlantic Monthly, January, 1959, H.F. Ellis, "The Niceties of Plagiarism," pp. 76, 78.

Christian Commonwealth, November 1, 1906, "An Interview with H. Rider Haggard," pp. 75-76.

Critic, February 12, 1887, H.B. (pseudonym of William Ernest Henley), review of *She: A History of Adventure,* pp. 78-79.

Dalhousie Review, fall, 1960, Morton N. Cohen, "Rudyard Kipling and Rider Haggard," pp. 297-322.

Fortnightly Review, March 1, 1890, James Runciman, "King Plagiarism and His Court," pp. 421-439.

Library Journal, October 1, 2001, Lee Arnold, review of *Diary of an African Journey: The Return of Rider Haggard,* p. 133.

London Mercury, November, 1924, Edward Shanks, "Sir Rider Haggard and the Novel of Adventure," pp. 71-79.

London Review of Books, September 20, 2001, E.S. Turner, "White Peril," pp. 33-34.

Outlook, July 1, 1911, Theodore Roosevelt, "Rider Haggard and the Salvation Army," pp. 476-477.

Race and Class, July-September, 2001, Barbara Harlow, review of *Diary of an African Journey,* p. 90.

Saturday Review, October 10, 1885, Andrew Lang, review of *King Solomon's Mines,* pp. 485-486.

Science Fiction Chronicle, May, 1998, review of *Smith and the Pharaohs, and Other Tales,* p. 42; February, 1999, review of *When the World Shook,* p. 43.

Spectator, August 19, 1882, "Our Sable Visitor," review of *Cetywayo and His White Neighbors; or, Remarks on Recent Events in Zululand, Natal, and the Transvaal,* pp. 1089-1090.

Times (London, England), August 8, 2001, F.W. de Klerk, review of *Diary of an African Journey,* p. 13.

Voice Literary Supplement, October, 1991, Geoffrey O'Brien, review of *She.*

Young Man, June, 1894, Frederick Dolman, "How I Write My Books" (interview with Haggard), pp. 21-23.

ONLINE

Rider Haggard Society Web site, http://www.riderhaggardsociety.org.uk/ (July 1, 2009).*

Lisi Harrison

■ Personal

Born July 29, 1975, in Toronto, Ontario, Canada. *Education:* Attended McGill University; Emerson College, B.F.A. (creative writing), M.A.

■ Addresses

Home—Laguna Beach, CA.

■ Career

Writer. Music Television Productions (MTV), New York, NY, senior director of production development, senior writer, 1992-2004, created and developed television programs, including *Room Raiders.* Former magazine columnist for *Jane.*

■ Writings

"CLIQUE" NOVEL SERIES

The Clique, Little, Brown (New York, NY), 2004.
Best Friends for Never, Little, Brown (New York, NY), 2004.
Invasion of the Boy Snatchers, Little, Brown (New York, NY), 2005.
Revenge of the Wannabes, Little, Brown (New York, NY), 2005.
The Pretty Committee Strikes Back, Little, Brown (New York, NY), 2006.
Dial L for Loser, Little, Brown (New York, NY), 2006.
It's Not Easy Being Mean, Little, Brown (New York, NY), 2007.
Sealed with a Diss, Little, Brown (New York, NY), 2007.
Bratfest at Tiffany's, Little, Brown (New York, NY), 2008.
P.S. I Loathe You, Little, Brown (New York, NY), 2009.

"CLIQUE SUMMER COLLECTION" SERIES

Massie, Little, Brown (New York, NY), 2008.
Dylan, Little, Brown (New York, NY), 2008.
Alicia, Little, Brown (New York, NY), 2008.
Kristen, Little, Brown (New York, NY), 2008.
Claire, Little, Brown (New York, NY), 2008.

"ALPHAS" NOVEL SERIES

Alphas, Poppy (New York, NY), 2009.

■ Adaptations

The Clique was adapted for a direct-to-DVD movie, 2008.

■ Sidelights

"Sartre with lip gloss" is the way *Time* reviewer Lev Grossman described the dynamics of the characters in Lisi Harrison's "Clique" series of novels, which follows a group of middle-school girls who learn about life while dealing with the typical social problems children face in school. In addition to the works in the "Clique" series, Harrison is also the author of the spin-off "Clique Summer Collection" books, which feature each of the five girls in separate volumes.

In an interview on the Warner Books Web site, Harrison noted that the first novel in the "Clique" series "was written for ages twelve years and up, but people of all ages seem to be getting something out it. I think that's because 'cliques,' 'bullying' and the need to 'fit in' happen at every age. Trust me, even adults feel it." Harrison's "Clique" books have

The plight of new-girl-in-school Claire Lyons plays out in Lisi Harrison's 2004 middle-grade novel *The Clique*.
(Little, Brown & Company, 2004. Cover photography by Carolyn Veith Krienke. Reproduced by permission.)

found a strong following among teen readers; in his review of series installment *The Pretty Committee Strikes Back*, Grossman concluded that the work is "unmistakably true to junior-high reality." Harrison's books have even spawned a movie version, *The Clique*, a direct-to-DVD film released in 2008.

Canadian Origins

Harrison was born in Toronto, Ontario, Canada, in 1975. After attending Montreal's McGill University, she transferred to Boston's Emerson College where she earned a bachelor of fine arts degree in creative writing. Soon after graduation she found work with MTV in New York City. She worked at the network for a dozen years, eventually becoming head writer and then senior director of production development, creating such popular programs as *Room Raiders* and *One Bad Trip*.

At the same time she began writing books for young readers featuring a clique of snooty seventh graders who have their rich-girl assumptions challenged by the arrival a new girl at school and in their lives. For inspiration Harrison took not so much her own experiences in middle school but rather her experiences with coworkers at MTV, especially in fleshing out the particulars of a seventh-grade wardrobe. As she remarked on her home page, "There were so many employees at MTV who would do and wear anything just to be accepted by the so-called 'cool people.' It reminded me so much of life in the seventh grade I had to write about it. And the rest is history."

Enter the "Clique"

In the series opener, *The Clique*, Claire moves with her family into the guest house of a family friend. The friend's daughter, Massie, is the snobbish leader of a school clique made up of similarly wealth, bratty kids. Although Massie's parents try to force her to befriend Claire, the two girls instead wage an ongoing battle; Massie and her friends see Claire as an outcast who dresses oddly and deserves all the torment they heap upon her. For her part, Claire is wise enough to figure out the perfect revenge. Olivia Durant, writing in *Kliatt*, called *The Clique* "a unique take on the popular 'chick lit' genre for teens." A *Publishers Weekly* contributor noted that the two main characters "stay pretty superficial, unchanged by their victories and defeats," and Diana Pierce, writing in *School Library Journal*, similarly cited "the shallowness of the characters [and] . . .

Cover of Harrison's novel *Invasion of the Boy Snatchers*, another novel in her "Clique" series. (Little, Brown & Company, 2005. Cover photography by Carolyn Veith Krienke. Reproduced by permission.)

the one-dimensional plot." Other reviewers offered more positive assessments, however. In her *Booklist* review, Hazel Rochman commented that Harrison "knows peer pressure, and her first novel has fun with the tyranny of brand names." Writing for *Teenreads.com*, Terry Miller Shannon noted of the "Clique" series: "Once you begin reading the first book . . . you'll be eager to get your hands on the next installments."

In *Best Friends for Never,* the cast of characters from the first novel returns, including Massie's fellow clique members Dylan Marvil, Kristen Gregory, and Alicia Rivera. This time the spoiled Massie decides to throw a coed Halloween party with the help of a professional party planner. As the battle between Massie and Claire continues, Massie finds herself struggling to keep her position as her clique's leader. Meanwhile, Claire seems to be gaining

ground in her competition with Massie over a potential boyfriend. Another subplot involves the clique previewing their party costumes, only to get in trouble for their choices. "This series continues to ooze fun and a delightfully charming insight into the world of the 'haves' and 'have nots' among the world of seventh grade preteens," wrote Livia Holton on the Romance Reader's Connection Web site.

In *Invasion of the Boy Snatchers* Claire and Massie become closer, literally, when Claire's family must move out of the guesthouse temporarily while it is being renovated. Now sharing her bedroom with Claire, Massie has little time for her feud with her new roommate: her position as alpha dog of the clique is being threatened by Nina, the attractive Spanish cousin of Alicia, over whom all the boys are now drooling. "The girls come off outwardly as unbelievably sophisticated, with their Manolo Blahnik shoes, highlighted hair, and limitless bank accounts," wrote *School Library Journal* reviewer Amanda MacGregor. "But when it comes down to it, they're typical junior high girls."

In the fourth series installment, *Revenge of the Wannabes,* the rich girls of Octavian Country Day School in Westchester, New York, continue to fight for the leadership of the clique. Alicia tampers with a ballot box so that her selection for a school uniform will win out over Massie's. Although readers may find the characters to be annoying at times, observed Alice DiNizo in a *School Library Journal* review, "the believability and humanity found in Claire and Kristen keep the story line moving." In *The Pretty Committee Strikes Back,* Kristen has to overcome the "tragedy" of a bad haircut, while Claire is made an official member of the clique. However, for their various escapades, clique members are expelled from school for a time.

Dial L for Loser finds the clique at first enjoying time away from school, but ultimately anxious to return. The five make their way to Hollywood to audition for a tween film, and Claire, surprisingly, beats out the other girls in the clique for the coveted role. Melissa Parcel, writing for *Curled Up with a Good Kid's Book,* described *Dial L for Loser* as "a fun, entertaining book that girls are sure to enjoy," despite the "great deal of brand-name dropping, which can get a little tedious." To Harrison, however, the use of brand names increases the authenticity of her stories. As she remarked to *New York Times* contributor Michael Winerip, "Details are what make the books seems so real for these girls. It feels very current, like one of them wrote it. It's actually the stuff they are talking about." Harrison further defended her choices to Winerip, noting that the focus on wealth and consumption is meant to be satirical, calling it "over-the-top absurdity."

Harrison continues the adventures and misadventures of the five young women in *It's Not Easy Being Mean, Sealed with a Diss, Bratfest at Tiffany's*, and *P.S. I Loathe You*. In *It's Not Easy Being Mean*, the girls are given clues to help them locate a legendary secret room in Octavian Country Day School, while in *Bratfest at Tiffany's*, the school is invaded by the boys of Briarwood. Suddenly, sports are so important that the male athletes might take over "most popular" status from the clique.

The Rich and the Spoiled

Harrison has also written from the point of view of each of her fictional protagonists in her "Clique Summer Collection" books, including *Massie* and *Claire*. The summer following their seventh grade, the girls part ways and have vastly different experiences. Massie is at an exclusive riding camp;

Dylan is off to Hawaii with her mother, a television host; Alicia travels to Spain; Kristen stays at home and tutors an eighth grader; and Claire returns to Orlando. Reviewing the five works in the series, *Teenreads.com* contributor Donna Volkenannt felt that the tone of each "is playful and breezy," and that "each one delivers a helpful and encouraging message for teenage girls." Harrison also began a new series in 2009, "Alphas," featuring another set of girls in an exclusive private school.

If you enjoy the works of Lisi Harrison, you may also want to check out the following books:

Meg Cabot, *How to Be Popular*, 2006.
Sarah Dessen, *Just Listen*, 2006.
Laura Peyton Roberts, *Queen B*, 2006.

Harrison, who remarked on her home page that she "was forbidden to wear anything made by anyone other than K-Mart or Hanes" while growing up, has sound advice for kids who find themselves in a cliquish school. "You have to understand why mean girls are mean," she counseled on the Hachette Book Group Web site. "They are insecure. I know that's hard to believe because they're probably pretty, popular, stylish, and outgoing. But trust me, it's true. Girls who put other girls down do it to feel better about themselves. So keep that in mind next time a pack of wild meanie weenies treats you like a loser."

Harrison's novel *Alicia* is part of her "Clique Summer Collection" of novellas. (Little, Brown & Company, 2008. Cover photography by Carolyn Veith Krienke. Reproduced by permission.)

■ Biographical and Critical Sources

PERIODICALS

Booklist, August, 2004, Hazel Rochman, review of *The Clique*, p. 1934.
Broadcasting and Cable, August 18, 2003, "MTV Networks," p. 24.
Kliatt, September, 2004, Olivia Durant, review of *The Clique*, p. 20: January 26, 2006, Amanda MacGregor, review of *Invasion of the Boy Snatchers*, p. 16.

THE CLIQUE
SUMMER COLLECTION
🌴🌴
CLAIRE
BY LISI HARRISON

THE #1 NEW YORK TIMES BESTSELLING SERIES

Popular "Clique" heroines Claire, Sarah, Sari, and Mandy are featured in Harrison's popular summer read *Claire.* (Little, Brown & Company, 2008. Cover photography by Carolyn Veith Krienke. Reproduced by permission.)

New York Times, July 13, 2008, Michael Winerip, "In Novels for Girls, Fashion Trumps Romance."

Publishers Weekly, May 24, 2004, review of *The Clique,* p. 63.

School Library Journal, June, 2004, Diana Pierce, review of *The Clique,* p. 143; May, 2005, Alice Di-Nizo, review of *Revenge of the Wannabes,* p. 128.

Teen People, November 1, 2004, Carolyn Juris, review of *Best Friends For Never,* p. 52.

Time, March 13, 2006, Lev Grossman, review of *The Pretty Committee Strikes Back,* p. 63.

ONLINE

Clique: Official Book Site, http://www.jointheclique.com/ (April 21, 2009).

Common Sense Media Web site, http://www.commonsensemedia.org/ (April 21, 2009), Pam Gelman, review of *Dial L for Loser.*

Curled Up with a Good Kid's Book Web site, http://www.curledupkids.com/ (April 21, 2009), Amanda Cuda, review of *The Clique;* Melissa Parcel, review of *Dial L for Loser.*

Hachette Book Group Web site, http://www.hachettebookgroup.com/ (April 21, 2009), "Author Interview: Lisi Harrison Answers Questions from Readers."

Lisi Harrison Home Page, http://www.lisiharrison.net (April 21, 2009).

Lisi Harrison Web log, http://www.lisiharrison.com/blah-g.php (April 21, 2009).

Romance Readers Connection Web site, http://www.theromancereadersconnection.com/ (May 5, 2005), Livia Holton, review of *Best Friends for Never.*

Teenreads.com, http://www.teenreads.com/ (April 1, 2005), "Author Talk: Lisi Harrison"; (April 21, 2009) Terry Miller Shannon, review of "The Clique" series; Donna Volkenannt, review of "The Clique Summer Collection" series.

Time-Warner Books Web site, http://www.twbookmark.com/ (May 5, 2005), interview with Harrison.*

Ishiro Honda

■ Personal

Born May 7, 1911, in Yamagata Prefecture, Japan; died February 28, 1993, in Tokyo, Japan, due to respiratory failure; son of Houkan (a Buddhist priest) and Miyo Honda; married, 1939; wife's name Kimi (a script director); children: Takako (daughter), Ryuji (son). *Education:* Graduated from Nihon University, 1933.

■ Career

Film director. PCL (Photography Chemistry Laboratory) studios (later Toho studios), Tokyo, Japan, cameraman and assistant director, 1933, assistant director, with Kajiro Yamamoto and Akira Kurosawa, c. 1930s-1940s; assistant director and creative consultant with Kurosawa, c. 1980s-1990s. Director of films, including *Co-Op of Living*, Toho, 1950; *Avi shinja (The Blue Pearl)*, 1951; *Zoku shishunki (Adolescence, Part II)*, Toho, 1953; *Taiheiyo no washi (The Eagle of the Pacific)*, Toho, 1953; *Saraba Rabauru (Farewell Rabaul)*, Toho, 1954; *Koi-gesho (Love Takeover)* Toho, 1955; *Oen-san (Cry-baby)*, Toho, 1955; *Jû jin yuki otoko (Beast Man Snow Man)*, Toho, 1955; *Tokyo no hito sayonara (People of Tokyo, Goodbye)*, Toho, 1956; *Rodan (Rodan, the Flying Monster)*, Toho, 1956; *Kono futari ni sachi are (Good Luck to These Two)*, Toho, 1957; *Waga mune ni niji wa kiezu (A Rainbow Plays in My Heart)*, Toho, 1957; *Chikyû Bôeigun (The Mysterians)*, Toho, 1957; *Hanayome sanjuso (Song for a Bride)*, Toho, 1958; *Bijo to Ekitainingen (H-Man)*, Toho, 1958; *Varan (Varan the Unbelievable)*, Toho, 1958; *Kodama wa yonde iru (An Echo Calls You)*, Toho, 1959; *Tetsuwan toshu inao monogatari (Inao: Story of an Iron Arm)*, Toho, 1959; *Uwayaku, shitayaku, godôyaku (Seniors, Juniors, Co-Workers)*, Toho, 1959; *Uchu daisenso (Battle in Outer Space)*, Toho, 1959; *Gasu ningen dai ichigo (The Human Vapor)*, Toho, 1960; *Mosura (Mothra)*, Toho, 1961; *Shinku no otoko (The Scarlet Man)*, Toho, 1961; *Yosei Gorasu (Gorath)*, Toho, 1962; *Kingu Kongu tai Gojira (King Kong vs. Godzilla)*, Toho, 1962; *Matango (Attack of the Mushroom People)*, Toho, 1963; *Kaitei gunkan (Atragon)*, Toho, 1963; *Mosura tai Gojira (Mothra vs. Godzilla)*, Toho, 1964; *Uchu daikaijû Dogora (Dagora, the Space Monster)*, Toho, 1964; *San daikaijû: Chikyû saidai no kessen (Ghidrah, the Three-headed Monster)*, Toho, 1964; *Furankenshutain tai chitei kaijû Baragon (Frankenstein vs. Baragon)*, Toho, 1965; *Kaijû daisenso (Godzilla vs. Monster Zero)*, Toho, 1965; *Oyome ni Oide (Come Marry Me)*, Toho, 1966; *Kingu Kongu no gyakushû (King Kong Escapes)*, Toho, 1967; *Ido zero daisakusen (Latitude Zero)*, Toho, 1969; *Gojira-Minira-Gabara: Oru kaijû daishingeki (All Monsters Attack)*, Toho, 1969; *Gezora, Ganime, Kameba: Kessen! Nankai no daikaijû (Yog, Monster from Space)*, Toho, 1970; *Mekagojira no gyakushu (Terror of MechaGodzilla)*, Toho, 1975; and (with others) *Dreams* ("The Tunnel" segment), Warner Brothers, 1990.

Assistant director of films, including *Enoken no senman choja (Enoken's Ten Millions)*, PCL, 1936; *Nadare (Avalanche)*, PCL, 1937; *Chinetsu (Subterranean Heat)*, Toho, 1938; *Uma (Horse)*, Toho, 1941; *Kato hayabusa sento-tai (Colonel Kato's Falcon Squadron)*, Toho, 1944; *Kaze no ko (Child of the Wind)*, Toho, 1949; *Nora Inu (Stray Dog)*, Toho, 1949; (and creative consultant) *Kagemusha*, Toho/Kurosawa/20th Century-Fox,

1980; (and director's counsel) *Ran*, Herald Ace/ Nippon Herald/Greenwich, 1985; (and creative consultant) *Dreams*, 1990; (and creative consultant) *Hachi-gatsu no kyôshikyoku* (*Rhapsody in August*), Shochiku, 1991; and (and directorial advisor) *Mada-dayo*, Toho, 1992. Director of television series, including *The Return of Ultraman*, Tsuburaya Productions; *Mirror Man*, Tsuburaya Productions; *Fireman*, Tsuburaya Productions; *Thunder Mask*; and *Urgent Command 104*. Actor in films, including *Nora inu*, 1949, and *Yarutokya yaruze*, 1987. *Military service:* Served in Japanese infantry, 1935-37, 1939-41, and 1944-45; repatriated in 1946 after serving as prisoner of war.

■ Writings

SCREENPLAYS

(And director) *Ise Shima* (documentary), Toho, 1949.
(And director) *Aoi shinju* (*The Blue Pearl*), Toho, 1951.

(And director) *Nangoku no hada* (*The Skin of the South*), Toho, 1952.

(And director) *Minato e kita otoko* (*The Man Who Came to Port*), Toho, 1952.

(With Takeo Murata; and director) *Gojira* (released internationally as *Godzilla*), Toho, 1954.

(With Ichiro Ikeda; and director) *Wakai ki* (*Young Tree*), Toho, 1956.

(With Hirosuke Takenaka; and director) *Wakare no chatsumi-uta* (*A Teapicker's Song of Goodbye*), Toho, 1957.

(With Hirosuke Takenaka; and director) *Wakare no chatsumi-uta shimai-hen: Oneesan to yonda hito* (*A Farewell to the Woman Called My Sister*), Toho, 1957.

(With Kaoru Mabuchi; and director) *Furankenshutain no kaijû: Sanda tai Gaira* (*The War of the Gargan-tuas*), Toho, 1966.

(With Kaoru Mabuchi; and director) *Kaijû sôshingeki* (*Destroy All Monsters*), Toho, 1968.

The battle between technology and prehistory plays out in Japanese film maker Ishiro Honda's 1956 film *Rodan, the Flying Monster.* (/The Kobal Collection/The Picture Desk, Inc.)

◼ Sidelights

Japanese filmmaker Ishiro Honda directed dozens of films and served as assistant director on several more, including some of the classics of modern Japanese cinema. He is known, above all, for one film: *Godzilla,* the 1954 release that became the king of all monster movies. "Honda will always be remembered as a director of monster movies, having helmed 25 special-effects pictures, including eight of the first 15 Godzilla movies," observed Steve Ryfle in *Japan's Favorite Mon-Star: The Unauthorized Biography of "The Big G."* "But he was much more than that. He was a visionary filmmaker who . . . transcended the limitations of the genre to create films that remain thoroughly entertaining, even today."

Godzilla—known in Japan as *Gojiro*—was an international smash and even spawned an entire Japanese film genre, *kaiju-eiga,* or monster films. Honda became a celebrity in Japan for *Godzilla* and the host of sequels he directed, each of them, in the opinions of many critics, more ridiculous than the last. Yet despite the popularity of the original *Godzilla,* Americans knew the film only in a drastically altered version until a restored version was released in the United States in 2004. That restoration clearly revealed Honda's intention to make an anti-nuclear statement with *Godzilla,* an aspect mostly lost when the film was re-cut for McCarthy-era American audiences. It became clear that the strange power of the "Godzilla" films, despite their often second-class production values, resided in a subtext of violence and war, phenomena with which Honda had been quite familiar in his own life.

An Early Love of Cinema

Honda was born in Yamagata Prefecture, Japan, on May 7, 1911. His father was a Buddhist priest. The young Honda loved to go to see silent films, at first because he was fascinated by the *benshi,* live narrators who were distinctive to the silent-film era in Japan. As he grew older, however, he began to think in career terms about his love of movies. "I watched movie theaters being built and regular theaters being turned into movie theaters, and eventually I realized there could be a pretty well-paying future for me in the business," he said in a *Tokyo Journal* interview. "It all came together. I enjoyed telling stories and could find work in an industry that was financially successful and artistic to boot."

At first, Honda enrolled at Nihon (or Nippon) University as an art student, but he soon signed up for a film apprenticeship program run by PCL (Photography Chemistry Laboratory), a studio that was an ancestor of the Japanese postwar moviemaking giant Toho. Honda did well in the program and was working as a cameraman by 1933, even before he graduated. He made two key contacts and friendships at PCL. One, Kajiro Yamamoto, was a director and film teacher who inspired a number of younger Japanese filmmakers. Honda rose in the PCL hierarchy and remained with the company as it was absorbed into Toho. He worked as an assistant director for Yamamoto in the late 1930s and early 1940s on such films as *Uma* (*Horse,* 1941). The other important acquaintance Honda made at PCL was Akira Kurosawa, considered one of the greatest directors in Japanese history. Honda and Kurosawa met in 1937.

By the time of his meeting with Kurosawa, Honda had been drafted into the Japanese army and sent to China to participate in Japan's invasion of that country. He served three tours of duty as an infantryman, returning to Tokyo in between tours to resume his film career. On one of these trips, he met his future wife Kimi, a Toho script assistant. Kimi would play an active role in her husband's career, often discussing his films with him as they were made. They raised a son and daughter. Honda kept a close watch on new developments in Japanese film, and he was impressed by the special effects in a 1942 Japanese war film called *The War at Sea from Hawaii to Malaya.* The following year, he worked for the first time with the earlier film's special effects coordinator, Eiji Tsuburaya, as the two assisted Yamamoto on Kato's *Flying Action Forces.* They did not get along at first, as Tsuburaya criticized the way Honda had staged a shot of some model fighter planes. Still, it was the beginning of a famous partnership.

War Experiences Influence Film Career

While serving in the military in China, Honda had often feared being ambushed by a large crowd, and that image became a motif in many of his films. In 1945 his fears were realized as he was seized and held as a prisoner of war for more than a year. He heard about the dropping of two atomic bombs on Japan from his prison cell. According to David Kalat, author of *A Critical History and Filmography of Toho's Godzilla Series,* "Honda's wartime experiences left an enduring psychological scar, which would later inform his directorial style." Released from imprisonment following Japan's surrender, he returned home and worked for a variety of studios.

In 1949 Honda was reunited with Kurosawa and signed on as assistant director for the note filmmaker's *Nora Inu* (*Stray Dog*), a police drama star-

Honda's film productions include the 1966 monster classic *The War of the Gargantuas.* (Toho/The Kobal Collection/The Picture Desk, Inc.)

ring frequent Kurosawa collaborator Toshiro Mifune. "I had Honda do mainly second-unit shooting," Kurosawa recalled in his book *Something like an Autobiography*. "Every day I told him what I wanted and he would go out into the ruins of postwar Tokyo to film it. There are few men as honest and reliable as Honda. He faithfully brought back exactly the footage I requested, so almost everything he shot was used in the final cut of the film. I'm often told that I captured the atmosphere of postwar Japan very well in *Stray Dog*, and if so I owe a great deal of that success to Honda." Honda also made two documentaries around 1950.

Successful work like this led to Honda's being given the chance, by Toho studio, to step behind the cameras himself for a major studio release. His first feature film, 1951's *Aoi shinju* (*The Blue Pearl*), focuses on female pearl divers. He became the first Japanese director to film under water, and the unusual movie was well received. Among the five

films Honda made over the next two years was *Minato e kita otoko* (*The Man Who Came to Port*), which likewise had an exotic environment. Set among Japanese whalers, it involved a sequence set at the South Pole. Eiji Tsuburaya, with whom Honda was now collaborating, did not film on location but simulated the Antarctic environment by using rear-screen projection. Honda and Tsuburaya reunited for the 1953 war film *Taiheiyo no washi* (*The Eagle of the Pacific*), and they worked together again on the romantic war story *Saraba Rabauru* (*Farewell, Rabaul*) the following year.

Enter Godzilla

Honda's participation in *Godzilla* came about almost by accident; he had been slated to direct another film called *Sanshiro the Priest*, but plans for that film

Honda goes slightly overboard in creating the squid-like creatures in *Yog, Monster from Space*, a film released in 1970.
(Toho/The Kobal Collection/The Picture Desk, Inc.)

A vast city is threatened by an oversized insect in Honda's *Mothra*, **which was released in its English-language version in 1961.** (Hulton Archive/Getty Images.)

fell through and he was moved to *Godzilla*, the idea for which had been hatched by Tsuburaya. The movie features an unstoppable dinosaur that had languished in hibernation since the era of the dinosaurs' extinction but is awakened and mysteriously strengthened by a hydrogen bomb test explosion. Godzilla is first seen attacking a small fishing boat, and this scene resonated with Japanese audiences who had recently heard about the illnesses of Japanese fishermen who had found themselves too close to the American H-bomb tests at Bikini Atoll in the Pacific.

More generally, Godzilla was seen as a symbol of the atomic bomb. During a visit to Hiroshima, Japan, Kalat stated, Honda "became fascinated with the nuclear holocaust, particularly the destructive power of an invisible substance (radiation). Honda felt compelled to translate the horrors of modern war into a film." Honda himself, as quoted by Brent Staples for the *New York Times*, said that he conceived of the fire-breathing dinosaur as a way of "making radiation visible," and he hoped to make an explicitly anti-nuclear statement. "Believe it or not, we naively hoped that the end of *Godzilla* was going to coincide with the end of nuclear testing," he was quoted as saying by Staples.

The famous scenes of Godzilla rampaging through Tokyo are primitive by modern special-effects standards, but they made a strong impact in a country that had experienced total devastation just nine years earlier. The film became a huge hit, and analytical articles in mainstream publications discussed the film for decades afterward in Japan. "In a devastated land where they still lived in great hardship," remarked London *Independent* critic James Kirkup, "Godzilla acted as a psychological cushion against the pain and confusion of post-war life, against the ever-present threats of earthquakes, volcanic eruptions and typhoons that have lent Japanese culture the strangely beautiful, evanescent quality of an impermanent 'floating world.' Godzilla became their Superman, reptilian, repulsive but all-conquering, belching out his radioactive furnace breath at wicked, unscrupulous enemies—frightening, but fun."

Honda was in many ways the ideal choice to direct *Godzilla*. In making the film he drew not on Japan's rich tradition of fantasy but on the plain, unsentimental style of military dramas, and on his own impressions of World War II. "Most of the visual images I got were from my war experience," he once stated in an interview, quoted by Ryfle. "After the war, all of Japan, as well as Tokyo, was left in ashes. . . . If Godzilla had been a big ancient dinosaur or some other animal, he would have been killed by just one cannonball. But if he were equal to an atomic bomb, we wouldn't know what to do. So, I took the characteristics of an atomic bomb and applied them to Godzilla."

Until the re-release of the original film in 2004, *Godzilla* was seen only in a distorted form in the U.S. version, with an entire new character, a reporter played by Raymond Burr, added in and with most of the references to the nuclear menace excised. Nevertheless, enough of the compelling quality of the film remained to make *Godzilla* a reference point in U.S. popular culture. The film's sequels were dubbed into English as quickly as Honda could make them and were staples of American movie theaters and then late-night television for decades.

The high point of the monster craze Honda created came in the 1960s. He introduced another memorable monster with *Mosura* (*Mothra*) in 1961, and pitted monsters against each other in *Kingu Kongu tai Gojira* (*King Kong vs. Godzilla*, 1962), *Mosura tai Gojira* (*Mothra vs. Godzilla*, 1964), and *Kaijû daisenso* (*Godzilla vs. Monster Zero*, 1965). Later "Godzilla" films were straight monster movies, lacking the nuclear commentary. Occasionally Honda rebelled against filling the Godzilla-director slot for Toho, making the romantic comedy *Oyome ni Oide* (*Come Marry Me*) in 1966. He refused to direct "Godzilla" films when he did not like the scripts, taking a break from filmmaking completely in the 1970s. "I'm not sure if the success of the Godzilla movies was a good thing or not," Kimi Honda was quoted as saying by Ryfle. "They were so popular that Mr. Honda became trapped. He had to work on them." Honda was a favorite among Japanese film-industry people, some of whom wished he could be given the chance to work on more artistic projects.

Honda got that chance to a degree in 1980 after several years of working in television directing

episodes of such series as *Return of Ultraman*. He returned to the "Godzilla" series in 1975 with *Mekagojira no gyakushu* (*Terror of MechaGodzilla*), a film centered on a robotic Godzilla double. He also reunited with his old friend Kurosawa, becoming assistant director on some of the Japanese master's most acclaimed films: *Kagemusha* (1980), *Ran* (1985), *Dreams* (1990), *Hachi-gatsu no kyôshikyoku* (*Rhapsody in August,* 1991), and *Madadayo* (1992). He also directed a segment of *Dreams,* a set of eight short stories; Honda's episode was a fantasy sequence in which a man meets figures from Japan's military past in a tunnel. It was perhaps as close as Honda came to returning to his wartime experiences as a filmmaker.

If you enjoy the works of Ishiro Honda, you may also want to check out the following films:

King Kong, starring Fay Wray, 1933.
Jurassic Park, directed by Steven Spielberg, 1993.
Cloverfield, written by Drew Goddard, 2008.

Honda died of respiratory failure in Tokyo on February 28, 1993, and was honored at a memorial service crowded with hundreds of his cinematic associates and capped by a eulogy from Kurosawa. Despite his ambivalent attitude toward his most famous creation in later life, he considered *Godzilla* his greatest film. As the monster's second half-century of existence began it was still his most familiar creation. In the words of John J. Pierce, writing in *The Official Godzilla Compendium,* while many film monsters were merely "special effects extras, . . . Godzilla was an *individual.* More than that, he had *soul.* . . . Godzilla lives on and on because he can always be reborn in whatever guise works best for the time, and be invested with whatever greater significance suits our psychological needs. Godzilla is, and always shall be, a monster for all seasons."

■ Biographical and Critical Sources

BOOKS

Galbraith, Stuart, IV, *The Toho Studios Story: A History and Complete Filmography,* Scarecrow Press (Lanham, MD), 2008.

Kalat, David, *A Critical History and Filmography of Toho's Godzilla Series,* McFarland (Jefferson, NC), 1997.

Kurosawa, Akira, *Something like an Autobiography,* Knopf (New York, NY), 1982.

Lees, J.D., and Marc Cerasini, *The Official Godzilla Compendium,* Random House (New York, NY), 1998.

Ryfle, Steve, *Japan's Favorite Mon-Star: The Unauthorized Biography of "The Big G,"* ECW Press (Toronto, Ontario, Canada), 1998.

PERIODICALS

Evolutionary Psychology, March, 2002, B.R. Smith, "Green Scales and Hot Breath: Godzilla! Again!," p. 11.

New York Times, May 1, 2005, Brent Staples, "Godzilla vs. the Giant Scissors: Cutting the Antiwar Heart out of a Classic."

Philadelphia Inquirer, April 27, 2006, Jeff Gammage, "'King of the Monsters' Marks 50 Years in Hollywood."

Tokyo Journal, April, 1991, interview with Honda.

World and I, May, 1998, Jerome F. Shapiro, "When a God Awakes: Symbolism in Japan's Mysterious Creature Movies," p. 182.

ONLINE

Japanese Giants Web site, http://www.japanesegiants.com/ (July 1, 2009), "Ishiro Honda."

Honda's best-known film, *Godzilla,* fascinated filmgoers when it arrived on the big screen in 1961. (Embassy Pictures/Getty Images.)

■ Obituaries

PERIODICALS

Daily Yomoiuri (Japan), March 2, 1993.
Globe & Mail (Toronto, Ontario, Canada), March 2, 1993, p. C1.

Independent (London, England), March 3, 1993, James Kirkup, "Ishiro Honda," p. 13.
New York Times, March 2, 1993.
Time, March 15, 1993, p. 23.
Times (London, England), March 12, 1993, p. 23.*

Norman Jewison

■ Personal

Born July 21, 1926, in Toronto, Ontario, Canada; son of Percy Joseph (a manager of a general store and post office) and Dorothy Irene Jewison; married Margaret Ann Dixon (a former model), July 11, 1953 (died November 26, 2004); children: Kevin Jefferie, Michael Philip, Jennifer Ann. *Education:* Graduated from Malvern Collegiate Institute, 1944; Victoria College (now University of Toronto), B.A., 1950. *Politics:* Liberal. *Religion:* Protestant. *Hobbies and other interests:* Skiing, yachting, tennis.

■ Addresses

Home—Caledon, Ontario, Canada. *Office*—Yorktown Productions, 18 Gloucester La., 4th Fl., Toronto, Ontario M4Y 1L5, Canada. *Agent*—Boaty Boatwright, International Creative Management, 10250 Constellation Way, 9th Fl., Los Angeles, CA 90067.

■ Career

Director, producer, actor, and writer. Director of films, including *The Fabulous Fifties,* 1960, *Send Me No Flowers,* 1964, *The Art of Love,* 1965, and *In the Heat of the Night,* 1967; director and producer of films, including *The Cincinnati Kid,* 1965, *The Russians Are Coming, the Russians Are Coming,* 1966, *The Thomas Crown Affair,* 1968, *Gaily, Gaily,* 1969, *Fiddler on the Roof,* 1970, *Rollerball,* 1975, *In Country,* 1989, *Other People's Money,* 1991, *Only You,* 1994, *Bogus,* 1996, *The Hurricane,* 1999, and *The Statement,* 2003; director and coproducer of films, including *Jesus Christ Superstar,* 1973, . . . *And Justice for All,* 1979, *A Soldier's Story,* 1984, *Agnes of God,* 1985, and *Moonstruck,* 1987. Director of television programs, including episodes of *Your Hit Parade,* 1958, and of specials, including *Tonight with Harry Belafonte,* 1959; director and producer of television programs, including *The Judy Garland Show,* 1963-64, and *Dinner With Friends,* Home Box Office, 2001. Affiliated with Canadian Broadcasting Corporation (CBC-TV), 1952-58; Columbia Broadcasting System (CBS-TV), producer and director, 1958-61; British Broadcasting Corporation (BBC-TV), actor and writer. Acted in several films and television shows, including *Canadian Pacific,* 1949, *Gräulein Berlin,* 1983; *The Stupids,* 1996; and *The Statement,* 2003. Institute for American Studies, Salzburg, Austria, faculty member, 1969; D'Avoriaz Film Festival, president, 1981—; Centre for Advanced Film Studies, former director, chairman emeritus, 1987-91. *Military service:* Royal Canadian Navy, 1945-46.

■ Member

Directors Guild of America (electoral board member), Academy of Motion Picture Arts and Scientists (former member of board of directors), Canadian Arts Council.

■ Awards, Honors

Academy Award nomination for best picture, Academy of Motion Picture Arts and Sciences, 1966, and Golden Globe Award for best motion picture, musical or comedy, 1967, both for *The Russians Are Coming, the Russians Are Coming;* British Academy of Film and Television Artists (BAFTA) UN Award for best foreign film, British Academy of Film and Television Arts, 1967, Academy Award nomination for best director, 1967, Golden Globe nomination for best director, 1968, and Sant Jordi Award (Spain) for best foreign film, 1969, all for *In the Heat of the Night;* Academy Award nominations for best picture and best director, both 1971, and Golden Globe Award for best motion picture, musical or comedy, and nomination for best director, 1972, all for *Fiddler on the Roof;* David di Donatello Award for Best Foreign Film, Accademia del Cinema Italiano, 1974, for *Jesus Christ Superstar;* LL.D., University of Western Ontario, 1974; director of the year, National Association of Theatre Owners, 1982; named officer, Order of Canada, 1982; honored by American Civil Liberties Union, 1984; Academy Award nomination for best picture, 1984, and Golden Prize, International Moscow Film Festival, 1985, both for *A Soldier's Story;* Golden Globe nomination for best film, Academy Award nominations for best film and best director, 1987, and Silver Berlin Bear for best director, 1988, all for *Moonstruck;* Genie Award for special achievement, Academy of Canadian Cinema and Television, 1988; Lifetime Achievement Award, Canadian Film Centre, 1998; Contribution to Cinematic Imagery Award, Art Directors Guild, 1998; Hollywood Film Award for outstanding achievement in directing, Hollywood Film Festival, 1998; Irving G. Thalberg Memorial Award, Academy of Motion Picture Arts and Sciences, 1999; Lifetime Achievement Award, Camerimage Film Festival, 1999; Robert Wise Director of Distinction President Award, Ft. Lauderdale International Film Festival, 1999; Prize of the Guild of German Art House Cinemas, Berlin Film Festival, and Golden Globe nomination for best director, both 2000, both for *The Hurricane;* Toarmina Arte Award, Toarmina International Film Festival, 2000; Lifetime Achievement Award, Canadian Film Centre, 2000; Opus Award, American Society of Composers, Authors, and Publishers (ASCAP), 2001; Award of Excellence, Banff Television Festival, 2001; Lifetime Achievement Award, Directors Guild of Canada, 2002; Board of Governors Award, American Society of Cinematographers, 2003; Governor General's performing arts award for lifetime achievement, 2003; Billy Wilder Award for excellence in directing, National Board of Review, 2003; King Vidor Memorial Award, San Luis Obispo Film Festival, 2005; honorary D.F.A., American Film Institute, 2008; Golden Eddie Filmmaker of the Year Award, American Cinema Editors, 2008.

■ Writings

(With Melvyn Bragg) *Jesus Christ Superstar* (screenplay), Universal, 1973.

This Terrible Business Has Been Good to Me: An Autobiography, foreword by John Patrick Shanley, Key Porter Books (Toronto, Ontario, Canada), 2004, Thomas Dunne Books (New York, NY), 2005.

The Norman Jewison Archive is housed at Victoria University, University of Toronto.

■ Sidelights

Over a long career spanning more than twenty-five films, Canadian director and producer Norman Jewison has earned seven Academy Award nominations, as well as the Academy's Irving Thalberg Award for lifetime achievement. His films range from romantic comedies to musicals to satires to dramas. He is best known for the 1987 critical and popular hit *Moonstruck,* as well as for a trio of films dealing with racial issues: 1968's *In the Heat of the Night,* 1984's *A Soldier's Story,* and 1999's *The Hurricane.* "I've always been interested in films that have something to say about us, to tell stories that have some relevance to where we are as a society and as a people," Jewison told Richard Natale of *Variety.*

Jewison enjoyed performing, even as a child. He studied piano and gave poetry recitals as a boy; while in college at Victoria University (now part of the University of Toronto), he joined the All-Varsity Revue and learned all he could about show business. He wrote skits, sang, danced, directed, wrote music, and even managed the sound and lighting. After graduating from college, he served in the Royal Canadian Navy for two years. While on leave in 1945, Jewison hitchhiked around the United States. The trip proved fascinating and disturbing; although he loved the friendly people, he was appalled by the discrimination he saw in the South. "That was my first experience with apartheid," he told Bob Thomas in the *Seattle Times.* "I was amazed that a black soldier could risk his life in battle, but he couldn't get a cup of coffee at Woolworth's." His trip would inspire Jewison to explore themes of racism and injustice in his films.

After leaving the military, Jewison traveled to England and broke into television with the British Broadcasting Corporation. When the fledgling Canadian Broadcasting Corporation started up back at home, he returned to Canada to work as a floor manager on a variety show. He later directed a children's puppet show and then the first weekly jazz show on North American television. By the late 1950s he was working for CBS-TV in New York City, directing the popular music show *Your Hit Parade.* When a sponsor ordered him to cancel an appearance by African-American singer Tommy Edwards, Jewison threatened to take the story to the *New York Times.* The sponsor gave in, and in 1959 Edwards became the first black singer to appear on *Your Hit Parade.* Soon Jewison was promoted to direct and produce variety specials, and worked with stars like Danny Kaye, Andy Williams, Harry Belafonte, and Judy Garland.

Begins Career in Film

Jewison broke into feature films when actor Tony Curtis was visiting the set of *The Judy Garland Show* and asked if he wanted to direct the actor's next movie. "I'd never dreamed of doing that. I was doing just fine in television," Jewison told Jon Silberg of the *Hollywood Reporter.* It required some on-the-job training, he added: "People like us started out making films, but there were no film schools at the time. We wanted to follow in the footsteps of the

Jewison explores the emotionally charged issue of racism in his powerful 1967 film *In the Heat of the Night*, **starring Sidney Poitier and Rod Steiger.** (Mirisch/United Artists/The Kobal Collection/The Picture Desk, Inc.)

Jewison's 1971 musical film *Fiddler on the Roof,* **which starred the actor Topol, showed the director's versatility.** (United Artists/The Kobal Collection/The Picture Desk, Inc.)

[great directors], but none of us came out of the movie industry. It was cameramen like Joe Mac-Donald, Phil Lathrop and Joe Biroc who taught me how to make movies." His first four features were romantic comedies starring superstars of the era, such as Curtis, Doris Day, Rock Hudson, and James Garner.

After directing the Steve McQueen poker drama *The Cincinnati Kid* in 1965, Jewison also served as producer for the 1966 satire *The Russians Are Coming, the Russians Are Coming.* Based on a novel by Nathaniel Benchley, the film follows what happens when a Russian submarine accidentally runs aground in coastal New England and panics the locals. It was a daring subject considering that it was the height of the cold war, but the film earned four Academy Award nominations, including one for best picture. The film also earned producer Jewison a Golden Globe award for best comedy/musical.

Jewison's next film earned him even more accolades. The 1967 drama *In the Heat of the Night* starred Rod Steiger as a Southern sheriff who is forced to rely on a big-city African-American detective (Sidney Poitier) to help solve a murder. "Its portrait of the professional respect that evolves between Rod Steiger's red-necked, small-town Southern sheriff and Sidney Poitier's Northern urban policeman, was made at a key juncture in the then-evolving civil rights movement," a critic noted in the *International Dictionary of Films and Filmmakers.* As the first film to depict an African American striking a white man, "it is a courageous film for its time." *In the Heat of the Night* won five Academy awards, including for best picture, and earned Jewison his first Oscar nomination for best director.

Starting with the 1968 bank-heist caper *The Thomas Crown Affair,* Jewison served as producer or co-producer on all his films. "You have more control over what you do. I guess it's all about control," he told Natale in *Variety.* In 1971 he was given the chance to produce and direct a film version of the enormously popular Broadway musical *Fiddler on the Roof,* which is set in a Russian Jewish village in 1905. "Everybody, of course, thought I was Jewish, which is why they offered me *Fiddler.* Then to their horror they found out I was a Methodist," the director told Mike McDaniel in the *Houston Chronicle*.

Nonetheless, *Fiddler on the Roof* was a popular and critical success, earning eight Oscar nominations, including for best director and best picture. Jewison shot many scenes on location in Croatia, expanding the scope of the musical in the process. He "turns the village of Anetevka into a real place . . . but retains the qualities that made the story such a hit on stage," George Perry observed on the British Broadcasting Corporation Web site. "In sequences such as Tevye's Dream, film proves even more effective than stage." The film also earned Jewison his second Golden Globe award for best comedy/musical.

Jewison's next film was also a musical, this time based on the popular album by composer Andrew Lloyd Webber and lyricist Tim Rice. *Jesus Christ Superstar* was filmed in Israel and Jewison's adaptation—which he co-wrote—contains only one line of spoken (not sung) dialogue. Featuring MTV-style cuts, as Jewison remarked in a *Washington Post* online chat, *Jesus Christ Superstar* became "the first hour and half rock video before the rock video was invented." *Jesus Christ Superstar* had been a music album before it became a Broadway play, and uses rock songs to tell the story of Christ's last days. The movie was a huge success with the viewing public, grossing nearly twenty million dollars, a large amount in 1973. Jewison's decision to film the movie on location in Israel was cited by critics as among the movie's strengths, as was its unusual and lavish production. The director has a special fondness for the project. Not only did he develop the film from a music album, but, "of all my films, I consider *Superstar* to be the most inventive and visually interesting," he wrote in *This Terrible Business Has Been Good to Me: An Autobiography*.

The crucifixion scene from Jewison's 1973 musical *Jesus Christ Superstar,* which was adapted from a soundtrack by Andrew Lloyd Weber and Tony Rice. (Universal/Robert Stigwood/The Kobal Collection/The Picture Desk, Inc.)

Jewison's 1989 film *In Country* starred Bruce Willis as an emotionally traumatized Vietnam veteran. (The Kobal Collection/The Picture Desk, Inc.)

Works with Hollywood's Best

Even though they were not huge hits, the director's next films explored his varied interests. 1975's *Rollerball* is a futuristic sci-fi story warning against corporate power; the 1978 film *F.I.S.T.* is a union melodrama starring Sylvester Stallone; 1979's . . . *And Justice for All* captures a sometimes-comic courtroom drama and earned star Al Pacino an Oscar nomination; and 1982's *Best Friends* is a romantic comedy starring Burt Reynolds and Goldie Hawn. Jewison returned to racial themes with his 1984 film, *A Soldier's Story*, which is notable for featuring future Oscar-winner Denzel Washington in his first prominent film role. Based on Charles Fuller's Pulitzer Prize-winning play, the film takes place during World War II on a Louisiana army base where an African-American sergeant has been shot to death and a black officer is sent to investigate. *New York Times* critic Lawrence Van Gelder noted of the film that Jewison "has opened up the play by using such interiors as the bar where the troops hang out and exteriors on and around the base. But perhaps most commendably, he has let Mr. Fuller's

drama speak for itself, applying the skills of a film maker to polish the facets that lent such substance to the drama." The film earned producer Jewison his third Oscar nomination for best picture.

After another play adaptation, the 1985 drama *Agnes of God*, Jewison produced and directed his most successful film, the 1987 romantic comedy *Moonstruck*. Set in Brooklyn amongst a close-knit Italian family, *Moonstruck* follows the widowed Loretta (Oscar-winner Cher) as she accepts the proposal of a man she does not really love and then falls for his younger brother. "Jewison gives the film, his deftest work in years, an irresistible romantic sheen," as *People* writer Peter Travers remarked, although John Simon noted in *Nation* that *Moonstruck* "is a series of set pieces, some of which work, some of which merely strain." "As directed by Norman Jewison . . . , it moves with the crack of sexual friction," Richard Corliss commented in *Time*, concluding that *Moonstruck* "proves there is life in movie comedy yet." The film was a box office hit and earned Oscar nominations for both best picture and best director, a rare achievement for a comedy.

Jewison's next few films, while not as successful as *Moonstruck*, demonstrated his broad range. They included the 1989 Vietnam drama *In Country*, the 1991 comedy *Other People's Money*, and the 1994 romance *Only You*. Jewison spent the next few years developing a true story about a former boxer who is wrongly convicted of murder and the young man who helps exonerate him, with the aid of his Canadian mentors. The result was 1999's *The Hurricane*, which starred Denzel Washington as boxer Ruben "Hurricane" Carter. "*The Hurricane* is the kind of old-fashioned liberal rabble-rouser that . . . Jewison . . . practically has a patent on," *Entertainment Weekly* critic Owen Gleiberman observed. In *Time* Richard Schickel found *The Hurricane* to be "a thoughtful and even inspiring film. That's not just because of the way it celebrates Carter's self-discipline," the critic added, "but because the director . . . enforces the contrast between his stoicism and the efforts of the unlikely team of '60s activists that eventually came to his rescue." As Bob Longino concluded in the *Atlanta Journal-Constitution*, *The Hurricane* is "fashioned with the kind of classic

Hollywood professionalism that's fast becoming a rarity at the movies. Like *In the Heat of the Night*, it knows racial injustice when it sees it—and lays it bare for all the world to witness." The film earned Golden Globe nominations for best director and best drama; controversy about whether the film was historically inaccurate cost it potential Oscar nods.

Jewison brought Donald Margulies's Pulitzer Prize-winning drama *Dinner with Friends*, which centers on the longtime relationship between two couples, to cable television in 2001. Calling the filmmaker "a skilled craftsman who knows how to tailor his approach for each project," Bruce Fretts observed in *Entertainment Weekly* that, "in fact, *Dinner* couldn't differ more from his last film, the unjustly indicted boxing docudrama *The Hurricane*." *New York Times* critic Anita Gates called Jewison's adaptation "a model of excellence." "Jewison is a wily veteran when it comes to transferring stage plays to film . . . ," Charlie McCollum observed in the *San Jose Mercury-News*. "He is equally crafty with *Dinner with Friends*, giving Margulies' sharp dialogue plenty of room to breathe and to be ap-

In 1987 Norman Jewison directed Cher and Nicholas Cage in the popular romantic comedy *Moonstruck*. (/The Kobal Collection/The Picture Desk, Inc.)

preciated." The film was nominated for an Emmy award for best television movie.

An Artist to the End

Even into his seventies, Jewison was producing and directing new films. He traveled to France to make the 2003 drama *The Statement.* The film is set in 1992 and stars Michael Caine as a former Nazi collaborator whose only way to avoid assassins may be to stand trial for his crimes during World War II. Kirk Honeycutt, writing in the *Hollywood Reporter,* observed that "the film certainly has the hallmarks of a top-notch Jewison production—splendid performances . . . , a pulse-quickening pace and production values that establish story and character within a distinct environment." Other critics found the film unsuccessful; *Daily Variety* contributor Scott Foundas called it a "lackluster pic [that] fails both as suspense and as character study." For *Denver Post* writer Lisa Kennedy, however, found *The Statement* serves as "an intriguing hybrid" that contains "a striking portrait of a man of faith's profound hypocrisy."

In his early eighties, Jewison still had no plans to retire and was developing several ideas for production. "I know I'm getting old," he told *New York Times* contributor Bernard Weinraub. "But I also know that it's worth it to keep going, worth it to keep fighting and hammering away." Whatever the subject, he always begins with a good script. "I believe my first obligation is to the writer and the material," Jewison told *Chicago Tribune* critic Julia Cameron. "Although there is a certain amount of natural improvisation that occurs when shooting a movie, if you don't have a strong script, one that's logical and definitive, then usually you get into trouble. So you see, it all starts with the writer and the writer's idea." His usual practice is to sit down with the screenwriter and read through the script together, listening for dialogue that can be improved or scenes that don't work. He then might suggest changes to improve pacing or increase tension. "The director is the only person who sees the whole movie in his mind from beginning to end," he told Jack Batten in *Toronto Life.* "So he's got to influence everybody else to give their best and still be in step with him."

Jewison took up writing duties himself when his biographer, Jay Scott, died from AIDS in 1993. Unable to complete the project, Scott made Jewison promise that he would finish his own life story. The result is *This Terrible Business Has Been Good to Me,* which details Jewison's extensive film career in movies through various chapters devoted to specific

If you enjoy the works of Norman Jewison, you may also want to check out the following films:

The Verdict, starring Paul Newman, 1982.
Glory, starring Denzel Washington and Matthew Broderick, 1989.
Chicago, starring Richard Gere and Renée Zellweger, 2002.

projects. Toronto *Globe & Mail* contributor Angela Baldassarre observed that "the gossip is kept to a minimum; it's not surprising that Jewison is considered a gentleman in the back-stabbing circles of the moviemaking business. Any criticism is reserved for himself, and the only person he truly despises turns out to be a real cad." A *Kirkus Reviews* contributor called *This Terrible Business Has Been Good to Me* "instructive, engaging, entertaining," and Whitney Scott, writing in *Booklist,* commented that Jewison's life is "presented with straightforward candor." A *Publishers Weekly* reviewer concluded that Jewison's autobiography was "a successful study of what it takes to triumph in Hollywood and achieve artistic satisfaction."

It has not been easy making a successful career in Hollywood, Jewison noted. "I have always felt tremendous pressure from studios," he revealed to David Ansen and Jeff Giles for *Newsweek.* "Maybe it's because my pictures haven't been that interesting. 'Can we cut to the chase? Can you put more chases in? Can you cut it down?' All of this is brought to bear upon the filmmaker. And all you are trying to do is try to tell a story you believe in." Despite the pressure, Jewison has been a successful storyteller, judging from the number of lifetime achievement awards he has received. Most major filmmaking guilds have honored him; on awarding him the Governors Award, the jury of the American Society of Cinematographers called Jewison "a complete filmmaker who is creating an extraordinary body of work," as Dave McNary reported in *Daily Variety.* "His films range from dark and intense dramas to uplifting fantasies and musicals produced for both television and cinema release," the jury added. "The common denominator is that he always touches your heart and soul."

Jewison is also one of the forces behind the creation of Toronto's Canadian Film Centre, described by Gayle MacDonald in the Toronto *Globe & Mail* as "a beacon for [Canada's] brightest creative minds." Whether making his own movies or helping to teach the next generation of filmmakers, Jewison has

Denzel Washington starred as Rubin "Hurricane" Carter in Jewison's 1999 film *The Hurricane*. (Universal/Beacon Communications/ The Kobal Collection/The Picture Desk, Inc.)

devoted his efforts to furthering his craft. "People always tell me, 'Gee, you direct so many movies,' as if that's an unusual thing to do," he told Batten in *Toronto Life*. "But I made my mind up when I was young in this business that what's important for a movie director is to keep working. Don't ever stop working. Because how else are you going to learn how to do new things, which, to me, is the whole point? So I make a lot of different kinds of movies, and I love them all."

■ Biographical and Critical Sources

BOOKS

Contemporary Theatre, Film, and Television, Volume 78, Gale (Detroit, MI), 2008.
International Dictionary of Film and Filmmakers, Volume 2: *Directors*, 4th edition, St. James Press, 2000.

Jewison, Norman, *This Terrible Business Has Been Good to Me: An Autobiography*, Key Porter Books (Toronto, Ontario, Canada), 2004, Thomas Dunne Books (New York, NY), 2005.

PERIODICALS

Atlanta Journal-Constitution, January 9, 2000, Bob Longino, "Director Jewison Storms Back with 'Hurricane,'" p. L1.
Booklist, September 1, 2005, Whitney Scott, review of *This Terrible Business Has Been Good to Me: An Autobiography*, p. 38.
Box Office, January, 1988, T. Matthews, interview with Jewison.
Chicago Sun-Times, January 1, 1971, Roger Ebert, review of *Fiddler on the Roof*.
Chicago Tribune, September 8, 1985, Julia Cameron, interview with Jewison.
Cinema, July-August, 1965, "Norman Jewison Discusses Thematic Action in *The Cincinnati Kid*."
Cinema Canada, September, 1985, C. Tadros, interview with Jewison.

Daily Variety, December 14, 2002, Dave McNary, "Jewison in ASC Governors Spotlight," p. 5; November 14, 2003, Scott Foundas, review of *The Statement,* p. 7.

Denver Post, January 9, 2004, Lisa Kennedy, "Acting Makes a Strong 'Statement,'" p. F1.

Entertainment Weekly, February 7, 1997, Ty Burr, review of *Bogus,* p. 76; January 7, 2000, Owen Gleiberman, review of *The Hurricane,* p. 44; August 10, 2001, Bruce Fretts, review of *Dinner with Friends,* p. 56; December 19, 2003, Owen Gleiberman, review of *The Statement,* p. 55.

Films and Filming, January, 1971, Gordon Gow, interview with Jewison; April, 1988, A. Hunter, interview with Jewison.

Globe & Mail (Toronto, Ontario, Canada), November 27, 2004, Angela Baldassarre, review of *This Terrible Business Has Been Good to Me,* p. D20; March 14, 2009, Gayle MacDonald, "Stoking Canada's Filmmaking Crucible," p. R5.

Hollywood Reporter, February 13, 2003, Jon Silberg, "Dialogue with Norman Jewison," p. 1; November 14, 2003, Kirk Honeycutt, review of *The Statement,* p. 10.

Houston Chronicle, September 13, 2007, Mike McDaniel, "Lights, Camera . . . Norman Jewison!," p. 6.

Kirkus Reviews, July 1, 2005, review of *This Terrible Business Has Been Good to Me,* p. 719.

Library Journal, August 1, 2005, Rosalind Dayen, review of *This Terrible Business Has Been Good to Me,* p. 88.

National Review, March 4, 1988, John Simon, review of *Moonstruck,* p. 53; November 7, 1994, John Simon, review of *Only You,* p. 76.

Newsweek, January 5, 1970, Paul D. Zimmerman, review of *Gaily, Gaily;* February 7, 2000, David Ansen and Jeff Giles, "The Envelope, Please," p. 58.

New York Times, September 14, 1984, Lawrence Van Gelder, review of *A Soldier's Story;* December 26, 1999, Bernard Weinraub, "A Veteran Director Still Fights the Good Fight"; August 10, 2001, Anita Gates, "Feeling the Ripple Effect of a Marriage Rent Asunder," p. B29.

People, January 18, 1988, Peter Travers, review of *Moonstruck,* p. 8; September 25, 1989, Ralph Novak, review of *In Country,* p. 16; October 17, 1994, Leah Rozen, review of *Only You,* p. 21.

Premiere, autumn, 1987, interview with Jewison; November, 1991, H. De Vries, "A Director's Story."

Publishers Weekly, July 11, 2005, review of *This Terrible Business Has Been Good to Me,* p. 80.

San Jose Mercury News, August 8, 2001, Charlie McCollum, "HBO's 'Dinner with Friends' Is a Feast for Viewers."

Seattle Times, October 27, 2005, Bob Thomas, "Director Jewison Recounts His Years in Hollywood," p. D3.

Time, August 25, 1986, Richard Corliss, review of *Agnes of God,* p. 64; January 11, 1988, Richard Corliss, review of *Moonstruck,* p. 80; October 2, 1989, Richard Corliss, review of *In Country,* p. 90; December 27, 1999, Richard Schickel, review of *The Hurricane,* p. 168.

Toronto Life, March, 2004, Jack Batten, "The Storyteller," p. 82.

Variety, March 1, 1999, Richard Natale, "Filmmaker with a Conscience," p. 50; December 20, 1999, Emanuel Levy, review of *The Hurricane,* p. 56; November 17, 2003, Scott Foundas, review of *The Statement,* p. 37.

ONLINE

British Broadcasting Corporation Web site, http:// www.bbc.co.uk/films/ (June 13, 2001), George Perry, review of *Fiddler on the Roof.*

Canada Heirloom Series Web site, http://collections.ic. gc.ca/heirloom_series/ (August 25, 2006), profile of Jewison.

Northern Stars: Canadians in the Movies Web site, http://www.northernstars.ca/ (August 25, 2006), profile of Jewison.

Vancouver International Writers Festival Web site, http://www.writersfest.bc.ca/ (August 25, 2006), profile of Jewison.

Washington Post Online, http://www.washington post.com/ (August 30, 2005), "Book World Live: Film Director Norman Jewison."

OTHER

The Life and Times of Norman Jewison (television series), Canadian Broadcasting Corporation, 1997.

John La Farge

(Photograph courtesy the Library of Congress.)

■ Personal

Born March 31, 1835, in New York, NY; son of Jean-Frédéric (a businessman) and Louisa (de Saint-Victor) La Farge; married Margaret Mason Perry, 1860; children: Christopher Grant, Oliver Hazard Perry, John, six others; died November 14, 1910, in Providence, RI. *Education:* Attended St. John's College (later part of Fordham University); Mount St. Mary's College (Emmitsburg, MD), graduated, 1853.

■ Career

Artist, painter, muralist, stained-glass designer, and writer.

■ Member

American Academy of Arts and Letters (inaugural member), National Society of Mural Painters (president, 1899-1904).

■ Awards, Honors

Legion of Honor, Government of France, 1889; medal of honor, Architectural League, 1909.

■ Writings

ART CRITICISM

Considerations on Painting, Macmillan (New York, NY), 1895.

Great Masters, McClure, Phillips (New York, NY), 1903.

The Higher Life in Art, McClure, Phillips (New York, NY), 1908.

(Editor, with August F. Jaccaci) *Concerning Noteworthy Paintings in American Private Collections*, A.F. Jaccaci (New York, NY), 1909.

One Hundred Masterpieces of Painting, Doubleday, Page (Garden City, NY), 1912.

The Gospel Story in Art, Macmillan (New York, NY), 1913.

Also author of pamphlet *The American Art of Glass*, 1893.

LETTERS AND MEMOIRS

An Artist's Letters from Japan, Century (New York, NY), 1897.

Reminiscences of the South Seas, Doubleday, Page (Garden City, NY), 1912, published as *An American Artist in the South Seas*, introduction by Kaori O'Connor, KPI (New York, NY), 1987.

■ Sidelights

American craftsman and writer John La Farge was one of the most versatile artists working at the turn of the twentieth century. He was a painter and watercolorist who became one of the country's first muralists. He was a designer of stained-glass windows who invented opalescent glass and pioneered its use. He was an art critic, memoirist, and friend to some of the era's foremost thinkers, including historian Henry Adams, psychologist and philosopher William James, and novelist Henry James. La Farge was so highly regarded by his peers that in 1904 they made him one of first seven members of the prestigious American Academy of Arts and Letters. "As an artist he was a Renaissance man in the true sense of the term," William Zimmer remarked in the *New York Times*.

John La Farge's oil painting "Wreath of Flowers" was completed in 1866. (Smithsonian American Art Museum, Washington, DC/ Art Resource, NY.)

La Farge was born in New York City on March 31, 1835, the son of a French military officer who came to America and became a successful hotel owner and businessman. His mother was also from a distinguished French family, and young La Farge grew up with a keen sense of pride in his heritage. He received a good education, reading widely in both English and French. As far as the arts, "the influences which I felt as a little boy were those of the paintings and works of art that surrounded me at home," he was quoted as saying in Royal Cortissoz's *John La Farge: A Memoir and Study*. "[The] very furniture and hangings of the Empire parlor did not belong to the Victorian epoch in which I was growing up. It so happened that my first teachings were those of the eighteenth century and my training has covered a century and a half."

La Farge graduated from Mount St. Mary's College in Emmitsburg, Maryland, in 1853, and studied law from 1854 to 1855. He went to Europe in 1856 to study, travel, and acquaint himself with his French relations. In Paris he met many prominent literary and artistic figures and studied painting briefly with Thomas Couture, although at the time he told Couture he did not intend to become a painter. He traveled outside of France, where he viewed rich collections of works by the Old Masters like Rembrandt, Titian, and Rubens. In England, La Farge met some of the Pre-Raphaelite painters and poets who wished to bring color and naturalistic detail back to painting. On his return to America in 1858 he read law for a time until he settled in affluent Newport, Rhode Island. At that time he gave up the law to study painting with William Morris Hunt. In 1860 La Farge married and settled in Newport.

Comes Late to Painting

Although La Farge wished to enlist in the Union Army, poor eyesight kept him at home during the U.S. Civil War. He devoted his time not just to painting, but to the scientific study of light and color. "I wished to apply principles of light and color of which I had learned a little," Cortissoz quoted La Farge as saying. "I wished my studies of nature to indicate something of this, to be free from *recipes,* as far as possible, and to indicate very carefully in every part, the exact time of day and circumstance of light." He used his new insights to paint both landscapes and still lifes, creating works almost impressionistic in style. Of his *Flowers in a Persian Porcelain Water Bowl* (1861), *Smithsonian* contributor—and close friend of La Farge—Henry Adams wrote: "With breathtaking skill and sensitivity, La Farge rendered the evanescent colored shadows on the billowing white curtain and captured the subtle variation in clarity and focus between indoors and out."

La Farge's painting "Diadem Mountain at Sunset, Tahiti," completed by the artist in 1891. (© Brooklyn Museum/Corbis.)

Other well-known early paintings include *Paradise Valley* (1866-68) and *Bishop Berkeley's Rock* (1868). Cortissoz lauded *Paradise Valley,* calling it "a picture of peculiar significance in the history of American art," and adding, "Impressionism, I knew, had come into American painting long after its date, and, besides, La Farge was not painting, at the moment, anything quite like it, nor had he done so for years. Yet here was a landscape, done in America while the Hudson River school was still active in the land, and preserving qualities of light and atmosphere to which that school had never even begun to attain. Also it was as emphatically modern as anything painted in the last quarter of a century."

During this time La Farge also worked as an illustrator; his famous engraving *Wolf Charmer* was widely viewed in *Riverside Magazine,* while his work also adorned an edition of *Enoch Arden* (1865) by English poet Alfred, Lord Tennyson. Cortissoz observed that "it is as a unit of imaginative design that *Wolf Charmer* bewilders and enchants. It produces an illusion as of something seen in a dream, poignantly realized while the dream lasts, and yet apprehended, as things are so often apprehended in a dream, with an indefinable consciousness of supernatural implications. It is as though the living world and the world of faery were made one in a kind of vision."

A Variety of Skills and Interests

By the mid-1870s La Farge had developed an interest in architecture and interior decoration. In 1876 he was invited by architect H.H. Richardson to beautify the inside of Boston's newly renovated Trinity Church. Working with a team of artists, La Farge covered the walls and ceilings of the church with religious and decorative images in only five months. His work was so admired that he soon gained many more commissions, including the home of railroad tycoon Cornelius Vanderbilt and the Minnesota State Capitol. In 1887 he executed the large, Renaissance-inspired *Ascension* mural for New York City's Church of the Ascension, producing what *Dictionary of American Biography* contributor Cortissoz called "indubitably the greatest mural painting of a religious subject produced anywhere in La Farge's time." *Smithsonian* writer Adams similarly observed that the mural "set a new direction in American art and initiated the movement now known as the American Renaissance."

Creates Masterworks in Glass

Around the same time, La Farge became involved in the production of stained glass at the request of an architect friend. He destroyed his first attempt at a decorative glass window for Harvard University's Memorial Hall as inadequate; then inspiration struck while he was bed-ridden and saw the light striking a colored bottle of toothpaste powder. This led him to develop opalescent glass: colored glass that was not perfectly clear and often fused several colors into one piece. "La Farge's new methods and new materials gave him such extraordinary control of color that he could duplicate the delicate texture of a peony blossom, the shimmer of light on a fish's scales . . . , or the iridescent splendor of a peacock's tail," Adams remarked in *Smithsonian*. Calling La Farge's work "among the best windows of his period," Wayne Craven surmised in *American Art: History and Culture* that the artist "perhaps felt a kinship with the medieval artisan who labored to produce handcrafted objects of beauty—a feeling very much in the spirit of the Arts and Crafts movement of La Farge's Day."

La Farge's first work in stained glass was the Battle Window at Harvard's Memorial Hall; he later produced three more windows for the building. Other stained-glass projects included windows for two Vanderbilt houses in New York City; four stained-glass windows for Boston's Trinity Church; and the "Peacock Window," his last work in the medium, which took him sixteen years to complete. When he exhibited the window in 1908, a *New York Times* critic called it "one of these imperative works of art that will not let one go in peace." La Farge's stained-glass work earned international acclaim, as well. A window he exhibited at the French Exhibition of 1889 earned him the Legion of Honor; the jury, as quoted in Cecelia Waern's *John La Farge: Artist and Writer*, released the following statement: "His work cannot be fully gauged here, where a single window represents a name the most celebrated and widely known in our Sister-Republic. He is the great innovator, the inventor of opaline glass. He has created in all its details an art unknown before, an entirely new industry, and in a country without traditions, he will begin one followed by thousands of pupils filled with the same respect for him that we have ourselves for our own masters. To share in this respect is the highest praise that we can give to this great artist."

La Farge was also an important figure in introducing Japanese art to America. He had long been an aficionado of Japanese painting—his first piece of art criticism was on the subject—and in 1886 La Farge and friend Henry Adams visited Japan. Upon his return La Farge painted several watercolors based on Japanese folklore, and later published his experiences in *An Artist's Letters from Japan*. In 1890 he and Adams traveled to the South Seas, arriving in Tahiti a few days before French Impressionist Paul Gauguin, who became famous for his painting of the people. La Farge's own South Seas paintings, done in both watercolor and oil, combine a sense of the exotic with the immediacy of precise anthropological observation, as in *Maua, Our Boatman* (1891).

Along with his varied artistic activities La Farge found time for writing and lecturing. His publications included *Considerations on Painting* (1895), *Great Masters* (1903), *The Higher Life in Art* (1908), and the posthumously published *Reminiscences of the South Seas* (1911), *One Hundred Masterpieces of Painting*, (1912), and *The Gospel Story in Art* (1913). La Farge died in Providence, Rhode Island, on November 14, 1910.

"The Necessity of Constant Work"

Throughout his artistic career, La Farge was constantly evolving, challenging himself to look at his subjects in fresh, unusual ways. This devotion to progress and self-discovery can be seen in his 1895 volume *Considerations on Painting*, in which he stated, "In all that we do freely, in our perception of things, we are obliged to join together, at every moment, thousands of former visual memories, recent or very old, to the perceptions of the moment. From the first movement of the hand to the last—even, as I said, from the first sight of the paper or the canvas on which the painter is to draw, every moment when he thinks of work, all the accumulated images come back to him, and have a right upon him." La Farge continued, "Hence the necessity of constant work; hence the necessity of constant purification of our memories; hence the use, not only of our own memories, but of the memories of others, such as are gathered about us. What we can feel sure of is that nothing has been done once for all—that all the illusions, the realities, have not yet been reproduced through other illusions, and that no matter how completely all has been done, all the more chance for you to do it again."

La Farge's "The Muse of Paintings" reflects the influence of the Pre-Raphaelite school led by Dante Gabriel Rossetti.
(Photograph. © Francis G. Mayer/Corbis.)

The stained-glass windows La Farge created for the Vanderbilt's New York City mansion are now being preserved for posterity by architectural conservationists. (Photograph © by James L. Amos/Corbis.)

If you enjoy the works of John La Farge, you may also want to check out the following:

The art of George Inness and James Mc-Neill Whistler, who were practitioners of tonalism.
The murals of celebrated Mexican artist Diego Rivera.
The stained-glass works of American artist Louis Comfort Tiffany and Irish artist Harry Clarke.

According to *Dictionary of American Biography* contributor Cortissoz, "What made [La Farge] ultimately a commanding figure in the American school was the fact that he saw his subjects beautifully as well as veraciously, that he had breadth of vision as well as control over the minute, passing effect, that he was a fine colorist and draftsman, and a skillful man with his hands." His work can still be seen today in buildings all over the Northeast, including several churches in New York City: the Church of the Ascension, the Church of the Incarnation, the Church of Saint Paul the Apostle, St. Paul's Chapel at Columbia University, and the Judson Memorial Church, which has over a dozen La Farge windows. La Farge's legacy is a large one, as Adams concluded in *Smithsonian:* "No other American artist of the 19th century so enriched American culture and none so inventively transformed an enormous range of media."

■ Biographical and Critical Sources

BOOKS

Cortissoz, Royal, *John La Farge: A Memoir and Study,* Houghton Mifflin (New York, NY), 1911.

Craven, Wayne, *American Art: History and Culture,* McGraw-Hill (New York, NY), 2003.

Dictionary of American Biography Base Set, American Council of Learned Societies (New York, NY), 1928-1936.

Encyclopedia of World Biography, 2nd edition, Gale (Detroit, MI), 1998.

Waern, Cecelia, *John La Farge: Artist and Writer,* Macmillan (New York, NY), 1896.

PERIODICALS

American Art Journal, spring, 1992, Julie L. Sloan and James L. Yarnall, "Art of the Opaline Mind," pp. 4-43; spring-fall, 1999, James L. Yarnall, "Adventures of a Young Antiquarian: John La Farge's 'Wanderjahr' in Europe, 1856-1857," p. 102.

Magazine Antiques, February, 1998, Julie L. Sloan and James L. Yarnall, "John La Farge and the Judson Memorial Church," p. 300.

New York Times, April 27, 1908, "An Imperative Work of Art," p. 6; December 9, 1990, William Zimmer, "La Farge: An Artist for the Gilded Age"; June 2, 1995, Pepe Karmel, "Art in Review."

Smithsonian, July, 1987, Henry Adams, "First 'A Marvel,' Then out of Fashion, a Fine Artist Returns," p. 46.

Southwest Review, winter, 2004, Patricia Vigderman, "Henry Adams in Japan," p. 147.*

(Photograph © by Jerry Bauer. Reproduced by permission.)

Ross Macdonald

■ Personal

Born Kenneth Millar (surname is pronounced "Miller"), December 13, 1915, in Los Gatos, CA; died of complications from Alzheimer's disease, July 11, 1983, in Santa Barbara, CA; son of John Macdonald (a newspaper editor) and Anne Millar; married Margaret Ellis Sturm (a mystery writer), June 2, 1938; children: Linda Jane. *Education:* University of Western Ontario, B.A. (with honors), 1938; University of Toronto, graduate study, 1938-39; University of Michigan, M.A., 1943, Ph.D. (English), 1951. *Politics:* Democrat.

■ Career

Mystery writer. Kitchener Collegiate Institute, Kitchener, Ontario, Canada, teacher of English and history, 1939-41; University of Michigan, Ann Arbor, teaching fellow, 1942-44, 1948-49; teacher of writing in adult education program, Santa Barbara, CA, 1957-59; *San Francisco Chronicle,* San Francisco, CA, book reviewer, 1957-60. Santa Barbara Natural History Museum, trustee, beginning 1970. *Military service:* U.S. Naval Reserve, served in the Pacific, 1944-46; became lieutenant junior grade.

■ Member

Mystery Writers of America (member of board of directors, 1960-61, 1964-65; president, 1965), American Civil Liberties Union, Authors League of America, Crime Writers Association, National Audubon Society, Sierra Club, Writers Guild of America West, Santa Barbara Audubon Society (publicity chair, 1965-66), Coral Casino.

■ Awards, Honors

Edgar Allan Poe Award, Mystery Writers of America, 1962, for *The Wycherly Woman,* and 1963, for *The Zebra-striped Hearse;* Crime Writers Association Silver Dagger, 1965, for *The Chill,* and Gold Dagger, 1966, for *The Far Side of the Dollar;* University of Michigan Outstanding Achievement Award, 1972; Grand Master Award, Mystery Writers of America, 1973; Popular Culture Association Award of Excellence, 1973; Life Achievement Award, Private Eye Writers of America, 1981; Robert Kirsch Award, *Los Angeles Times,* 1982; the Kenneth Millar Memorial Fund was established in 1983 by the Foundation for Santa Barbara City College.

■ Writings

NOVELS

(As John Ross Macdonald) *The Drowning Pool,* Knopf (New York, NY), 1950, published under name Ross Macdonald, Garland Publishing (New York, NY), 1976.

(As John Ross Macdonald) *The Way Some People Die* (also see below), Knopf (New York, NY), 1951, published under name Ross Macdonald, State Mutual Book (New York, NY), 1982.

(As John Ross Macdonald) *The Ivory Grin,* Knopf (New York, NY), 1952, published under name Ross Macdonald, Bantam (New York, NY), 1984, published as *Marked for Murder,* Pocket Books (New York, NY), 1953.

(As John Ross Macdonald) *Meet Me at the Morgue,* Knopf (New York, NY), 1953, published as *Experience with Evil,* Cassell (London, England), 1954.

(As John Ross Macdonald) *Find a Victim,* Knopf (New York, NY), 1954.

The Barbarous Coast (also see below), Knopf (New York, NY), 1956, published under pseudonym John Ross Macdonald, Cassell (London, England), 1957.

The Doomsters (also see below), Knopf (New York, NY), 1958, published under pseudonym John Ross Macdonald, Cassell (London, England), 1958.

The Galton Case (also see below), Knopf (New York, NY), 1959, published under pseudonym John Ross Macdonald, Cassell (London, England), 1960, reprinted, Bantam (New York, NY), 1980.

The Ferguson Affair, Knopf (New York, NY), 1960, reprinted, Bantam (New York, NY), 1980.

The Wycherly Woman, Knopf (New York, NY), 1961, reprinted, Vintage Crime (New York, NY), 1998.

The Zebra-striped Hearse (also see below), Knopf (New York, NY), 1962, reprinted, Vintage Crime (New York, NY), 1998.

The Chill (also see below), Knopf (New York, NY), 1964.

The Far Side of the Dollar, Knopf (New York, NY), 1965, reprinted, Bruccoli Clark (Columbia, SC), 1982.

Black Money (also see below), Knopf (New York, NY), 1966.

Archer in Hollywood (contains *The Moving Target, The Way Some People Die,* and *The Barbarous Coast*), Knopf (New York, NY), 1967.

The Instant Enemy (also see below), Knopf (New York, NY), 1968.

The Goodbye Look, Knopf (New York, NY), 1969, reprinted, Vintage Crime (New York, NY), 2000.

Archer at Large (contains *The Galton Case, The Chill,* and *Black Money*), Knopf (New York, NY), 1970.

The Underground Man, Knopf (New York, NY), 1971.

Sleeping Beauty, Knopf (New York, NY), 1973, reprinted, Vintage (New York, NY), 2000.

The Blue Hammer, Knopf (New York, NY), 1976.

Archer in Jeopardy (contains *The Doomsters, The Zebra-striped Hearse,* and *The Instant Enemy*), Knopf (New York, NY), 1979.

(As John Ross Macdonald) *The Lew Archer Omnibus,* Volume 1 (includes *The Drowning Pool, The Chill,* and *The Goodbye Look*), Allison & Busby (London, England), 1993.

(As John Ross Macdonald) *The Lew Archer Omnibus,* Volume 2 (includes *The Moving Target, Barbarous Coast,* and *Far Side of the Dollar*), Allison & Busby (London, England), 1994.

CRIME NOVELS AS KENNETH MILLAR; EXCEPT AS NOTED

The Dark Tunnel, Dodd (New York, NY), 1944, published under name Ross Macdonald, Gregg (Boston, MA), 1980, published as *I Die Slowly,* Lion (New York, NY), 1955.

Trouble Follows Me, Dodd (New York, NY), 1946, published as *Night Train,* Lion (New York, NY), 1955.

Blue City, Knopf (New York, NY), 1947.

The Three Roads, Knopf (New York, NY), 1948.

(Under pseudonym John Macdonald) *The Moving Target* (also see below), Knopf (New York, NY), 1949, published under name Ross Macdonald, Vintage (New York, NY), 1998, published as *Harper,* Pocket Books (New York, NY), 1966.

STORY COLLECTIONS

(Under pseudonym John Ross Macdonald) *The Name Is Archer,* Bantam (New York, NY), 1955.

Lew Archer, Private Investigator, Mysterious Press (New York, NY), 1977.

Early Millar: The First Stories of Ross Macdonald and Margaret Millar, Cordelia Editions (Santa Barbara, CA), 1982.

Strangers in Town: Three Newly Discovered Stories, Crippen & Landru (Norfolk, VA), 2001.

OTHER

(Editor) William F. Nolan, *Dashiell Hammett: A Casebook,* McNally & Loftin (Charlotte, NC), 1969.

(Editor) *The Santa Barbara Declaration of Environmental Rights,* January 28 Committee (Santa Barbara, CA), 1969.

(Author of introduction) Matthew J. Bruccoli, compiler, *Kenneth Millar/Ross Macdonald: A Checklist,* Gale (Detroit, MI), 1971.

On Crime Writing, Capra (Santa Barbara, CA), 1973.

(Editor) *Great Stories of Suspense,* Knopf (New York, NY), 1974.

A Collection of Reviews, Lord John (Northridge, CA), 1980.

Self-Portrait: Ceaselessly into the Past, edited by Ralph Sipper, Capra (Santa Barbara, CA), 1981.

Also contributor to *The Queen's Awards, 1946,* Little, Brown (Boston, MA), 1946; *Murder by Experts,* Ziff-Davis, 1947; *Maiden Murders,* Harper (New York, NY), 1952; *Ellery Queen's Awards, Honors: Ninth Series,* Little, Brown, 1954; *A Choice of Murders,* Scribner (New York, NY), 1958; *Best Detective Stories of the Year,* Dutton (New York, NY), 1962; *Best Detective Stories of the Year,* Dutton, 1966; *Essays Classic and Contemporary,* Lippincott (Philadelphia, PA), 1967; *Afterwords,* Harper, 1969; and *Crimes and Misfortunes,* Random House (New York, NY), 1970. Contributor to *Ellery Queen's Mystery Magazine, Cosmopolitan, Esquire, Argosy, Sports Illustrated, Saturday Night, Antaeus,* and *San Francisco Chronicle.*

Author's manuscript collected at the University of California—Irvine Library.

■ Adaptations

The Moving Target was filmed as *Harper* by Warner Bros. in 1966; *The Underground Man* was filmed for television by Paramount in 1974; *The Drowning Pool* was filmed by Warner Bros. in 1975; *Archer,* a National Broadcasting Company (NBC) television series in 1975, was based on several of Macdonald's short stories featuring private detective Lew Archer; *The Three Roads* was filmed as *Double Negative,* 1980; *Blue City* was filmed for a movie of the same title, 1986; *The Ferguson Affair* was adapted as the television movie, *Criminal Behavior,* 1992.

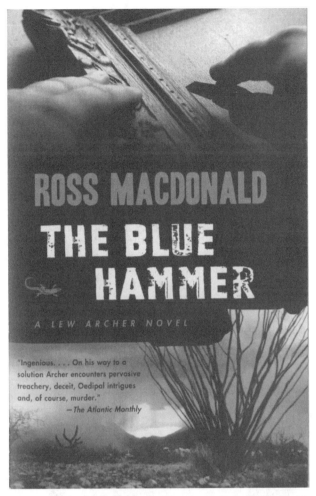

Cover of Ross Macdonald's 1976 novel *The Blue Hammer,* featuring Detective Lew Archer. (Copyright © 2008 by Vintage Books. Cover photographs (top) © Arthur Turner/Alamy; (bottom) © Loomis Dean/Time Life. Used by permission of Alfred A. Knopf, a division of Random House, Inc.)

■ Sidelights

"If Dashiell Hammett can be said to have injected the hard-boiled detective novel with its primitive force, and Raymond Chandler gave shape to its prevailing tone, it was Ken Millar, writing as Ross Macdonald, who gave the genre its current respectability, generating a worldwide readership that has paved the way for those of us following in his footsteps." Thus wrote mystery author Sue Grafton in her introduction to *Ross Macdonald: A Biography.* Indeed, Macdonald is considered by many to be one of the great masters of twentieth-century detective fiction, linked to his predecessors Hammett and Chandler to comprise "the big three . . . of the American hard-boiled detective novel," according to Matthew J. Bruccoli in the *Dictionary of Literary Biography Yearbook: 1983.*

With his eighteen novels featuring rock-solid private investigator Lew Archer, Macdonald has been credited with transforming detective fiction into serious literature through his explorations of character and social issues. A *Los Angeles Magazine* contributor described Archer as "a lone crusader whose jaundiced eye and hard-boiled comments incompletely mask a tender heart . . . a warrior monk, compassionate and detached." Archer is a keen observer of mankind, and does not shy away from psychology. By infusing his whodunits with literary style, complex, character-driven plots, and moral and psychological ambiguity, Macdonald, via Archer, broadened the concerns of the detective genre. Throughout his life Macdonald won recognition for his mystery novels featuring Archer, a character he created in 1949. The "Lew Archer" books, William Goldman famously stated in the *New York Times Book Review,* are "the finest series of detective novels ever written by an American." Ten years before he died, Macdonald was honored with the Grand Master Award, the most prestigious citation given by the Mystery Writers of America.

Despite such acclaim, Macdonald's legacy has been a contested one. As the *Los Angeles Magazine* contributor noted, "Raymond Chandler scolded· Macdonald for dropping $3 metaphors into dime novel plots." Other contemporary critics also voiced similar concerns. After Macdonald's death in 1983, some reviewers further took his work to task for employing pop psychology and continuously revisiting a similar plot trope. Writing in the *New York Times Book Review,* Terry Teachout argued that Macdonald's reputation was inflated by a concerted effort on the part of critics such as Goldman, who was a personal friend of the novelist. Until Goldman's review of *The Goodbye Look* in 1969, "the literary establishment, to the extent that it was aware of Millar at all, seems to have regarded him as a bit of a hack," Teachout noted, the critic adding that, after Goldman's positive review, Macdonald's novel "spent 14 weeks on the best-seller list, and until his death at the age of 67 in 1983, Millar was treated not as a hack but as a serious writer."

Similarly, Tom Nolan, in his study *Ross Macdonald: A Biography,* assayed Macdonald's rise to fame: "In 1969, when most literate readers thought detective stories beneath consideration and mystery fiction rarely appeared on best-seller lists, a handful of New York journalists conspired to push a California writer of private-eye novels to the front rank of American letters." Writing in the *Boston Globe* in 2003, Leonard Cassuto noted of Macdonald's longevity, "Unlike Chandler, Macdonald has since slipped to the back shelves. Fewer than half of his books remain in print. And although American crime fiction now receives unprecedented attention from literary scholars, Macdonald's reputation lags behind that of contemporaries such as Jim Thompson and Patricia Highsmith." Contested or not, Macdonald's reputation lingers, and several of the best of his "Lew Archer" books continue to find an avid readership even when competing against more modern and graphic mystery novels.

Beginnings of a Novelist

Macdonald was born Kenneth Millar in 1915, an only child of transplanted Canadians. He spent his first four years of life in California, where his itinerant newspaper-editor father and nurse mother were then working. In 1919 the family moved to Vancou-

ver, British Columbia. The elder Millar was now working as a harbor pilot, and the family lodged in a hotel along the waterfront. Macdonald's parents separated for a time when he was four years old; a year later the break was permanent when his father abandoned his wife and son. As Macdonald's mother was a semi-invalid, mother and son thereafter became charity cases. This trauma affected the rest of Macdonald's life. He had to beg on the streets at one point; at another time, his mother almost placed him in an orphanage. Finally, he and his mother moved to Ontario where her relatives lived. He saw little of his father while growing up, but remained attached emotionally to the man who had rejected him. For the next fifteen years, Macdonald and his mother shuttled between one relative and the other. As he told *Newsweek* contributor Raymond

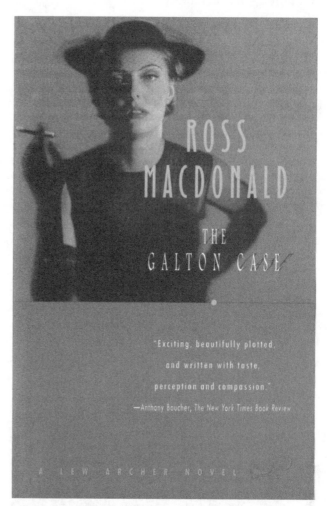

Macdonald's popular sleuth Lew Archer follows the trail of a missing man that is two decades old in his 1959 novel *The Galton Case.* (Copyright © 1996 by Vintage Books. Cover photograph © Darrell Eager. Used by permission of Alfred A. Knopf, a division of Random House, Inc.)

A. Sokolov, "I felt uprooted from the time my parents separated. It was a good background for a novelist, but not for anything else I can think of." The one secure place in his life during those years of constant upheaval was the local public library, where he found solace in books.

In 1930 Macdonald read *The Maltese Falcon* by Hammett; he was greatly influenced by it and began writing his own stories. When he was fifteen years old Macdonald published his first story in the annual of the Kitchener-Waterloo Collegiate and Vocational School. As he wrote in his introduction to *Kenneth Millar/Ross Macdonald: A Checklist,* the story "was a parody of Conan Doyle written in the obvious influence of Leacock." His father's death in 1932 brought Macdonald a small legacy that he used to attend college. Devastated by his mother's death in 1935, he dropped out of school for a time, cycling through Europe. In 1939, he graduated from the University of Western Ontario; the day after graduation he married Margaret Ellis Sturm, a young woman he had known since his high school days.

In 1939, about a year after he married Margaret, Macdonald recalled, "I became at the same time the father of a daughter and a professional writing for money. My main market was the Toronto political and literary weekly, *Saturday Night.* I lightly bombarded the editor, B.K. Sandwell, with verses and humorous sketches, and my first few realistic stories. *Saturday Night* came out on Saturday morning, and [Margaret and I] used to walk up Bloor Street to see if anything of mine had been printed that week. Payment was just a cent a word, but the early joys of authorship were almost as sweet as sex."

Macdonald cites his wife as a major impetus at the beginning of his writing career. Confined to bed for six months due to a heart ailment, Margaret Millar began to read mystery novels and, eventually, to write one of her own. The book was published, and she began a writing career. Her success led Macdonald to try his own hand at writing. His first few efforts were published under his real name, but to avoid confusion with his wife, he adopted the pseudonym John Macdonald, derived from his father's name. Confusion with John D. Macdonald, the author of the "Travis McGee" mystery novels, then led him to use John Ross Macdonald and, finally, Ross Macdonald. Speaking of his wife's influence on his early career, Macdonald recounted in *Kenneth Millar/Ross Macdonald:* "By going on ahead and breaking trail, she helped to make it possible for me to become a novelist, as perhaps her life with me had helped to make it possible for her."

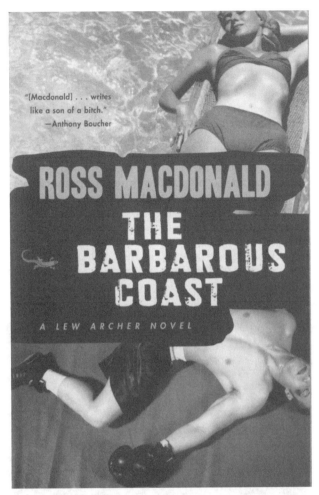

The 1956 novel *The Barbarous Coast* was one of the first books to be published using the Ross Macdonald pseudoynm. (Copyright © 2007 by Vintage Books. Used by permission of Alfred A. Knopf, a division of Random House, Inc.)

In tribute to his wife, Macdonald made their wedding anniversary date, June 2, Lew Archer's birthday.

Macdonald wrote his first novel while on fellowship at the University of Michigan, in the fall of 1943, "at night in one of the offices of the main classroom building, and the book preserves some of the atmosphere of that empty echoing pile." He also observed in *Kenneth Millar/Ross Macdonald* that "part of the terror that permeates the book" was derived from his fear of writing a lengthy work, his experiences in a two-month visit to Nazi Germany, and his initial rejection from the U.S. Naval Reserve. Macdonald documented the genesis of his next three works: "My second book was written a year or so later aboard an escort carrier in the Pacific. Then I came home to California, where Margaret and our daughter now lived, and between March 1946 and the end of that year, in a kind of angry rapture, wrote *Blue City* and *The Three Roads.*"

Enter Lew Archer

Hammett and Chandler had a tremendous influence on Macdonald's early writings. The hard-boiled detective genre the two men helped to create struck the newly minted writer as "a popular and democratic literature. . . . [Hammett's and Chandler's] heroes seemed to continue in highly complicated urban environments the masculine and egalitarian frontier traditions of Natty Bumppo. . . . Their abrupt and striking scenes seemed to reflect the disjunctions of an atomized society. Their style, terse and highly figured, seemed not quite to have reached the end of its development." Macdonald

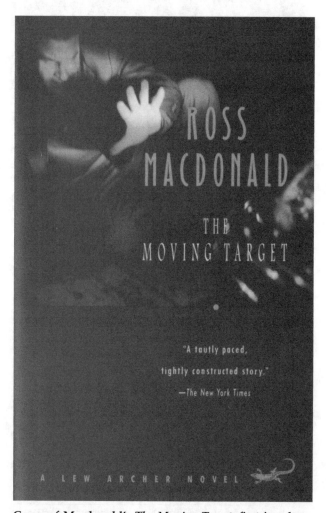

Cover of Macdonald's *The Moving Target*, first in a long series of mysteries featuring hard-edged sleuth Lew Archer. (Copyright © 1998 by Vintage Books. Cover photograph © Charles R. Smith, Jr. Used by permission of Alfred A. Knopf, a division of Random House, Inc.)

was so impressed with Hammett's work in particular that he named Lew Archer in honor of Miles Archer, a character in Hammett's classic detective novel *The Maltese Falcon.*

Archer's first appearance was in the 1949 novel, *The Moving Target.* Writing in the *New York Times Book Review,* Anthony Boucher found the book to be "the most human and disturbing novel of the hard-boiled school in many years." Macdonald began to write the "Lew Archer" novels at the rate of one a year for a few years. There followed *The Drowning Pool* from 1950, *The Way Some People Die* from 1951, and *The Ivory Grin* from 1952. Macdonald was, at the same time, finishing his dissertation on British poet and critic Samuel Taylor Coleridge at the University of Michigan. Earning his doctorate in 1952, he and his wife and daughter thereafter returned to Santa Barbara, California, which became the fictional Santa Teresa of his novels.

Slowly, Macdonald began to build a loyal fan base. Although he wrote detective novels in the hard-boiled tradition of Hammett and Chandler, beginning with *The Galton Case* of 1959, Macdonald took the genre into new territory by exploring its psychological dimensions. His novels after *The Galton Case* featured a recurring theme: the resolution of family conflicts through a psychological search of the past. The typical Macdonald novel begins with Lew Archer being hired to find a missing family member. Sometimes the missing person seems to have been kidnapped; other times he or she is a runaway. Archer's investigation soon becomes a search into the family's past to determine the reasons for the disappearance. Archer discovers that an old crime—usually a murder—is the hidden cause of the present trouble. This discovery leads to new violence in the present. "The origins of present crime, of present distress," Charles Champlin wrote in the *Los Angeles Times Book Review,* "are found to be a generation or more in the past, in a tangle of greeds, fears, hatreds and betrayals that will not stay buried." Archer grows obsessed with the case as it unfolds, even seeming to relive past events himself. "As other people's pasts and plots metamorphose into Archer's," George Grella explained in the *New Republic,* "[Lew Archer] becomes a participant in the sequence of events, its victim, even its perpetrator." When Archer ultimately solves the crime, it is often, Grella noted, "by some flash of irrational and illogical thought, by intuition or dream." Grella went on to call Macdonald in this 1974 article "the most distinguished living practitioner of what has become known as 'hard-boiled' detective fiction and a worthy successor to Dashiell Hammett and Raymond Chandler."

Macdonald's obsession with traumatic family history had its roots in his own troubled childhood.

He was finally able to deal with this material in *The Galton Case,* a novel in which a woman hires Archer to find her long-lost son. The trail Archer follows leads back to Canada and to many of the sites of Macdonald's own childhood. The book takes the autobiographical material that Macdonald could not handle earlier and successfully reworks it into a detective novel. *The Galton Case* "was a watershed book," Joe Gores wrote in the *Dictionary of Literary Biography Yearbook: 1983,* "the one in which [Macdonald] shook free of the Chandler influence and began to speak in his own unique voice." Champlin believed that the novel marked "a new dimension in the Ross Macdonald body of work."

In subsequent novels Macdonald continued to explore his childhood, and Lew Archer became, Champlin stated, "more a surrogate for the author." John Leonard quoted Macdonald's description of Archer in the *New York Times Book Review* as "a welder's mask enabling us to handle dangerously hot material." Archer plays this pivotal role in Macdonald's later novels. He asks the questions that reveal, in bits and pieces, the hidden events of the past. He then fuses these events into a coherent whole, revealing not only the solution to the mystery but the truth about the family past as well. Champlin also quoted Macdonald, who said that Archer is "less a doer than a questioner, a consciousness in which the meanings of other lives emerge." Archer's investigations, John Vermillion maintained in the *Dictionary of Literary Biography:* "force people to examine themselves and their links to the past, and to recognize that they are bound by past events which have fashioned their lives and will fashion their futures."

Ironically, it is Archer's own lack of a private life that allows him to uncover the private lives of others. Divorced and with few friends, Archer has the time to devote himself to his work. Michael Wood, writing in the *New York Times Book Review,* found Archer to be "a wise, tired, divorced, and lonely private eye." As Vermillion pointed out, Archer "is very much his own man, a man who has come to grips with his own deficiencies, a man for whom life is lonely and frequently painful, but nonetheless strangely satisfying." Noting that Archer evolves over the course of the book series, Eudora Welty wrote in the *New York Times Book Review* that Macdonald's fictional sleuth "matured and deepened in substance. . . . Possessed even when young of an endless backlog of stored information, most of it sad, on human nature, he tended once . . . to be a bit cynical. Now he is something much more, he is vulnerable. . . . He cares. And good and evil both are real to him." Unlike the hardboiled detectives of Hammett and Chandler, Archer is "the sensitive observer, watching the human tragedy, grieving for the victims," Champlin believed. Lew Archer was judged to be "a masterful creation" by Bruce Cook in *Catholic World* and a "distinguished creation" by Welty.

Because all of the "Lew Archer" books involve a search into the past, several critics were moved to question their value. Cook maintained that Macdonald was "rewriting the same novel over and over again. . . . As his plots continue to move backward in time and through the generations, they have also . . . become rather baroque in their development—terribly involved and complicated." Jean White, writing in the *Washington Post Book World,* also noted the repetition of plot in the "Lew Archer" books. Perhaps, White mused, "Archer is a trifle weary himself as case after case leads him to some terrible crime from the past that explodes to shatter a family a generation or two later. By now, you pick up a new Lew Archer novel and immediately begin trying to piece together tangled kinships and hidden family secrets." White also found that, despite the familiarity of the pattern, Macdonald's books remain satisfying: "Macdonald does it well, if again and again. He is an honest writer, a talented craftsman. He adds a psychological and social dimension to mystery writing."

California as Setting and Metaphor

Like Hammett and Chandler before him, Macdonald set his novels in California, and his ability to evoke the contemporary West Coast scene was especially praised by several critics. "Nobody," Goldman asserted, "writes southern California like Macdonald writes it." Lew Archer's cases take him from his modest two-room office into the wealthy suburbs and the dangerous underworld of Los Angeles. "The setting is always California," Julian Symons wrote in *Mortal Consequences: A History—From the Detective Story to the Crime Novel,* "sometimes its rich face and often its dirty backside." Archer's southern California, White believed, is "the land of the new rich with their houses and egos clinging precariously to the hillsides; the land of restless, rootless human beings lost in a technological society. Macdonald's crime novels give a better feel for this life and the people than a lot of serious fiction."

After the first burst of creativity in the 1950s, Macdonald slowed his pace in producing the "Lew Archer" novels, publishing one about every two years. His last non-Archer novel, *The Ferguson Affair,* was published in 1960. Thereafter he wrote only novels featuring Lew Archer. Some of the best of

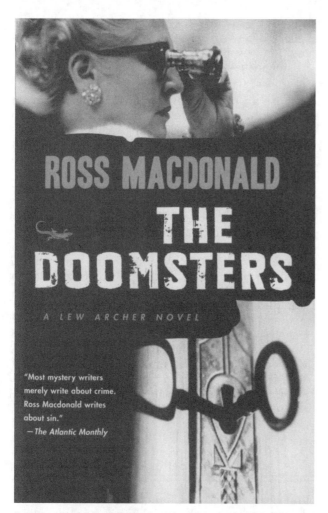

ROSS MACDONALD

THE DOOMSTERS

A LEW ARCHER NOVEL

"Most mystery writers merely write about crime. Ross Macdonald writes about sin."
— The Atlantic Monthly

In Lew Archer's outing in *The Doomsters*, Macdonald takes readers to small-town California and a secret that threatens to bring down a family dynasty. (Copyright © 2007 by Vintage Books. Used by permission of Vintage Books, a division of Random House, Inc.)

his later works were *The Goodbye Look, The Underground Man,* and *Sleeping Beauty.* Jerry Speir, author of the biography *Ross Macdonald,* called *The Underground Man* the author's "greatest achievement because it constructs a world view that incorporates the author's well-love themes of human pain and suffering within a vast sweep of sympathetic natural forces."

In 1976 Macdonald released *The Blue Hammer,* his final novel. As the contributor for *Los Angeles Magazine* noted, *Blue Hammer* "left little doubt that an era was over. At the book's end Archer, if not exactly married off by his fond progenitor, has been allowed to embark on a promising relationship with a young newspaperwoman. It's a farewell more poignant than readers realized."

A deep concern for the environment is evident in much of Macdonald's work. In private life he picketed on behalf of environmental groups against industrial polluters. He was also active in efforts to save the California condor from extinction. In such novels as *Sleeping Beauty,* in which the Santa Barbara oil spill of 1969 is prominently featured, Macdonald made clear his "view of California as a place of immense beauty made ugly by man," to quote Symons. Additionally, his own troubled parenthood worked its way into the books. Macdonald's daughter, Linda, was involved in a vehicular homicide as a teenager. She subsequently underwent psychological therapy, as did Macdonald himself at the time. In college in 1959, Linda disappeared in Reno for a couple of weeks, the result of her continuing guilt feelings over the earlier incident. In *The Wycherly Woman* from 1961, Archer is hired to find just such a tormented missing daughter. Macdonald's daughter ultimately died in 1970 at age thirty-one. It was one of the great tragedies of his life.

The Legacy

Macdonald died of Alzheimer's disease in 1983, and some two decades later many of his "Lew Archer" books are still in print. In fact, some work that he deemed not worth of publication was also posthumously published, including the story collection *Strangers in Town: Three Newly Discovered Stories.* The three stories in *Strangers in Town* come from the early part of Macdonald's career and are of most interest as "milestones in the gifted author's development," noted a contributor in *Kirkus Reviews,* who described the book as the "last crumbs from the master's table."

In the *St. James Guide to Crime and Mystery Writers,* Larry N. Landrum summarized the author's work: "Macdonald's sensitivity to people who are caught in the conflicts of social change is apparent throughout his fiction. . . . [Macdonald's characters] live illusions in order to conceal from themselves and others their own inadequacies and carry with them petty grievance that they have steadfastly refused to place in perspective. Archer is often spectator to arguments that have been worn down through repetition, but which are repeated once more for a new audience." Landrum continued: "The guilt that emerges in the novels is rarely traced to one person, but usually involves the full or partial commitments of several people at one stage or another. In many of the novels the identities of characters are interchanged, unexpected parenthood is revealed, or new identities have been assumed. The plots resulting from these complexities are intricate, the dialogue is a studied vernacular. . . . The process of demystification that occurs as Archer conducts his investigations creates resonances within the reader that urge him toward self-recognition."

Macdonald's standing as a detective novelist, as Frank MacShane wrote in the *New York Times Book Review,* "lay in the psychological insights he added to the tradition that had been handed down to him by Hammett and Chandler." Outside of the detective genre, MacShane believed, Macdonald ranked as "one of the best writers of his generation." Similarly, Bruccoli made the distinction that "an attempt to assess [Macdonald's] career properly must judge him as a novelist who wrote mysteries, not as a mystery writer—that is, against the whole field of American fiction." William McPherson, writing in the *Washington Post Book World,* made an interesting comparison: "Macdonald resembles another artist obsessed with guilt and retribution: Nathaniel Hawthorne, moved ahead a century and waking up in California, there to unravel the tangled past in the hope of exorcising it."

If you enjoy the works of Ross Macdonald, you may also want to check out the following books:

Dashiell Hammett, *The Maltese Falcon,* 1930.
Raymond Chandler's "Philip Marlowe" novels, including *Farewell, My Lovely,* 1940.
Robert Crais's "Elvis Cole" series, including *The Forgotten Man,* 2005.

Regarding Macdonald's legacy, Grella, writing in the *Reference Guide to American Literature,* observed that the novelist's "own place in the continuum of American detective fiction is as solid as that of Hammett and Chandler." Grella went on to note, however, that Macdonald's "influence on later writ-

Paul Newman starred as Lew Archer in the 1975 film adaptation of Macdonald's novel *The Drowning Pool.* (Warner Bros./The Kobal Collection/The Picture Desk, Inc.)

ers, beyond the superficial levels of the host of writers who imitate some of his mannerisms and themes, is more difficult to determine. . . . What cannot be doubted is that Macdonald's greatest influence has been to add to the literary richness and possibility of his form." "Those who read [Macdonald's] works in the future may find some accurate creation of a special time and place," Grella further noted, "but it is more likely that in Macdonald's fiction they will be instructed in the harsh lessons of an inner reality."

■ Biographical and Critical Sources

BOOKS

Bruccoli, Matthew J., compiler, *Kenneth Millar/Ross Macdonald: A Checklist*, Gale (Detroit, MI), 1971.

Bruccoli, Matthew J., *Kenneth Millar/Ross Macdonald: A Descriptive Bibliography*, University of Pittsburgh Press (Pittsburgh, PA), 1983.

Bruccoli, Matthew J., *Ross Macdonald*, Harcourt Brace Jovanovich (New York, NY), 1984.

Contemporary Literary Criticism, Gale (Detroit, MI), Volume 1, 1973, Volume 2, 1974, Volume 3, 1975, Volume 14, 1980, Volume 34, 1985, Volume 41, 1987.

Dictionary of Literary Biography, Gale (Detroit, MI), Volume 2: *American Novelists since World War II*, 1978, Volume 226: *American Hard-boiled Crime Writers*, 2000.

Dictionary of Literary Biography Documentary Series, Volume 6: *Hardboiled Mystery Writers: Raymond Chandler, Dashiell Hammett, Ross Macdonald*, Gale (Detroit, MI), 1989.

Dictionary of Literary Biography Yearbook: 1983, Gale (Detroit, MI), 1984.

Macdonald, Ross, *Self-Portrait: Ceaselessly into the Past*, edited by Ralph Sipper, Capra (Santa Barbara, CA), 1981.

Nolan, Tom, *Ross Macdonald: A Biography*, Scribner (New York, NY), 1999.

Reference Guide to American Literature 3rd edition, Gale (Detroit, MI), 1994.

St. James Guide to Crime and Mystery Writers, 4th edition, Gale (Detroit, MI), 1996.

Sipper, Ralph, editor, *Inward Journey: Ross Macdonald*, Cordelia Editions (Santa Barbara, CA), 1984.

Speir, Jerry, *Ross Macdonald*, Ungar (New York, NY), 1978.

Symons, Julian, *Mortal Consequences: A History—From the Detective Story to the Crime Novel*, Harper (New York, NY), 1972.

Weinkauf, Mary S., *Hard-boiled Heretic: The Lew Archer Novels of Ross Macdonald*, Brownstone (Madison, IN), 1994.

Wolfe, Peter, *Dreamers Who Live Their Dreams: The World of Ross Macdonald's Novels*, Bowling Green University (Bowling Green, OH), 1977.

PERIODICALS

Armchair Detective, January, 1977, Zahava K. Dorinson, "Ross Macdonald: The Personal Paradigm and Popular Fiction," p. 43.

Booklist, March 15, 2001, Wes Lukowsky, review of *Strangers in Town*, p. 218.

Boston Globe, November 2, 2003, Leonard Cassuto, "The Last Testament of Ross Macdonald."

Catholic World, October, 1971, Bruce Cook, review of *Underground Man*.

Christian Science Monitor, February 27, 1968, review of *Instant Enemy*, p. 9.

Commentary, September, 1971, review of *Underground Man*.

Esquire, June, 1972, John Carroll, "Ross Macdonald in Raw California," p. 148.

Harper's, July, 1966, review of *Black Money*, p. 86.

Hudson Review, spring, 1966, review of *Black Money*, p. 124.

Kirkus Reviews, November 1, 1965, review of *Black Money*, p. 1138; December 15, 1966, review of *Archer in Hollywood*, p. 1310; December 1, 1967, review of *Instant Enemy*, p. 1441; February 15, 2001, review of *Strangers in Town: Three Newly Discovered Stories*, p. 218.

Library Journal, February 1, 1966, review of *Black Money*, p. 719; May 1, 1967, review of *Archer in Hollywood*, p. 1857; February 1, 1968, review of *Instant Enemy*, p. 574.

Los Angeles Magazine, April, 2008, "Gravity's Angel" p. 85.

Los Angeles Times Book Review, November 21, 1982, review of *Self-Portrait*; January 19, 1985, Charles Champlin, review of *Inward Journey*, p. 1.

National Observer, January 10, 1966, review of *Black Money*, p. 27.

New Leader, April 11, 1966, Henry A. Woodfin, "Desperation in the Suburbs," review of *Black Money*, p. 26.

New Republic, July 26, 1975, George Grella, "Evil Plots," p. 24.

Newsweek, July 28, 1969, review of *The Goodbye Look*, p. 82; March 22, 1971, Raymond A. Sokolov, "The Art of Murder," p. 101.

New Yorker, January 22, 1966, review of *Black Money*, p. 112; April 6, 1968, review of *Instant Enemy*, p. 180.

New York Times, July 6, 1968, review of *Instant Enemy*, p. 19.

New York Times Book Review, April 3, 1949, Anthony Boucher, review of *The Moving Target*; January 9, 1966, review of *Black Money*, p. 36; February 19, 1967, review of *Archer in Hollywood*, p. 46; March 3, 1968, review of *Instant Enemy*, p. 37; June 1, 1969, William Goldman, review of *The Goodbye Look*, p. 1; June 1, 1969, John Leonard, "Ross Macdonald, His Lew Archer and Other Secret Selves," pp. 2, 19; February 14, 1971, Eudora Welty, review of *The Underground Man*, p. 1; May 20, 1973, Crawford Woods, review of *Sleeping Beauty*, p. 55; June 13, 1976, Michael Wood, review of *Blue Hammer*, p. 13; December 18, 1977, Frank MacShane, review of *Lew Archer, Private Investigator*, p. 25; March 14, 1999, Terry Teachout, "The Coleridge Scholar Who Took on Marlowe."

Observer (London, England), August 14, 1966, review of *Black Money*, p. 18; August 11, 1968, review of *Instant Enemy*, p. 23.

Publishers Weekly, December 12, 1966, review of *Archer in Hollywood*, p. 50; December 11, 1967, review of *Instant Enemy*, p. 40.

Punch, September 11, 1968, review of *Instant Enemy*, p. 381.

Saturday Review, January 29, 1966, review of *Black Money*, p. 37; March 25, 1967, review of *Archer in Hollywood*, p. 35.

Times Literary Supplement, April 2, 1982, review of *Self-Portrait*, p. 369.

Washington Post Book World, May 20, 1973, Jean White, review of *Sleeping Beauty*; June 27, 1976, William McPherson, review of *Blue Hammer*; May 20, 1984, review of *The Far Side of the Dollar*, p. 12.

ONLINE

Detnovel.com, http://www.detnovel.com/ (April 20, 2009), William Merling, "Ross Macdonald (Kenneth Millar)."

January Magazine Online, http://januarymagazine.com/ (September 1, 1998), J. Kingston Pierce, "The Private Eye of Ross Macdonald"; (April 1, 1999) J. Kingston Pierce, "Fifty Years with Lew Archer."

Thrilling Detective Web site, http://www.thrilling detective.com/ (April 20, 2009), "Authors and Creators: Ross Macdonald."

■ **Obituaries**

PERIODICALS

Chicago Tribune, July 14, 1983.
Detroit News, July 13, 1983.
Newsweek, July 25, 1983.
New York Times, July 13, 1983.
Publishers Weekly, July 29, 1983.
Rolling Stone, September 1, 1983.
Time, July 25, 1983.
Times (London, England), July 14, 1983.
Washington Post, July 13, 1983.*

D.J. MacHale

■ Personal

Born Donald James MacHale, March 11, 1956, in Greenwich, CT; married; wife's name Evangeline; children: Keaton (daughter). *Education:* New York University, B.F.A. *Hobbies and other interests:* Running, playing guitar.

■ Addresses

Home—Manhattan Beach, CA. *Agent*—Richard Curtis, Richard Curtis Assoc., 171 E. 74th St., Fl. 2, New York, NY 10021. *E-mail*—djmac@thependragon adventure.com.

■ Career

Writer, film director, and executive producer of television programming. Worked variously as a filmmaker, freelance writer/director, and teacher of photography and film production. Cocreator and producer of television series, including *Are You Afraid of the Dark?*, Nickelodeon, and *Flight 29 Down*, Discovery Kids/NBC.

■ Awards, Honors

CableAce Award nomination for Best Writer, for "The Tale of Cutter's Treasure" (episode of *Are You Afraid of the Dark?*); Gemini Award nomination for Best Director, for "The Tale of the Dangerous Soup" (episode of *Are You Afraid of the Dark?*); CableAce Award for Best Youth Series, for *Chris Cross*; CableAce Award nomination, for *Encyclopedia Brown, Boy Detective* (television program); Gemini Award for Best Youth Series, for *Are You Afraid of the Dark?*; Director's Guild of America award nomination for Best Children's Program, and Writers Guild of America Award, 2008, both for *Flight 29 Down.*

■ Writings

"PENDRAGON" SERIES; YOUNG-ADULT NOVELS

The Merchant of Death, Aladdin (New York, NY), 2002.

The Lost City of Faar, Aladdin (New York, NY), 2003.

The Never War, Aladdin (New York, NY), 2003.

The Reality Bug, Aladdin (New York, NY), 2003.

Black Water, Aladdin (New York, NY), 2004.

(With Victor Lee and Peter Ferguson) *Pendragon: The Guide to the Territories of Halla* (atlas of places from the novels in the series), Aladdin (New York, NY), 2005.

The Rivers of Zadaa, Simon & Schuster (New York, NY), 2005.

The Quillan Games, Simon & Schuster (New York, NY), 2006.

The Pilgrims of Rayne, Simon & Schuster (New York, NY), 2007.

Raven Rise, Simon & Schuster (New York, NY), 2008.

The Soldiers of Halla, Simon & Schuster (New York, NY), 2009.

"THE TRAVELERS" SERIES; YOUNG-ADULT NOVELS

(With Carla Jablonski), *Pendragon before the War: Book One,* Simon & Schuster (New York, NY), 2009.

(With Walter Sorrells) *Pendragon before the War: Book Two,* Simon & Schuster (New York, NY), 2009.

(With Walter Sorrells) *Pendragon before the War: Book Three,* Simon & Schuster (New York, NY), 2009.

OTHER

(Reteller), *East of the Sun, West of the Moon,* Rabbit Ears (Westport, CT), 1991, with illustrations by Vivienne Flesher, Abdo (Edina, MN), 2006.

The Monster Princess (picture book), illustrated by Alexandra Boiger, Aladdin Paperbacks (New York, NY), 2010.

Scriptwriter for television programs, including *ABC Afterschool Special; Ghostwriter,* PBS; and *Encyclopedia Brown, Boy Detective,* HBO. Writer and director of *Are You Afraid of the Dark?* (television series), and Disney television movie *Tower of Terror.* Cocreator and writer of television series, including *Chris Cross,* Showtime, and *Flight 29 Down,* Discovery Kids/ NBC. Coauthor of *The Tale of the Nightly Neighbors.*

■ Adaptations

The "Pendragon" series has been adapted for audiobook by Brilliance Audio. *The Merchant of Death* has been adapted for a graphic novel by Carla Speed McNeil.

■ Sidelights

"Imagine what it would be like to discover you aren't the person you thought you were," author D.J. MacHale encouraged readers of his home page. "That's what happened to Bobby Pendragon. He was living the life of a normal 14 year old guy, until his Uncle Press came by one night to say: 'I need your help.' From that moment on, nothing was the same." Thus, the "Pendragon" saga began. A collec-

tion of ten young-adult novels, MacHale's hugely popular "Pendragon" series relates a tale of adventure as Bobby joins other Travelers—beings who can travel through space and time—to secure the territories of Halla from the evil doings of the shape-shifting Saint Dane.

With over three million copies in print, the "Pendragon" books are more adventure than science fiction, as Bobby must rely not on magic or superhuman powers but rather on his skills and acumen to foil the plots of Saint Dane. MacHale focused on this realistic aspect of the fantasy series in an interview for the Simon & Schuster Web site: "I believe Bobby's appeal comes from the fact that he never loses sight of the person he was before the adventure began. When he's faced with a challenge, he reacts the way a regular person would. I believe readers put themselves into Bobby's shoes, imagining how they would deal with the same challenges." MacHale added that, while "the stories may technically be fantasies, . . . Bobby's experience is very real-world." Another aspect of the series that keeps readers hooked is the fact that Bobby would much rather be at home in Connecticut, shooting hoops and hanging out with his family. The problem is that once he became a Traveler, his family disappeared. Part of the mystery of "Pendragon" story is why Bobby specifically was chosen to become a Traveler, as well as what happened to his family.

A Career in Television

Born Donald James MacHale in 1956, the author grew up in Greenwich, Connecticut. As a child he enjoyed reading, telling *Writers Write* online interviewer Claire E. White: "I had an odd history in that I went from Dr. Seuss, straight to Ian Fleming. I'm sad to say that I missed out on the wealth of terrific 'middle reader' literature that was out there. But I believe that reading the adventure thrillers written by Ian Fleming and Alistair McLean developed my love for the genre." By high school, however, MacHale's focus had turned to filmmaking. He also played football and ran track. In college he floundered for a time searching for a major, but remembered his enjoyment with filmmaking. Ultimately he graduated from New York University with a degree in fine arts and film.

After college, MacHale began work filming advertisements and public-service announcements. "But the whole time I was writing screenplays and teleplays and trying to break into entertainment," he remarked to White. "It wasn't until I started writ-

Featuring artwork by Carla Speed McNeil, MacHale's first "Pendragon" novel was adapted into graphic-novel format as *The Merchant of Death Graphic Novel.* (Illustration © 2008 by Carla Speed McNeil. Reproduced by permission of Aladdin Paperbacks.)

ing for kids, that my stories started to sell. So . . . I guess you could say that through trial and error, I eventually found my true calling." MacHale forged a successful career in television, directing, producing, writing, and creating children's content for channels from Nickelodeon to Discovery Kids. He was the cocreator and writer behind such television shows as *Are You Afraid of the Dark? Flight 29 Down,* and *Chris Cross.*

Through his work in television, MacHale gained experience writing for children. When asked about his turn from screen to printed page, he explained to White: "Any screenwriter will tell you that as satisfying and wonderful a career as that is, outside of the people you work with, nobody actually reads what you write. Your writing goes through a process, touched by multiple dozens of people, until it becomes a finished piece of film. . . . Writing a book is much more pure than that, and I wanted to experience it."

The World of "Pendragon"

MacHale had long planned to write the story at the heart of the "Pendragon" books, but he soon came to realize that the depth of detail involved was not appropriate for television. Instead, in 2001, he began to write the story in book form. The result was *The Merchant of Death.* Content with his basketball career, his girlfriend, and his suburban Connecticut life, fourteen-year-old Bobby receives the shock of his life when his Uncle Press explains to the teen that they are both actually Travelers: beings able to make the leap between parallel realities and on whom many worlds depend. Uncle Press now asks Bobby to travel with him to the territory of Denduron, a medieval civilization that is about to experience civil war. In Denduron the two uncover the identity of the vicious Saint Dane, a shape changer who hopes to take over all of the worlds the Travelers have sworn to protect. Reviewing *The Merchant of Death* for *School Library Journal,* Celeste Steward recommended the series as "perfect for reluctant readers."

Bobby's adventures continue in further books in the "Pendragon" series, among them *The Lost City of Faar, The Never War,* and *The Reality Bug.* In each book he travels to a new world via an interplanetary wormhole, visiting underwater cities, parallel Earths, and unusual societies. Along the way the teen meets fellow Travelers, including Spader and Loor, and sends his journals to his best friends back home in Connecticut. MacHale tells each of the stories by combining a third-person narrative with

Bobby's viewpoint as noted in the letters he sends home. "With Pendragon," he told White, "I've tried very hard to have the stories feel as if they are being told by Bobby, directly to the reader. I wanted to make Bobby as accessible as possible, so that readers will feel as if he could actually be somebody they know in real life, which then adds to the whole wonder of the experience because the reader can then imagine what it would be like to have someone they know off on an impossible adventure."

In *The Lost City of Faar,* Bobby and Uncle Press travel to the watery world of Cloral, hoping there to locate a legendary city beneath the waves before Saint Dane can gain control of it and wreak havoc on the territories of Halla. Reviewing the second book of the series, a *Kirkus Reviews* critic noted that MacHale "displays a flair for action-packed pacing," and a *Publishers Weekly* critic recommended *The Lost City of Faar* to fans of Jules Verne's adventures, writing that the author "embellishes his science fiction with just enough silly touches to leaven the mood."

The Never War, one of MacHale's personal favorites in the series, finds Bobby, along with his buddy Spader, on a variant of Earth in 1937. Gangsters rule New York City, and the duo must dodge bullets to stop Saint Dane's latest evil plot. Reviewing this novel for *Blog Critics* online, Mel Odom termed it "a fascinating and fast-paced tale." Odom further remarked that "MacHale's sense of timing and pacing is excellent" and his "dialogue is fantastic and sounds real." Writing about *The Never War,* Sharon Rawlins noted in *School Library Journal* that while the book "may not be great literature," readers will enjoy its "fast pace, suspenseful plotting, and cliffhanger chapter endings."

With book four, *The Reality Bug,* Bobby travels to Veelox, a world that appears to be deserted because all of the inhabitants are living a sort of virtual reality, escaping into their own dream worlds. It seems a peaceful place, but Bobby knows that Saint Dane has malevolent plans for Veelox. Book five, *Black Water,* takes Bobby and friends to the territory of Eelong, a jungle world populated by huge and ferocious cats. White found this installment "a fast-paced, exciting adventure that has an underlying theme of choice."

In *The Rivers of Zadaa* the Travelers come to the home world of Loor, the young warrior woman who has become Bobby's fellow soldier in the fight against Dane as well as his romantic interest. Here they discover that the once peaceful relationship between the two civilizations, the subterranean Rokadors (who supply water above ground) and the Batu (who in turn protect the Rokador from invasion by uncivilized tribes), are now at each other's throats because of a drought. Dane, meanwhile, is thwarting every peace initiative between the two, attempting to turn the altercation into death-dealing war. "The Travelers are faced with a seemingly impossible task, especially with Saint Dane countering their every move," wrote James Blasingame in a *Journal of Adolescent & Adult Literacy* review of book number six. Blasingame went on to comment that *The Rivers of Zadaa* "is as good if not better than its predecessors," comparing Bobby to "Harry Potter, Frodo Baggins, and a host of other characters." Writing in *School Library Journal*, Walter Minkel remarked, "The action never stops for long, and Zadaa is sure to hold the interest of fans of the series."

According to *Kliatt* reviewer Deirdre Root, the seventh book in the saga, *The Quillan Games*, shows that, with each new adventure, the "Pendragon" series "gets better and better." Here Bobby and his friends discover a world on the brink of destruction. Holding the territory together are the Quillan Games of the title, masterminded by a strange pair: Veego and LeBerge. The games, which mix sport and combat, are played to the death for the amusement of the game masters. Bobby knows that the only way to save Quillan is by competing in the games and defeating Veego and LeBerge.

The eighth book in the series, *The Pilgrims of Rayne*, marks a change of pace for the series; the first book of a trilogy within the series, it takes "Pendragon" to its conclusion. Here, and in *Raven Rise* and *Soldiers of Halla*, Bobby and the Travelers must battle Saint Dane as he attempts to take over all of the territories. *The Pilgrims of Rayne* is set on the seemingly blissful world of Ibara but, as Bobby soon discovers, it is blissful only because its leader is hiding a dreadful secret. After battling Saint Dane through eight worlds, it appears in *Raven Rise* that Bobby and the Travelers have lost the war for control of the territories. Now Bobby, Uncle Press, and the others must liberate Halla.

Before and Beyond Halla

On the Simon & Schuster Web site, MacHale addressed the question of whether the "Pendragon" saga would positively end with book ten, *Soldiers of Halla*: "I'll never say never to anything, but as of right now I can't see how the series will go beyond ten books. Once all the questions are answered and the final battle plays out, it will be pretty clear that the story has ended. It has to, or my brain might explode." Instead, MacHale planned to produce

MacHale's ninth "Pendragon" novel, *Raven Rise*, features cover art by Dawn Austin. (Illustration copyright © 2008 by Dawn Austin. Reproduced by permission of Simon & Schuster Books for Young Readers and Dawn Austin.)

various trilogies, series, and picture books based on the series. Among these is the "Travelers" series, a group of three novels that serve as a prequel to the "Pendragon" books, as well as a fantasy series for middle-grade readers and a supernatural series for older readers.

If you enjoy the works of D.J. MacHale, you may also want to check out the following books:

K.A. Applegate, *Mystify the Magician*, 2001.
Charles Stross, *The Hidden Family*, 2005.
Paul Park, *The White Tyger*, 2007.

Speaking with White, MacHale noted a recurrent theme in all his writings, whether for television or print. "One consistent theme in all of my work, is the notion of self-empowerment," he observed. "I portray characters, usually kids, kids who are faced with dilemmas, and who do not have an adult around to show them the right thing to do." MacHale also offered advice for aspiring writers: "Write about what you know. That way your writing will be real and people will respond to it. It's as simple as that. And never give up."

■ Biographical and Critical Sources

PERIODICALS

Journal of Adolescent & Adult Literacy, October, 2006, James Blasingame, review of *The Rivers of Zadaa,* p. 161.

Kirkus Reviews, January 1, 2003, review of *The Lost City of Faar,* p. 63.

Kliatt, July, 2003, Deirdre B. Root, review of *The Never War,* p. 33; May, 2006, Deirdre Root, review of *The Quillan Games,* p. 11;.

PR Newswire, February 28, 2009, "Simon & Schuster Children's Publishing Signs Multi-Book Deal with New York Times Bestselling Author D.J. MacHale."

Publishers Weekly, December 2, 2002, review of *The Lost City of Faar,* p. 53; May 30, 2005, review of *Pendragon: The Guide to the Territories of Halla,* p. 62.

School Librarian, summer, 2003, review of *The Merchant of Death,* p. 100.

School Library Journal, November, 2002, John Peters, review of *The Merchant of Death,* p. 173; May, 2003, Susan L. Rogers, review of *The Lost City of Faar,* p. 156; July, 2003, Sharon Rawlins, review of *The Never War,* p. 133; July, 2005, Walter Minkel, review of *The Rivers of Zadaa,* p. 106.

Voice of Youth Advocates, April, 2003, review of *The Lost City of Faar,* p. 66; October, 2003, review of *The Never War,* p. 325.

ONLINE

Blog Critics Web site, http://blogcritics.org/ (February 8, 2008), Mel Odom, review of *The Never War.*

D.J. MacHale Home Page, http://www.thependragon adventure.com (April 20, 2009).

Kidzworld Web site, http://www.kidzworld.com/ (April 20, 2009), interview with MacHale.

Powell's Books Web site, http://www.powells.com/ (November 26, 2006), interview with MacHale.

Scholastic Web site, http://www2.scholastic.com/ (May 5, 2007), Aaron Broder, "A Talk with D.J. MacHale."

Simon & Schuster Web site, http://authors.simon andschuster.com/ (April 20, 2009), interview with MacHale.

Writers Write Web site, http://www.writerswrite. com/ (October 1, 2004), Claire E. White, "A Conversation with D.J. MacHale."*

Jack McDevitt

(Miller Photography. Reproduced by permission of Jack McDevitt.)

■ Personal

Born April 14, 1935, in Philadelphia, PA; son of John A. (a refinery worker) and Elizabeth (a homemaker) McDevitt; married Maureen McAdams (a teacher's aide), December 16, 1967; children: one daughter, two sons. *Education:* LaSalle College, B.A. 1957; Wesleyan University, M.A.L.S., 1971. *Hobbies and other interests:* Chess, bridge, astronomy.

■ Addresses

Home—Brunswick, GA. *Agent*—Ralph Vicinanza, 111 8th Ave., Ste. 1501, New York, NY 10011. *E-mail*—cryptic@gate.net.

■ Career

Writer, novelist, short-story writer, and educator. Woodrow Wilson High School, Levittown, PA, theater director and instructor in English and history, 1963-68; Mount St. Charles Academy, Woonsocket, RI, instructor in English, history, and theater,

1968-71; Newfound Memorial High School, Bristol, NH, English department chair, 1971-73; U.S. Customs Service, customs inspector in Pembina, ND, 1975-82, regional training officer in Chicago, IL, 1982-85, supervisor and management trainer specializing in motivational techniques and leadership at Federal Law Enforcement Training Center, Glynco, GA, 1985-95; full-time writer, 1995—. *Military service:* U.S. Navy, 1958-62; served in naval security group; earned commission.

■ Member

U.S. Chess Federation, Science Fiction Writers of America, Military Officers Association of America.

■ Awards, Honors

Locus Award, and Philip K. Dick Special Award, both 1987, both for *The Hercules Text;* Hugo Award nomination for best short story, 1988, for "The Fort Moxie Branch"; UPC Award, 1992, for novella "Ships in the Night," and 1994, for "Time Travellers Never Die"; Homer Award, 1997, for *Time Travellers Never Die;* Nebula Award nomination, 1997, for *Ancient Shores,* 1998, for *Moonfall,* 2000, for *Infinity Beach,* 2003, for *Chindi,* 2005, for *Polaris,* 2007, for *Odyssey,* and 2008, for *Cauldron;* Nebula Award nomination, and John W. Campbell Award for best novel, both

2004, both for *Omega;* Nebula Award for best novel, 2006, for *Seeker;* lifetime achievement award, Southeastern Science Fiction Achievement Awards; Phoenix Lifetime Achievement Award.

■ Writings

"ACADEMY" NOVELS

The Engines of God, Ace Books (New York, NY), 1994.
Deepsix, HarperCollins (New York, NY), 2001.
Chindi, Ace Books (New York, NY), 2002.
Omega, Ace Books (New York, NY), 2003.
Odyssey, Ace Books (New York, NY), 2006.
Cauldron, Ace Books (New York, NY), 2007.

"ALEX BENEDICT" NOVELS

A Talent for War, Ace Books (New York, NY), 1989.
Polaris, Ace Books (New York, NY), 2004.
Seeker, Ace Books (New York, NY), 2005.
The Devil's Eye, Ace Books (New York, NY), 2008.

OTHER

The Hercules Text, Ace Books (New York, NY), 1986.
Ancient Shores, HarperCollins (New York, NY), 1996.
Standard Candles (short-story collection), Tachyon Publications (San Francisco, CA), 1996.
Eternity Road, HarperCollins (New York, NY), 1997.
Moonfall, HarperCollins (New York, NY), 1998.
Hello Out There (contains revision of *The Hercules Text* and *A Talent for War*), Meisha Merlin (Atlanta, GA), 2000.
Infinity Beach, HarperCollins (New York, NY), 2000.

Contributor of short stories to magazines, including *Isaac Asimov's Science Fiction, Magazine of Fantasy and Science Fiction, Twilight Zone,* and *Full Spectrum.*

■ Sidelights

Jack McDevitt, a former English teacher, naval officer, taxi driver, and customs official, is the author of such highly regarded science-fiction novels as *The Hercules Text, Omega,* and the Nebula Award-winning *Seeker.* In his character-driven works, McDevitt examines themes of authority, religion, technology, and, most especially, loss. "It's compel-

ling," he author told *SciFi.com* interviewer John Joseph Adams. "I can't think of anything that locks in the emotions quite like the sense of something valuable, something utterly irreplaceable, that goes missing, that disappears. Whether it's a lost lover, or Atlantis, or how Egyptian engineers got those large blocks of stone across the Nile. It's the electric train set you had when you were a kid and foolishly gave away and wish now you still owned. It's that first car."

Born in 1935 in Philadelphia, Pennsylvania, McDevitt developed an interest in the mysteries of space at an early age. "Science fiction caught me when I was about four," he remarked to Charles Tan on the Nebula Awards Web site. "Inspired me to look above the South Philadelphia rooftops. I can remember a time, during the 50's, when UFO's were hot, when the kids in my neighborhood hoped a UFO would land on the vacant lot at the north end of the street. The UFO never came. But if it does show up, I hope to be there." The works of legendary author Ray Bradbury were another strong influence on the young McDevitt. "He got to me when I was 12, and demonstrated what a capable SF writer could do," he stated to Adams. "My all-time favorite book is *The Martian Chronicles.* Years ago, when I was teaching high school, I used it to win over students who thought books were mainly a hassle."

A Variety of Occupations

After graduating from LaSalle College in 1957, McDevitt joined the U.S. Navy, serving in a naval security group. He later taught high-school English, theater, and history for some ten years before joining the U.S. Customs Service in 1975, where he worked as a customs inspector, training officer, and supervisor. Although one of his childhood ambitions was to become a science-fiction writer, McDevitt did not realize his dream until he was in his forties. Prompted by his wife, Maureen, he wrote a short story, "The Emerson Effect," which was purchased by *Twilight Zone* magazine. Since then, he has produced more than a dozen novels, as well as several more story contributions to periodicals.

Until 1995, McDevitt did his writing while also working full-time for the Customs Service. In fact, his job in customs revived his interest in science fiction. While working the night shift as an inspector at his first post in Pembina, North Dakota, McDevitt stayed awake by reading science-fiction novels. A town with a population of just 600, Pembina was fictionalized as Fort Moxie in several of McDevitt's short stories as well as in his novel *Ancient Shores.*

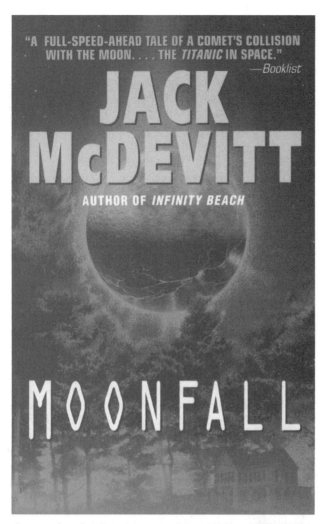

Cover of Jack McDevitt's 1998 novel *Moonfall*, which imagines the disaster that will occur when a comet shatters Earth's moon. (.Copyright © 1998 by Cryptic, Inc. Reprinted by permission of HarperCollins Publishers Inc.)

McDevitt is considered a "humanist" science-fiction writer, as his stories typically place an ordinary person in unusual, sometimes threatening situations that often result from encounters with the unknown. "For me, the pleasure to be derived from SF comes largely not from putting, say, a spectacle on display," the author told *SciFi.com* interviewer John Joseph Adams. "It's not the simple act of using a starship to watch a collision between two stars. Rather, it's watching the reactions of the characters who get to live the experience. It's watching people react to the notion that the edge of the universe runs through their dining room, or that the guy next door has a nuclear-powered refrigerator. That's what I'm interested in."

McDevitt's first novel, *The Hercules Text*, finds protagonist Harry Carmichael involved in a race with cold-war Soviet scientists to decode information transmitted by extra-galactic aliens from a source in the Hercules constellation. Speculation that the transmission's data could have military applications has caused each government to scramble for the answers. Among the scientists assisting Carmichael in the processing of the information is a Roman Catholic priest whose involvement with science may have cost him his faith. "The book," wrote *Twentieth-Century Science-Fiction Writers* contributor F. Brett Cox, "is a splendid example of what Algis Budrys has called the 'science-procedural novel,' concerning itself with the process of decoding the alien text and the power struggles that ensue as various scientific and governmental factions vie for control of the information contained in the transmission." Although the emphasis in *The Hercules Text* "is on problem-solving," Cox added that "McDevitt does not neglect his characters, giving all the major figures believable lives whose individual quirks and problems are fully integrated into the central problem of the Hercules Text."

McDevitt's novel *Ancient Shores* features a plot that is set in motion by an ordinary man's discovery of a quite remarkable artifact. While clearing a field, a North Dakota wheat farmer unearths a sea-going vessel in perfect condition. Scientific tests reveal that the boat has a carbon number so high that its materials will never decompose. "Within weeks," wrote Carl Hays in *Booklist*, "the boat becomes a media sensation coveted by prospective buyers and scientists." In a very short time, "the national economy verges on collapse because the materials from which the artifacts are made seem to wear forever: obsolescence in goods made from the stuff will be obsolete," Hays concluded. "Right up to the climax," stated a *Publishers Weekly* critic, "McDevitt . . . tells his complex and suspenseful story with meticulous attention to detail, deft characterizations, and graceful prose."

Eternity Road is set in a future world that has been decimated by a viral plague and describes an expedition to recover some of the knowledge left behind by the people who built the great road system of North America. "McDevitt redeems the possible overfamiliarity of his quest plot," stated Roland Green in *Booklist*, "with a large cast of well-handled, original characters, starting with the principal protagonist, silversmith Chaka Milana." *Eternity Road*, Green concluded, "is eminently readable and a real credit to McDevitt."

"In *Infinity Beach*, "McDevitt explained, "humans have decided that either intelligent species are extremely rare, or that humanity is alone. But a mission that went out twenty years ago *may* have found

Cover of McDevitt's futuristic novel *Eternity Road*, featuring artwork by Joe Danisi. (Copyright © 1997 by Cryptic, Inc. Reprinted by permission of HarperCollins Publishers Inc.)

logically sound and filled with hubristic, foolish people" whose choices are concerned more with image and the opinion of history rather than the actual benefit to society, commented a *Publishers Weekly* reviewer. *Infinity Beach* "is a wonderful mix of science-based fiction, mystery, and romance, with loads of action" and suspense, remarked *School Library Journal* reviewer Pam Johnson.

The "Academy" Series

The Engines of God, the first book in McDevitt's "Academy" series featuring starship pilot Priscilla "Hutch" Hutchins, revolves around a people's search for understanding of seemingly inexplicable events, this time the discovery of a mysterious formation on a moon orbiting a distant world. In *Deepsix*, it is the twenty-third century and the world is about to witness a spectacular celestial event: the collision of planet Maleiva III (also known as Deepsix) with a rogue gas giant, Morgan's World. A collection of scientists, civilians, tourists, and reporters have gathered to observe the planetary impact. A previous mission to Deepsix, intended to search for intelligent life, was aborted when it was attacked by vicious birds. In the face of the impending collision and destruction, new findings suggest that not only life, but an established civilization exists on the surface of Deepsix. Hutchins, a trained archaeologist, leads a mission to investigate the landmarks on Deepsix before its destruction. When an earthquake destroys the mission lander, the team is stranded on the world, and faces a harrowing trip across the planet's surface to locate a workable lander that was left by the previous expedition nearly two decades earlier. In the meantime, they must still do all they can to solve the mystery of the world's apparently vanished civilization. "McDevitt's captivating scenario plays out in a surprisingly relaxed, straightforward manner," remarked *Booklist* critic Bryan Baldus in a review of *Deepsix*. "McDevitt puts his characters into predictable jeopardies while methodically solving the conundrum of the missing aliens," commented a *Publishers Weekly* contributor. Paul Brink, writing in *School Library Journal,* noted that the novel's "well-rounded characters grow through their adventures, without that growth seeming trite or inevitable," and *Library Journal* critic Jackie Cassada commented favorably on McDevitt's "expert sense of pacing and . . . knack for cliffhanging suspense."

Chindi, the sequel to *Deepsix*, finds Hutchins on board for another mission. A brief transmission from the vicinity of a neutron star has attracted the attention of the Contact Society, which believes the

something. If so, it's being kept quiet." In the novel, scientist Kim Brandywine is quite familiar with the ill-fated mission of the starship *Hunter*. She is suspicious that the explorers on the vessel found extraterrestrial life but the discovery is being suppressed for reasons unknown. She also suspects that the *Hunter* mission is somehow connected to the disappearance of her clone-sister, and that a strange presence appearing on the planet Greenway also has connections to the troubled starship. To answer the questions that haunt her, Brandywine must risk her life, her lover, and her reputation in a determined search for the truth. "Exquisitely timed revelations maximize suspense, and fine characterization and world building also hold the reader's interest," noted Roland Green in a *Booklist* review. In *Infinity Beach* McDevitt has "created a future that is techno-

broadcast must have come from an intelligent alien source. Hutch is selected to act as pilot and archaeologist for the mission. When the expedition arrives at the neutron star, its members confirm the transmission but find no aliens. Instead, three hidden satellites are discovered to be sending data to an unknown source in a distant star system. As the story unfolds, more of these stealth satellites are discovered orbiting other worlds, including Earth. When a friend of Hutch's snags one of the satellites and takes it on board for inspection, the ship is destroyed by its explosion. Determined to uncover the mystery behind the satellites, Hutch and a group of colleagues set out on a mission where they find a world suffering from the aftermath of nuclear war. Inexplicably, in a far-flung star system, they explore a moon where they find a seemingly normal house containing objects, books, and a grave. Along with these strange findings, they also detect a huge, ominously silent alien spaceship refueling in the vicinity.

"First contact is McDevitt's favorite theme, and he's also good at creating large and rather spectacular astronomical phenomena," observed a contributor to *Publishers Weekly* in a review of *Chindi*. Within the novel, "the puzzles wrapped in explanations within mysteries and cliffhanging resolution are well up to McDevitt's previous high standards," commented a *Kirkus Reviews* contributor. In his assessment of the novel, Green mused that *Chindi* "is really quite splendid," and *Library Journal* reviewer Jackie Cassada called the novel a "first-rate sf adventure" characterized by "smooth, well-plotted storytelling."

Omega, set in the same future universe as *Deepsix* and *Chindi,* brings Earth and other inhabited worlds into contact with the massively destructive "Omega cloud": huge waves of energy with the power to destroy entire planets and devastate civilizations. An Omega cloud is discovered heading toward Earth, though its arrival is many years distant, giving scientists the opportunity to discover ways to divert it. Meanwhile, another cloud approaches a known populated world inhabited by the Korbikkan, a primitive but intelligent alien species. A desperate and daring expedition sets out from Earth in hopes of saving the endangered world, and also with the intention of finding out enough about the Omega effect to create a workable defense for Earth. McDevitt explores the ethical nature of altruism as the population of Earth wonders if it can spare the resources to save the Korbikkan in the face of its own impending peril. McDevitt "forges out of ethical dilemmas a plot as gripping as any action fan could want," commented Green in *Booklist*. McDevitt's characters "succeed in imposing their compassion on the void," observed a *Publishers Weekly* reviewer.

"The logical heir to Isaac Asimov and Arthur C. Clarke. . . . You're going to love it."
Stephen King

JACK McDEVITT
INFINITY BEACH

In *Infinity Beach* McDevitt spins a futuristic story about cloning, Extra-terrestrials, and a missing starship crew.

In *Odyssey,* the fifth work in McDevitt's space-adventure series featuring Hutchins, journalist Gregory MacAllister leads a media campaign to halt the Academy's deep-space missions and divert the funding to much-needed programs on Earth, such as global warming. After numerous sightings of alien spacecraft known as "moonriders," officials send the starship *Salvator* to investigate, despite Hutch's misgivings. To their astonishment, members of the crew, including MacAllister, pilot Valya Kouros, and Amy Taylor, a senator's daughter, discover that the moonriders are changing the course of a wandering asteroid and directing it toward an orbiting hotel. In *Booklist,* Carl Hays complimented the novel's "energetic, character-driven prose," and Jackie Cassada remarked in *Library Journal* that in *Odyssey* McDevitt's characters "put a human face on scientific speculation."

Cauldron centers on physicist Jon Silvestri, who convinces the Prometheus Foundation to fund a risky interstellar drive that will allow a mission headed by Hutchins to investigate the mysterious and deadly omega clouds terrorizing the galaxy. According to Cassada, the novel showcases McDevitt's "talent for character building and seamlessly blending hard science with sf action/adventure."

Introduces Alex Benedict

With *A Talent for War,* McDevitt begins his "Alex Benedict" series. Set thousands of years in the future, the novel introduces a young antiquities dealer named Alex Benedict who seeks the truth about an adored war hero, whom he suspects was a fraud. "The bulk of the novel," Cox explained, "traces Benedict's journey from planet to planet as he investigates the problem; as he pieces the puzzle together, the most important people are not the soldiers who fought the war, as much as the historians and poets who witnessed the events and recorded them."

Polaris presents "another space mystery for antiquarian sleuths to resolve," noted a *Kirkus Reviews* contributor. The starship *Polaris,* populated with a group of scientists, celebrities, and other notables, has traveled to observe the spectacular cosmic event of an ordinary sun being torn apart by a dense neutron star. The ship is later reported to be returning home to Earth by pilot Maddy English, but it never arrives. Later, the *Polaris* is found adrift, its artificial intelligence systems shut off and all personnel gone. Six decades later, artifacts from the storied ship have turned up for sale. Antiquities dealer Benedict buys a few, but the rest are destroyed in a suspicious explosion. Later, Alex's house is burglarized, with the thief managing to steal a blouse once owned by Maddy English. As the story progresses, Benedict realizes that someone has a great interest in artifacts from the *Polaris,* and is going to great lengths to find and recover them even while carefully concealing his or her identity. As Benedict and assistant Chase Kolpath step up their investigation of the fate of the starship's passengers, they find their lives in danger. "This SF mystery's smooth and exciting surface makes it difficult to appreciate how exceptionally good it is at combining action and ideas," commented a *Publishers Weekly* reviewer.

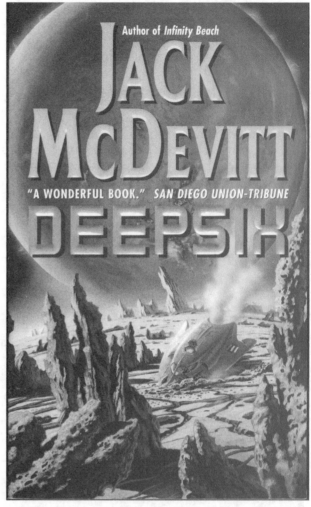

Deepsix takes readers to 2204 and McDevitt's tale of a scientific team's race against the clock to study a planet destined for destruction. (Copyright © 2001 by Cryptic, Inc. Reprinted by permission of HarperCollins Publishers Inc.)

Cassada, in a *Library Journal* review, observed that the novel is characterized by "stellar plotting, engaging characters, and a mastery of storytelling."

In *Seeker,* Benedict and Kolpath encounter an ancient artifact that leads them to investigate the fate of a vanished, possibly legendary, colony of Earth people from nine millennia in the past. When Benedict finds an unusual old cup inscribed with English characters, he believes it is from the *Seeker,* one of two transport ships that supposedly carried a group of 5,000 colonists away from Earth's religious dictatorship in the twenty-seventh century. Almost ninety centuries later, most believe the *Seeker* and the colonists' destination, the planet Margolia, to be a myth. However, Benedict and Kolpath uncover information that leads them to believe that the *Seeker* exists and was discovered by two space-survey employees who concealed their discovery but died in an accident before they could take any further steps. Benedict asks the assistance of the telepathic alien Mutes to recover the *Seeker*'s original log. With determined effort, he and Kolpath manage to pinpoint the location of the *Seeker*, now an ancient derelict adrift with destroyed engines. More intriguing, however, is the fact that the star system where the *Seeker* drifts also contains a habitable world that may be the mysterious Margolia. "This novel delivers everything it promises—with a galactic wallop," remarked a *Publishers Weekly* reviewer.

A famous author contacts Benedict and then mysteriously vanishes in *The Devil's Eye*, the fourth work in the "Alex Benedict" series. After Alex receives a cryptic message from horror writer Vicki Greene, he learns that the author has voluntarily had her memory erased, although she has left him an enormous sum of money, without explanation. Benedict and Kolpath track Greene to a remote planet on the edge of the galaxy, where they uncover a massive political cover-up of a deadly catastrophe. In the words of a *Publishers Weekly* critic, *The Devil's Eye* "turns into commentary on government reaction to emergencies and the values of openness," and in *Booklist* Roland Green asserted that McDevitt blends "fast pacing, unforgettable world building, and nerve-tingling suspense."

If you enjoy the works of Jack McDevitt, you may also want to check out the following books:

Frederik Pohl, *The Other End of Time*, 1996.
C.J. Cherryh, *Forge of Heaven*, 2004.
Ray Hammond, *The Cloud*, 2007.

Commenting on the human and spiritual elements in his stories, McDevitt told a *Locus* interviewer: "I would expect that if you could go back far enough with any intelligent species, assuming there are others, you'd find religious systems. The real question might be, what becomes of the religious systems, in time? Maybe you toss those over the side. If science is the new religion, science fiction is maybe the new mythology. I think science fiction is a more noble effort at resolving some of these issues than religion ever was anyhow." Summarizing his career, McDevitt remarked to Tan, "I was old enough when I started—in my 40's—to realize how fortunate I'd

been. You start when you're 22, I think you take everything for granted. But I have no preference. I'm happy writing either short or long fiction. As long as I have a good idea."

■ Biographical and Critical Sources

BOOKS

Twentieth-Century Science-Fiction Writers, 3rd edition, St. James Press (Chicago, IL), 1991.

PERIODICALS

Booklist, September 15, 1994, Carl Hayes, review of *The Engines of God*, p. 118; April 15, 1996, Carl Hays, review of *Ancient Shores*, p. 1425; May 15, 1997, Roland Green, review of *Eternity Road*, p. 1567; April, 1998, John Mort, review of *Moonfall*, p. 1307; February 15, 2000, Roland Green, review of *Infinity Beach*, p. 1091; February 15, 2001, Bryan Baldus, review of *Deepsix*, p. 1122; July, 2002, Roland Green, review of *Chindi*, p. 1833; October 15, 2003, Roland Green, review of *Omega*, p. 399; November 1, 2004, Roland Green, review of *Polaris*, p. 472; November 1, 2005, Roland Green, review of *Seeker*, p. 32; October 1, 2006, Carl Hays, review of *Odyssey*, p. 45; November 1, 2007, Carl Hays, review of *Cauldron*, p. 33; November 1, 2008, Roland Green, review of *The Devil's Eye*, p. 30; December 1, 2008, Regina Schroeder, review of *Cryptic: The Best Short Fiction of Jack McDevitt*, p. 37.

Florida Times Union, May 29, 1997, Ann Hyman, "Reaching for the Stars," p. D1.

Kirkus Reviews, April 15, 2002, review of *Chindi*, p. 533; September 15, 2004, review of *Polaris*, p. 896; September 1, 2005, review of *Seeker*, p. 947; September 15, 2006, review of *Odyssey*, p. 934; September 15, 2007, review of *Cauldron*.

Library Journal, May 15, 1997, Susan Hamburger, review of *Eternity Road*, p. 106; April 15, 1998, Jackie Cassada, review of *Moonfall*, p. 118; February 15, 2000, Jackie Cassada, review of *Infinity Beach*, p. 201; March 15, 2001, Jackie Cassada, review of *Deepsix*, p. 110; January, 2002, Rex Klett, Jackie Cassada, and Kristin Ramsdell, review of *Deepsix*, p. 51; July, 2002, Jackie Cassada, review of *Chindi*, p. 127; November 15, 2003, Jackie Cassada, review of *Omega*, p. 101; November 15, 2004, Jackie Cassada, review of *Polaris*, p. 54; October 15, 2005, Jackie Cassada, review of *Seeker*, p. 50; October 15, 2006, Jackie Cassada, review of *Odys-*

sey, p. 54; November 15, 2007, Jackie Cassada, review of *Cauldron,* p. 53; November 15, 2008, Jackie Cassada, review of *Cryptic,* p. 63.

Locus, February, 1995, interview with McDevitt, p. 4.

New York Times Book Review, March 7, 2004, Gerald Jonas, review of *Omega.*

Publishers Weekly, March 25, 1996, review of *Ancient Shores,* p. 67; April 21, 1997, review of *Eternity Road,* p. 65; February 23, 1998, review of *Moonfall,* p. 56; January 31, 2000, review of *Infinity Beach,* p. 86; February 26, 2001, review of *Deepsix;* June 24, 2002, review of *Chindi,* p. 44; October 13, 2003, review of *Omega,* p. 62; September 20, 2004, review of *Polaris,* p. 50; September 5, 2005, review of *Seeker,* p. 39; September 24, 2007, review of *Cauldron,* p. 49; September 22, 2008, review of *The Devil's Eye,* p. 42; December 8, 2008, review of *Cryptic,* p. 48.

School Library Journal, July, 2000, Pam Johnson, review of *Infinity Beach,* p. 128; August, 2001, Paul Brink, review of *Deepsix,* p. 209.

ONLINE

Jack McDevitt Home Page, http://jackmcdevitt.com (July 1, 2009).

Nebula Awards Web site, http://www.nebulaawards. com/ (August 6, 2008) Charles Tan, interview with McDevitt; (March 10, 2009), Charles Tan, interview with McDevitt.

SciFi.com, http://www.scifi.com/ (January 1, 2007), John Joseph Adams, "Jack McDevitt Investigates the Mysteries of the Universe, Searches for Lost Things, and Ponders the Future of Space Flight as He Embarks upon His Latest Odyssey."*

Graham McNamee

■ **Personal**

Born in Toronto, Ontario, Canada.

■ **Addresses**

Home—Vancouver, British Columbia, Canada.

■ **Career**

Writer.

■ **Awards, Honors**

Best Book for Young Adults designation, and Quick Picks for Reluctant Readers selection, both American Library Association (ALA), Austrian Children's Book Award, and Governor General's Award nomination, all 1999, all for *Hate You*; PEN/Phyllis Naylor Working Writer fellowship, 2001, for *Sparks*; Best Book for Young Adults selection, ALA, Edgar Award for Best Young-Adult Mystery, Mystery Writers of America, and Arthur Ellis Award, all 2003, all for *Acceleration*.

■ **Writings**

YOUNG-ADULT NOVELS

Hate You, Delacorte Press (New York, NY), 1999.

Nothing Wrong with a Three-legged Dog, Delacorte Press (New York, NY), 2000.

Sparks, Wendy Lamb Books (New York, NY), 2002.

Acceleration, Wendy Lamb Books (New York, NY), 2003.

Bonechiller, Wendy Lamb Books (New York, NY), 2008.

■ **Adaptations**

Acceleration was adapted for audiobook, Listening Library, 2005.

■ **Sidelights**

Canadian young-adult author Graham McNamee has garnered numerous honors for his often edgy novels. He won the Austrian Children's Book Award for his debut title, *Hate You*, was the first recipient of the PEN/Phyllis Naylor Working Writer fellowship in 2001 for his third novel, *Sparks*, and took the Edgar Award for Best Young-Adult Mystery and the Arthur Ellis Award for his fourth work, *Acceleration*. The rousing success of his work is often surprising to the author. As he stated in an interview for the Random House Web site, "After I write a novel and it comes out in stores, I always shake my head and say—'Man, I wrote a book?'"

Tales of Despair and Redemption

In 1999 the Toronto-born McNamee published his first book, *Hate You*. This story centers on a young girl's hatred for her father after he choked her so hard it permanently destroyed her vocal chords. Nearly a decade later, she accepts an offer to meet with her dying father and deals with her feelings of hatred with the help of her boyfriend and music. A reviewer in *Publishers Weekly* had mixed thoughts on the book, stating that "McNamee offers a biting account of domestic violence, but he never moves out of the problem-novel arena." In a *Booklist* review, Karen Simonetti had reservations about the ending, but concluded that *Hate You* "is a powerful first-person narrative about the truth, relationships, and the sadness of a lost childhood."

Cover of Graham McNamee's futuristic middle-grade novel *Acceleration*, featuring artwork by Sandy Young.
(Cover illustration by Sandy Young. Used by permission of Wendy Lamb Books, an imprint of Random House Children's Books, a division of Random House, Inc.)

Nothing Wrong with a Three-legged Dog tells the story of Keath, a young white child in a predominantly black school who is bullied. His only friends include Lynda, a biracial girl, and Leftovers, her three-legged, one-eared dog. A *Publishers Weekly* reviewer wrote that "McNamee's narrative voice is dead-on, filled with winning touches of wry humor." Sharon McNeil liked the characterizations, but commented in her review for *School Library Journal* that, "with its focus on issues, *Nothing Wrong with a Three-legged Dog* . . . sometimes becomes thin in plot." To *Booklist* reviewer John Peters, however, McNamee's "issues-heavy story" is supported by "likeable characters, healthy doses of humor, and a cast of slobbery, appealing canines."

Sparks introduces Todd Sparks, a boy who was recently promoted from his special-needs group into a mainstream fifth-grade class. The story deals with issues of bullying, acceptance, self-esteem, and the general difficulties of preteen children. Writing in *School Library Journal*, Alison Grant commented that "McNamee crafts a warm and humorous story about a boy's struggle to overcome his learning difficulties and his own self-doubt." Evette Berry, in her review of the book for *Resource Links*, found *Sparks* to be "a warm, funny story" and called Todd "a very endearing character." In a separate review in *Resource Links*, John Dryden noted that "the writing has been crafted very well," and that "the reader can truly feel the awkward position that Todd is put in" in McNamee's tale.

Of Monsters Urban and Rural

In 2003 McNamee published *Acceleration*, "a well-written, read-it-in-one-gulp thriller," in the words of a *Kirkus Reviews* contributor. "I love a good suspense novel," the author stated in his Random House on-line interview, adding that he hoped to recreate the thrills and chills found in such films as *The Silence of the Lambs*. "I wanted [*Acceleration*] to read like a movie, real visual and atmospheric, and to be something you could sink into, like quicksand." The work centers on seventeen-year-old Duncan, who works in the lost-and-found section of the Toronto Transit Commission. One day Duncan comes across a notebook that outlines techniques of animal cruelty and a potential murder. After the police dismiss his concerns, he tries to figure out the mystery owner of the notebook to thwart his potential crime. For Duncan, who once failed to save a drowning girl, a successful mission would be a vindication of sorts, and could help him ease his guilt. Joining him on his search for a potential serial killer are his buddies, Vinny and Wayne.

Acceleration earned strong reviews. Sara Ann Shettler commented in a review for the *Journal of*

Adolescence and Adult Literacy that "McNamee not only creates an interesting plot, but he also creates a well-developed protagonist." Hillias J. Martin enjoyed the pace of the book, commenting in a *School Library Journal* review that *Acceleration* "will keep readers on the edge of their seats." A critic for *Publishers Weekly* called the story "a well-tuned thriller" in which "the timing never falters, and the dialogue stays crisp." *Canadian Review of Materials* contributor Joanne Peters had further praise for *Acceleration,* noting that McNamee's "writing is, by turns, suspenseful, brilliant and witty." Peters went on to observe that the story "pulls you along and gathers speed just as an accelerant in a fire speeds up combustion." Similarly, Jeffrey Canton, reviewing the novel in *Quill & Quire,* noted of *Acceleration:* "It's a perfectly paced thriller that propels the reader through the story at break-neck speed. At the same time, it paints emotionally charged portraits of Duncan and his friends, which give the novel real depth."

Bonechiller, McNamee's next title, was based on a nightmare that involved one of the author's childhood memories. McNamee would often spend summers at a lakeside cottage owned by his uncle; when his family decided to visit the cottage one winter to do some ice fishing, they found themselves stranded after a bad snowstorm. The howling winds so frightened McNamee that, when he finally fell asleep, he imagined a terrifying creature with silver eyes and sharp teeth was chasing him through the icy countryside. "And when it caught me—it always caught me—all I could do was stare at my own reflection in those hideous, silver-mirrored eyes. And scream until I screamed myself awake," he wrote on the Random House Web site.

Bonechiller is set in a place known to Canadians as the "Big Empty," a place far north of Ontario. It is here, at the marina of Harvest Cove on the shores of a frozen lake, that Danny's father takes a job as caretaker. Danny has not had an easy time of it since the death of his mother. He has been to several different schools and never seems to fit in. Now his father is trying to start a new life for them both. During the course of one of the coldest winters in years, Danny is joined by three new friends in a battle against a beast that the local Native Americans call the "bonechiller." This demon supposedly haunts the lake and, during especially cold winters, makes teens disappear. Such has been the case for a thousand years. Danny thinks this is the stuff of legend until one night he is attacked by the monster while hurrying home. Stung, he is now haunted by visions of the beast in his dreams. Now he knows it is only a matter of time until the monster draws him into its power. Aided by his intelligent new friend Howie, who has also been stung by the can-

Danny encounters a strange creature in the snowy wilds of rural Canada in McNamee's thrilling novel *Bonechiller.* (Jacket art copyright © 2008 by Greg Capullo. Used by permission of Wendy Lamb Books, an imprint of Random House Children's Books, a division of Random House, Inc.)

nibalistic beast, as well as by Howie's brother Pike and the beautiful half-native female boxer Ash, Danny races against time to destroy the creature before it destroys him and his friends.

A *Kirkus Reviews* contributor noted of *Bonechiller* that McNamee's "first-person, present-tense narration is taut, fast-paced and stylish," adding: "Read this intense horror story in big gulps, and don't forget to breathe." Writing in *Booklist,* Heather Booth termed *Bonechiller* a "page-turning thriller . . . with an eerie supernatural edge that will appeal to fans of psychological horror." Likewise, *School Library Journal* reviewer Caroline Tesauro concluded, "The unrelenting pace, short chapters, and the idea of teenagers taking on a monster with a large amount of weaponry will certainly appeal to fans of horror novels." *Quill & Quire* contributor John Wilson added to the praise, remarking that in *Bonechiller*

"McNamee has crafted a fine thriller that offers more than simple serial gore and pointless frights."

If you enjoy the works of Graham McNamee, you may also want to check out the following books:

Michael Cadnum, *Calling Home,* 1991.
Jerry Spinelli, *Stargirl,* 2000.
Joyce Carol Oates, *Freaky Green Eyes,* 2003.

In his Random House online interview, McNamee addressed the aspect of violence in some of his works: "I'm not really smart enough to say anything about violence and society. I mean, what do I know? Except maybe this—there's a dark place in the human heart that can go undiscovered your whole life, where an animal capacity for violence lives. Maybe it's hidden in that oldest reptilian core of our brains—the instinct that to fight is to live another day, to kill is to survive."

■ **Biographical and Critical Sources**

PERIODICALS

Booklist, February 1, 1999, Karen Simonetti, review of *Hate You,* p. 969; August, 2000, John Peters, review of *Nothing Wrong with a Three-legged Dog,* p. 2141; October 15, 2002, Hazel Rochman, review of *Sparks,* p. 407; September 15, 2003, Stephanie Zvirin, review of *Acceleration,* p. 232; November 1, 2008, Heather Booth, review of *Bonechiller,* p. 33.

Canadian Review of Materials, April 23, 2004, Joanne Peters, review of *Acceleration;* October 24, 2008, Tanya Boudreau, review of *Bonechiller.*

Journal of Adolescent and Adult Literacy, May, 2004, Sara Ann Shettler, review of *Acceleration,* p. 708.

Kirkus Reviews, June 15, 2002, review of *Sparks,* p. 885; September 15, 2003, review of *Acceleration,* p. 1179; August 15, 2008, review of *Bonechiller.*

Kliatt, January, 2004, Claire Rosser, review of *Acceleration,* p. 10.

Publishers Weekly, January 11, 1999, review of *Hate You,* p. 73; July 31, 2000, review of *Nothing Wrong with a Three-legged Dog,* p. 95; August 7, 2000, review of *Hate You,* p. 97; August 5, 2002, review of *Sparks,* p. 73; November 10, 2003, review of *Acceleration,* p. 63.

Quill & Quire, August, 2003, Jeffrey Canton, review of *Acceleration;* July, 2008, John Wilson, review of *Bonechiller.*

Resource Links, December, 2002, John Dryden, review of *Sparks,* p. 26; February, 2004, Evette Berry, review of *Sparks,* p. 18.

School Library Journal, September, 2000, Sharon McNeil, review of *Nothing Wrong with a Three-legged Dog,* p. 234; August, 2002, Alison Grant, review of *Sparks,* p. 194; November, 2003, Hillias J. Martin, review of *Acceleration,* p. 142; January, 2009, Caroline Tesauro, review of *Bonechiller,* p. 110.

ONLINE

Random House Web site, http://www.randomhouse.com/ (April 17, 2009), interview with McNamee.

TeenReads.com, http://www.teenreads.com/ (April 17, 2009), Tali Rasis, review of *Acceleration.**

(Photo courtesy of Blake Nelson.)

■ Personal

Born August 31, 1960, in Chicago, IL; married. *Education:* Earned bachelor's degree. *Hobbies and other interests:* Books, movies, music.

■ Addresses

Home—Portland, OR. *Agent*—Jodi Reamer, Writers House, LLC, 21 W. 26th St., New York, NY 10010. *E-mail*—blake@blakenelsonbooks.com.

■ Career

Novelist. Also served as humor columnist for *Details* magazine.

■ Awards, Honors

Best Books for Young Adults selection, American Library Association, 2005, for *Rock Star, Superstar.*

Blake Nelson

■ Writings

NOVELS FOR YOUNG ADULTS

The New Rules of High School, Viking (New York, NY), 2003.
Rock Star, Superstar, Viking (New York, NY), 2004.
Gender Blender, Delacorte (New York, NY), 2006.
Paranoid Park, Viking (New York, NY), 2006.
Prom Anonymous, Viking (New York, NY), 2006.
They Came from Below, Tor (New York, NY), 2007.
Destroy All Cars, Scholastic Press (New York, NY), 2009.

NOVELS FOR ADULTS

Girl, Simon & Schuster (New York, NY), 1994.
Exile, Scribner (New York, NY), 1997.
User, Versus Press (San Francisco, CA), 2001.

■ Adaptations

Girl was adapted as a motion picture, 1998; *Paranoid Park* was adapted as a motion picture, directed by Gus Van Sant; *Gender Blender* has been optioned for film by Nickelodeon.

■ Sidelights

"Beginner's luck is real," author Blake Nelson noted in an online interview for *WriteandPublishYou Book. com.* "That's one thing I guess I would tell begin-

ning writers. That first book is going to have a fresh-
ness and vitality to it you may never have again.
Don't screw it up!" These words of advice come
from experience, for Nelson's own first book, the
1994 novel *Girl,* made his career—for a time. Critically acclaimed, *Girl* was subsequently published in
eight countries and made into a feature film.
However, after publishing two other adult novels,
Nelson turned to writing for young adults, producing novels such as *The New Rules of High School* and
Paranoid Park. The latter title was also adapted for
an award-winning feature film by Gus Van Sant.

In an interview with *Powells.com,* Nelson explored
some of the reasons he chose to write for a younger
audience: "I write mostly for older teens, people in
that difficult age from 15 to 19. I think that's a tough
time and I admire kids for struggling through it
and so it's kind of my attempt to show them: I
remember, it's hard, get through it and you'll be
fine." Nelson further noted that in his works for
teen readers he does not provide a clear-cut message or moral instruction: "Books aren't supposed
to be simplistic. TV is simplistic. Movies are
simplistic. Books are supposed to be challenging
and complicated. As complicated as life itself."

A Portland Author

Though he was born in Chicago, Illinois, Nelson
grew up in Portland, Oregon. In an online interview
for *Children's Literature,* he remarked on the influence his childhood had, especially regarding environmental concerns: "Growing up I lived on the
edge of a big woods that I played in and built forts
in. This forest was composed of tall evergreen trees
that would sway majestically in the wind. My fond-
est memories of growing up was during stormy
nights my buddies and I would hike through these
woods while the trees whispered above us." On his
home page, Nelson also noted the importance of
the city of Portland in his novels: "Most of my writing, especially for teens and younger kids is set in
Portland. I think Portland has that perfect all
American quality, so I'm lucky to have my childhood memories there, and I go there enough that I
can fill in the gaps in between my memories and
the current reality."

Although Nelson did develop an early interest in
literature, more important at the time was music,
and throughout his teens and twenties he played in
a number of bands. Nelson studied history at Wesleyan University and after graduation he continued
playing in alternative bands until he found a job
penning humor pieces for *Details* magazine. He

Cover of Blake Nelson's young-adult novel *The New
Rules of High School.* (Cover illustration copyright © 2003 by Hadley
Hooper. Reproduced by permission of Speak, a division of Penguin Putnam Books for
Young Readers.)

wrote on trendy social topics from dating a feminist
to living poor in New York City. At the same time
he also began work on a story about a young
woman living in Portland and trying to make sense
out of her life. Nelson's fiction began generating
interest from publishers after excerpts from his first
novel appeared in the popular teen magazine *Sassy.*

Nelson's well-regarded debut, *Girl,* was written in
the first person. The novel focuses on Andrea Marr,
a high-school student living in Portland who is
struggling to find her identity. The reader follows
this quest from Andrea's sixteenth birthday to the
time she is ready to depart for college. Nelson deals
with events in Andrea's life from high school socializing to her initiation into sex. "I *am* the Andrea
type," Nelson commented to an interviewer on
Teenreads.com. "I didn't realize it at first. I tried at

the beginning to make Andrea a clueless mall chick, but she quickly became more of an observer (like me!) and she did what I did in high school, which is become friends with a lot of different people from different cliques and especially befriend the weirdest, most creative people." A *Publishers Weekly* reviewer had praise for this first novel, noting that, "while making Andrea neither victim nor victimizer, Nelson captures this young woman's fears and joys in subtle and often uncannily accurate ways." Commenting on the publisher's comparison of *Girl* with J.D. Salinger's classic *Catcher in the Rye, Write Stuff* contributor Giles Hugo noted: "For starters its first-person subject, Andrea Marr, is extremely funny and sad—often simultaneously. This seeming contradiction echoes Holden Caulfield's bitter-sweet dwelling on the heinous crimes of the hordes of phoneys who both anger and depress him." Hugo went on to observe, "Nelson's strength is in his ability to speak directly from within the troubled being of a young girl whose angst and awakening we share."

Nelson followed *Girl* with two more novels for adults: *Exile* and *User.* At the center of *Exile* is Mark West, a writer who survived the poetry slam scene in New York and now earns a poet-in-residence position at a college in Oregon. Mark indulges in his twin passions—heroin and women—until a visit from an old friend makes him realize how he has wasted his gifts. A *Publishers Weekly* reviewer was not impressed by this second novel, terming it a "sophomoric effort." Nelson followed *Exile* with *User,* another "sex and drugs book," as the author described it on his home page. This novel did not fare well, either.

At a career crossroads, Nelson decided to review his options. As he noted in an interview for *WriteandPublishYourBook.com:* "People had told me for a long time that my style was a Young Adult style, kind of minimal and simplistic. . . . I thought, well I'll just write a great YA book and then it really wasn't that easy. You don't want to think of yourself as naive but I was shocked how competitive and how good the other YA books out there were." Nelson may also have remembered the words of the *Publishers Weekly* contributor who reviewed his first novel, *Girl.* Absent the obscenities of that novel, the critic opined, *Girl* "could be YA fiction at the very top of the genre."

Enters Young-Adult Market

After reviewing the fiction that was available to teen readers, Nelson set out on his own effort in that genre, relying on his memories of what high school was like. In his *Teenreads.com* interview, Nelson stated, "I guess in some part of my brain I have always been younger than I really am. I love high school. I think it is a great time in a person's life, an epic time, when love seems absolute and infinite and there's still room for heroism and bravery and romance."

The New Rules of High School, Blake's first work for teen, follows Max Caldwell, an overachieving high-school senior. Max appears to have it all: he serves as editor-in-chief of the school newspaper and captain of the debate team, earns straight A's in the classroom, and dates a beautiful girl. When the pressure to live up to such high standards becomes too much for him, however, Max begins to self-destruct, first dumping his girlfriend and then jeopardizing his other close relationships. "Thus begins an intense journey of self-discovery, told in an achingly honest narrative," observed a critic in *Publishers*

When Tom and Emma collide on a trampoline, the two friends change places in Nelson's entertaining novel *Gender Blender.* (Jacket illustration copyright © 2006 by Molly Zakrajsek. Used by permission of Dell Publishing, a division of Random House, Inc.)

Weekly. "Nelson skillfully reveals Max's character and problems in 'show-don't-tell' style," noted a *Kirkus Reviews* contributor, and Gillian Engberg, writing in *Booklist,* stated that "there's a refreshing honesty in his 'averageness' and in his bewildered disconnection." "Whether Max is grieving over his breakup or testing the waters of singledom," wrote *School Library Journal* critic Vicki Reutter, "readers are empathetic to his emotional vulnerability."

A teenager takes his shot at fame and fortune in *Rock Star, Superstar,* "a brilliant, tender, funny, and utterly believable novel about music and relationships," in the opinion of *School Library Journal* contributor Miranda Doyle. Pete, a talented bass player whose parents were also musicians, is asked to join the Tiny Masters of Today, a rock band on the verge of hitting it big. Despite reservations about his bandmates' devotion to their craft, Pete agrees to tour with his new group, learning some hard les-

sons about the music industry along the way. He also enters an intense, complicated relationship with Margaret, his first true love. "Nelson paints Pete as endearingly clueless," remarked a critic in *Publishers Weekly,* "yet the teen proves his loyalty throughout the book—to his girlfriend, to his dad and ultimately to his music."

A pair of sixth graders learns firsthand what it is like to be a member of the opposite sex in Nelson's humorous *Gender Blender.* After colliding on a trampoline, Tom Witherspoon and Emma Baker discover that they have magically swapped bodies. Forced to impersonate each other, Tom must learn the intricacies of wearing a bra while Emma copes with her counterpart's goofy friends and their childish pranks. According to a *Kirkus Reviews* contributor, the teens "find that others' expectations and their own physical and emotional makeup shape their experiences." "Throughout the novel," remarked a *Publishers Weekly* critic, "Nelson demonstrates his keen understanding of peer pressure and gender stereotyping."

Edgier Material: From Skateboards to Cars

A skateboarder's journey to a rough-and-tumble neighborhood goes terribly wrong in *Paranoid Park,* a "deeply disturbing cautionary tale," in the words of a *Kirkus Reviews* critic. When the unnamed sixteen-year-old narrator decides one night to visit Paranoid Park, which has a reputation as a sketchy, dangerous place, he meets Scratch, a street kid who convinces him to hop a train. Confronted by a vicious security guard, the narrator lashes out with his skateboard and watches in horror as the guard falls beneath the train. "Written in the form of a confessional letter," a *Publishers Weekly* contributor noted, "the book details the narrator's moral dilemma after the incident." "Gritty and aching, the narrative will have readers pondering what they might do under the circumstances," according to *Kliatt* reviewer Paula Rohrlick.

In *Prom Anonymous,* a high-school junior hopes to reunite with two old friends on the night of the big dance. Although Laura has drifted apart from Chloe and Jace, she is determined to play matchmaker for them; unfortunately, she begins to ignore her own boyfriend in the process. "Yes, it's a who-will-date-whom story," noted a *Kirkus Reviews* contributor, "but with laughter and surprising depth." "As might be expected, prom night is filled with crises, but creative resolutions make for a gratifying all's-well-that-ends-well conclusion," noted a critic reviewing *Prom Anonymous* for *Publishers Weekly.*

Cover of Nelson's novel *Paranoid Park,* featuring artwork by Emilian Gregory. (Jacket illustration copyright © 2006 by Emilian Gregory. Reproduced by permission of Viking, a division of Penguin Putnam Books for Young Readers.)

Nelson's novel *Paranoid Park* was adapted for film in 2007. (Photograph courtesy of MK2/The Kobal Collection/The Picture Desk, Inc.)

A change of pace for Nelson, *They Came from Below* is a science-fiction and fantasy novel featuring two teenage girls looking for fun while on summer vacation on Cape Cod. What they find are two young men, outwardly handsome and fun, who turn out to be aliens who can heal people with only a glance. The girls, Emily and Reese, connect with Steve and Dave on a deeper level, and Emily's father, a scientist, ends up helping the two aliens. A *Kirkus Reviews* contributor praised the book's "compelling musings on humanity's connection to the earth and each other," and termed *They Came from Below* "fun, interesting and perfectly pitched to many YA readers." Similarly, *School Library Journal* contributor Ann Robinson noted that "the environmental message is front and center in this story," while *Kliatt* reviewer Claire Rosser called it "smart, witty, and suspenseful."

In *Destroy All Cars* Nelson presents something of an anti-consumerist romance. The novel centers on James Hoff, a seventeen year old who is fond of criticizing contemporary Western culture with its consumer culture. He is also critical of his former girlfriend, Sadie, whose efforts to improve society,

such as organizing a community food drive, are not radical enough for his tastes. As the novel progresses, James comes to see that his nihilistic stance and passionate rants have little effect on the world, and he realizes that he must make a true commitment to change. In *Destroy All Cars*, Nelson "offers an elegant and bittersweet story of a teenager who is finding his voice," according to a *Publishers Weekly* contributor.

If you enjoy the works of Blake Nelson, you may also want to check out the following books:

Rob Thomas, *Slave Day*, 1997.
Robert Cormier, *The Rag and Bone Shop*, 2001.
Gordon Korman, *Born to Rock*, 2006.

"I enjoy the intimacy of writing," Nelson once commented. "Of all the art forms, it feels the most immediate to me, the most direct in its communication. Reading a good book is like having a good talk with an interesting person. It is about the most rewarding way to spend time I can think of." Asked if he had any advice for aspiring authors, Nelson remarked on his home page, "You have one life. What are you gonna do with it? If you go into the arts, that's a big risk. There's no certain reward. You are really sort of throwing yourself at the mercy of the fates. But if that's really what you feel called to do, then you do it."

■ Biographical and Critical Sources

PERIODICALS

Booklist, August, 2003, Gillian Engberg, review of *The New Rules of High School*, p. 1972; November 1, 2004, Todd Morning, review of *Rock Star, Superstar*, p. 476; March 1, 2006, Jennifer Mattson, review of *Gender Blender*, p. 88; April 1, 2006, Anne O'Malley, review of *Prom Anonymous*, p. 37; September 1, 2006, Ilene Cooper, review of *Paranoid Park*, p. 115; June 1, 2009, Ian Chipman, review of *Destroy All Cars*, p. 50.

Kirkus Reviews, June 1, 2003, review of *The New Rules of High School*, p. 809; August 1, 2004, review of *Rock Star, Superstar*, p. 746; February 15, 2006, review of *Gender Blender*, p. 188, and review of *Prom Anonymous*, p. 189; August 1, 2006, review of *Paranoid Park*, p. 793; June 1, 2007, review of *They Came from Below*.

Kliatt, September, 2006, Paula Rohrlick, review of *Paranoid Park*, p. 16; July, 2007, Claire Rosser, review of *They Came from Below*, p. 19.

New York Times, March 2, 2008, Blake Nelson, "Back in Portland, The Latest Outsider Has a Skateboard," p. AR6.

Publishers Weekly, August 1, 1994, review of *Girl*, p. 74; May 12, 1997, review of *Exile*, p. 58; June 23, 2003, review of *The New Rules of High School*, p. 68; September 20, 2004, review of *Rock Star, Superstar*, p. 63; February 6, 2006, reviews of *Gender Blender* and *Prom Anonymous*, p. 70; August 21, 2006, review of *Paranoid Park*, p. 69; May 25, 2009, review of *Destroy All Cars*, p. 59.

School Library Journal, June, 2003, Vicki Reutter, review of *The New Rules of High School*, p. 148; October, 2004, Miranda Doyle, review of *Rock Star, Superstar*, p. 173; March, 2006, Morgan Johnson-Doyle, review of *Prom Anonymous*, p. 228; April, 2006, Laurie Slagenwhite, review of *Gender Blender*, p. 145; November, 2006, Joel Shoemaker, review of *Paranoid Park*, p. 144; August, 2007, Ann Robinson, review of *They Came from Below*, p. 124.

Voice of Youth Advocates, October, 2004, Patrick Jones, review of *Rock Star, Superstar*, p. 306.

ONLINE

Blake Nelson Home Page, http://www.blakenelson books.com (April 16, 2009).

Children's Literature, http://www.childrenslit.com/ (April 16, 2009), "Blake Nelson."

Powells.com, http://www.powells.com/ (April 17, 2009), "Author Q&A: Blake Nelson."

Teenreads.com, http://www.teenreads.com/ (February 26, 2002), interview with Nelson.

Write and Publish Your Book Web site, http://www. writeandpublishyourbook.com/ (September 26, 2006), "Blake Nelson on Writing Young Adult Novels and Film Options."

Write Stuff Web site, http://www.the-write-stuff. com.au/ (May 26, 1997), Giles Hugo, review of *Girl*.*

Katherine Hall Page

(Photograph by Jean Fogelbert. Courtesy of Katherine Hall Page.)

■ Personal

Born July 9, 1947, in NJ; daughter of William Kingman (a hospital administrator) and Alice (an artist) Page; married Alan Hein (a professor and psychologist), December 6, 1975; children: Nicholas William. *Education:* Wellesley College, B.A., 1969; Tufts University, Ed.M., 1974; Harvard University, Ed.D., 1985.

■ Addresses

Home—Lincoln, MA. *Agent*—Faith Hamlin, Sanford J. Greenburger Associates, Inc., 55 5th Ave., New York, NY 10022.

■ Career

Writer, educator, and consultant. Worked as a teacher of English and history, and as a director of programs for adolescents with special emotional needs, 1969-80; writer, 1980—. Educational consultant, 1985—.

■ Member

North American International Association of Crime Writers, Mystery Writers of America, Sisters in Crime, Malice Domestic, American Crime Writers League.

■ Awards, Honors

Agatha Award for best first mystery novel, Mystery Writers of America, 1991, for *The Body in the Belfry*, and 2006, for *The Body in the Snowdrift*; Edgar Allan Poe Award nomination, for *Christie and Company Down East*; Agatha Award for best short story, 2001, for "The Would-Be Widower"; Agatha Award nomination for best mystery novel, 2003, for *The Body in the Bonfire*; Agatha Award nomination for best short story, 2005, for "The Two Marys."

■ Writings

"FAITH FAIRCHILD" MYSTERY NOVELS

The Body in the Belfry, St. Martin's Press (New York, NY), 1990.

The Body in the Kelp, St. Martin's Press (New York, NY), 1991.

The Body in the Bouillon, St. Martin's Press (New York, NY), 1991.

The Body in the Vestibule, St. Martin's Press (New York, NY), 1992.

The Body in the Cast, St. Martin's Press (New York, NY), 1993.

The Body in the Basement, St. Martin's Press (New York, NY), 1994.

The Body in the Bog, St. Martin's Press (New York, NY), 1996.

The Body in the Fjord, Morrow (New York, NY), 1997.

The Body in the Bookcase, Morrow (New York, NY), 1998.

The Body in the Big Apple, Morrow (New York, NY), 1999.

The Body in the Moonlight, Morrow (New York, NY), 2001.

The Body in the Bonfire, Morrow (New York, NY), 2002.

The Body in the Lighthouse, HarperCollins (New York, NY), 2003.

The Body in the Attic, Morrow (New York, NY), 2004.

The Body in the Snowdrift, Morrow (New York, NY), 2006.

The Body in the Ivy, Morrow (New York, NY), 2006.

The Body in the Gallery, Morrow (New York, NY), 2008.

The Body in the Sleigh, Morrow (New York, NY), 2009.

Also author of short stories. Contributor to anthologies, including *Malice Domestic X,* Avon Books (New York, NY), 2001.

"CHRISTIE AND COMPANY" YOUNG-ADULT MYSTERY NOVELS

Christie and Company, Avon (New York, NY), 1996.

Christie and Company Down East, Avon (New York, NY), 1997.

Christie and Company in the Year of the Dragon, Avon (New York, NY), 1997.

Bon Voyage, Christie and Company, Avon (New York, NY), 1999.

OTHER

(With others) *Mistletoe and Mayhem,* Avon Books (New York, NY), 2004.

Club Meds (young-adult novel), Simon Pulse (New York, NY), 2006.

■ Sidelights

"Katherine Hall Page's cozy domestic mysteries are set in the nutshell world of a young minister's wife," according to Marilyn Stasio in the *New York Times Book Review.* Faith Fairchild—who in addition to being wed to a minister is also a caterer—is the amateur sleuth at the heart of Page's series, begun in 1990 with *The Body in the Belfry.* Since that time Page has written over a dozen other mysteries set either in the small town of Aleford, Massachusetts, or in locations ranging from Vermont to France. Interestingly, these novels are laced with the recipes Faith puts to use in her catering business.

Page has described the "Faith Fairchild" series as featuring traditional village mysteries in the spirit

Cover of *The Body in the Belfry,* a novel by Katherine Hall Page that finds sleuth Faith Fairchild relocating to a sleepy New England town. (Copyright © 1990 by Katherine Hall Page. All rights reserved. Reprinted by permission of HarperCollins Publishers Inc.)

of Agatha Christie. "I don't think you can be a writer without being a reader," Page noted on her home page. "When I wrote my first mystery, *The Body in the Belfry,* I set out to write the kind of book I liked to read: suspenseful, with a good puzzle, an interesting sleuth, a strong sense of place, humor, and food," the author noted on her home page. "Agatha Christie, Rex Stout, Dorothy L. Sayers, Virginia Rich, and non-mystery writers Nancy Mitford, and M.F.K. Fisher were all influences."

Page is also the author of the young-adult novel *Club Meds,* which focuses on Attention Deficit Hyperactivity Disorder (ADHD). Additionally, she wrote a four-book mystery series aimed at young readers that features three eighth-grade girls known as Christie and Company. The threesome's adventures include a healthy teenage concern for such things as hairstyles, boys, and clothing.

Time Abroad Leads to Change

Born and raised in New Jersey, Page was one of three children of a father who was executive director of the Kessler Institute for Rehabilitation and a mother who was an artist. The family's favorite vacation haunt was in Maine, a location Page later used in her "Faith Fairchild" series. She earned her bachelor's degree in English from Wellesley College and went on to receive a master's in education from Tufts and a doctorate in administration from Harvard University. For over a decade, Page directed a program within a Massachusetts high school aimed at helping students with substance-abuse problems, low self-esteem, behavioral issues, and motivation difficulties. This was followed by a career as an English and history teacher at the high-school level.

Page's lifestyle changed dramatically when the family spent a year in France while her husband, an experimental psychologist at the Massachusetts Institute of Technology, was on sabbatical. This was not long after the birth of the couple's son, and in France—with her son in nursery school and her husband pursuing research projects—Page had time on her hands. As she told a contributor for the Tufts University Web site, "I always wanted to write a novel and knew I was never going to have time like that again, because when we got back to the United States I was going to look for a job as an assistant superintendent for a school district." She began a mystery novel, finished it that year, and, after returning to the United States, found an agent. When *The Body in the Belfry* was published by St. Martin's Press it earned an Agatha award for best first mystery novel from the Mystery Writers of America.

Page's debut work introduces Faith, Faith's minister husband Tom, and their son Benjamin, who live in fictional Aleford, Massachusetts. Though she is not overly attracted to the townsfolk of Aleford, Faith (originally a caterer in Manhattan) wants to be a good neighbor, and she decides to try to find the murderer of Cindy Shepherd, whose body she discovers in the church belfry. Cindy is the niece of neighbors Patricia and Robert Moore. Soon Cindy's boyfriend is arrested for the crime, but Faith believes otherwise; her investigation ends up endangering her and her family.

Page was surprised when her publishers asked for a second novel featuring Faith, but she set dutifully to work. The result was *The Body in the Kelp,* in which Faith comes upon a corpse while walking along the beach on an island off the coast of Maine. The plot involves a mysterious quilt and the contested inheritance of a mansion on the island. The third novel in the series, *The Body in the Bouillon,* finds Faith working as a caterer and investigating the mysterious deaths of several residents at an exclusive retirement community. In *The Body in the Vestibule* the action moves to France, where Faith's husband is researching his dissertation. Faith, four months pregnant with her second child, discovers the body of a homeless man in the vestibule of their apartment house and once again cannot resist trying her hand at solving the crime. A contributor to *Publishers Weekly* found this installment in the series an "engrossing adventure."

In *The Body in the Cast,* Faith is hired to cater the meals for a film crew working on a new film adaptation of Nathaniel Hawthorne's novel *The Scarlet Letter.* When a series of seeming pranks begins to plague the production, Faith investigates, finding hidden links between the film crew's troubles and a particularly nasty local race for town council. A reviewer in *Publishers Weekly* praised the story for its "spirited characterization and energetic plotting."

Several of the "Faith Fairchild" books also feature Faith's neighbor, friend, and part-time employee Pix Miller. In *The Body in the Basement,* Pix and her daughter visit the site of Faith's new summer home, which is under construction, to check up on the development of the project. When the pair discover that a body has been buried in the house's unfinished basement, Pix works to unravel the mystery, all the while keeping Faith informed of both the progress of her investigation and of the construction project. The mystery centers on a strange blue "X" stitched into the quilt wrapped around the murdered man's body. A *Publishers Weekly* contributor called *The Body in the Basement* a "leisurely tale" and added that the "down-to-earth, eminently likable Pix . . . proves an enjoyable stand-in for Faith."

Faith investigates the murder of a birdwatcher in *The Body in the Bog*, "another delightful installment in a charming series," according to *Booklist* reviewer Stuart Miller. Pix returns in *The Body in the Fjord*, this time journeying to Norway to see about the missing granddaughter of a close family friend. The granddaughter's fiancée has turned up dead, floating in a fjord, and the missing girl is tied to possible stolen artifacts. GraceAnne A. DeCandido commented in *Booklist* that the "real treat here is the detailed and totally engaging tour of the fjords of Norway," especially "the evocative descriptions of Norway's physical beauty and culinary triumphs."

Another Recipe for Murder

With *The Body in the Bookcase* murder comes close to home when Faith discovers the body of her friend Sarah, killed in the course of a robbery. Faith balances family and business obligations to track down the culprit. Emily Melton, reviewing the title in *Booklist*, noted that it "effectively mixes modern-day moral dilemmas with charm, warmth, and humor." Similar praise came from a *Publishers Weekly* reviewer who concluded that Page "braids her various storylines neatly and briskly, right up to the enticing conclusion in which Faith confronts the brains behind the burglaries."

Faith Fairchild's other appearances include a prequel, *The Body in the Big Apple*, which details her life before her marriage and relocation to Massachusetts. The story involves a politician's wife who seeks Faith's help in thwarting a blackmail attempt. "New Yorkers and suburbanites alike should enjoy this fast-paced mystery," declared a *Publishers Weekly* contributor. In *The Body in the Moonlight*, Faith caters the annual Murder Mystery benefit, which turns all too real when an actual murder takes place. Suspicion falls on Faith, and now she must play detective with added gusto to clear her good name. *The Body in the Bonfire* takes Faith to an exclusive boarding school, and *The Body in the Lighthouse* concerns the murder of a developer on a pristine Maine island. A *Publishers Weekly* contributor called *The Body in the Lighthouse* "absorbing" and further commented that it is "an ideal beach read for cozy fans heading for the shore this summer."

In *The Body in the Attic* Faith finds herself in Cambridge, Massachusetts, while her minister husband, Tom, accepts a temporary post at Harvard Divinity School. Living in an old house, Faith has an uneasy feeling that is exacerbated when she finds an old diary in the attic. The book reveals that the

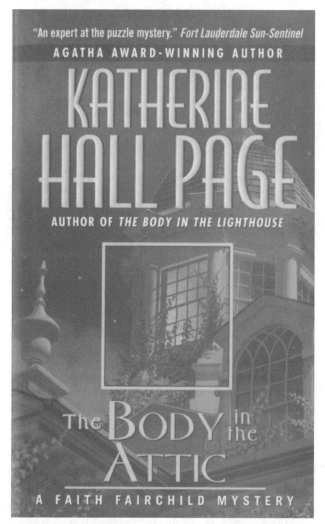

"An expert at the puzzle mystery." *Fort Lauderdale Sun-Sentinel*

AGATHA AWARD-WINNING AUTHOR

KATHERINE HALL PAGE

AUTHOR OF *THE BODY IN THE LIGHTHOUSE*

The BODY in the ATTIC

A FAITH FAIRCHILD MYSTERY

Boston is the setting for Page's fourteenth "Faith Fairchild" mysteries, *The Body in the Attic*. (Copyright © 2005 by Katherine Hall Page. All rights reserved. Reprinted by permission of HarperCollins Publishers Inc.)

woman who wrote it had been held captive in the house by her abusive husband. As Faith investigates who this woman was and what her life was like, her own life becomes further complicated when an old boyfriend suddenly reappears. "As Faith explores the byways of Boston and Cambridge . . . both cities come to vivid life," observed a *Publishers Weekly* contributor. GraceAnne A. DeCandido, writing in *Booklist*, noted that "Faith becomes an ever more interesting character" in this installment in the series.

In *The Body in the Snowdrift*, Faith and Tom visit a failing Vermont ski resort as part of a family reunion honoring the birthday of Tom's father, Dick. However, Dick is depressed because his old friend, Boyd Harrison, has died from a heart attack while skiing.

As Faith takes over the cooking duties for the family and tries to resolve a number of family issues, a body is found in the water used for the resort's snow-making machine. A *Publishers Weekly* contributor noted that *The Body in the Snowdrift* has "an attractive setting, great characters, good food and murder most foul."

Page pays homage to Agatha Christie's classic mystery novel *Ten Little Indians* in her next "Faith Fairchild" mystery titled *The Body in the Ivy*. Trapped on a remote New England island with guests at the house of noted author Barbara Bailey Bishop, Faith, who was asked to cater the affair, suddenly finds that she has numerous suspects in the murder of one of the guests. After some probing, she learns that the murder may be related to the guests' school days. They were all students at Pelham College in the 1970s when Barbara's sister supposedly committed suicide there. "Readers of the series will relish this addition," a *Publishers Weekly* contributor remarked. Connie Fletcher, writing in *Booklist,* called *The Body in the Ivy* a "romantic mystery, filled with country-house atmosphere and cookery."

The seventeenth installment of the series, *The Body in the Gallery,* appeared in 2008. Although busy with her husband, children, and her catering business, the amateur sleuth now takes over management of the coffee shop at the Ganley Art Museum. Here Faith hopes to help her friend Patsy, who is on the board of the museum, find the culprit who has replaced a valuable artwork with a copy. The investigation turns nasty when a body is found at an art opening and Faith learns that the crime may be connected to the art forgery. A *Kirkus Reviews* contributor felt that, like other titles in the same series, "this one is stronger on domesticity and culinary skills than on criminal behavior." A *Publishers Weekly* reviewer noted of *The Body in the Gallery* that, "along with fun foodie details, Page provides an entertaining subplot involving Faith's rebellious teenage son, Ben." High praise for *The Body in the Gallery* also came from a *Mystery News* contributor who wrote that in the book "Page does what she does best: creates a tightly woven story using a small cast of well developed characters, all within a closed community."

Turns to Juvenile and Young-Adult Fiction

Page has used her experience as a high-school teacher to craft several books for younger readers. Her "Christie and Company" series features a trio of teenage detectives: Christie and her school friends Maggie and Vicky. In the opening book of the series, *Christie and Company,* the three sleuths work to uncover the identity of a thief who is stealing valuable items from the students at their Massachusetts boarding school. A contributor in *Publishers Weekly* praised the novel's well-drawn protagonists, stating that Page "works into the plot details about their family backgrounds, shaping credible, distinct portraits of each girl." *Christie and Company Down East* finds the three girls in Maine for a month-long summer stay at an inn owned by Maggie's parents. While working at the inn as waitresses, the girls begin investigating "seemingly unrelated but progressively more serious events designed to ensure the resort's demise," as Susan

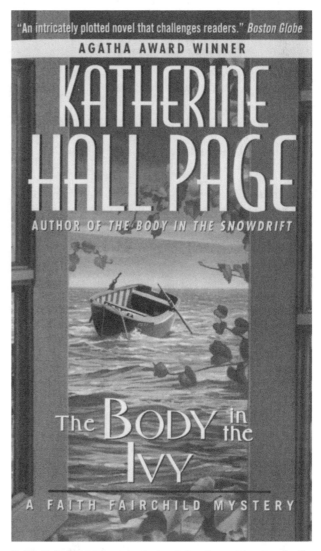

"An intricately plotted novel that challenges readers." *Boston Globe*

AGATHA AWARD WINNER

KATHERINE HALL PAGE

AUTHOR OF *THE BODY IN THE SNOWDRIFT*

The BODY in the IVY

A FAITH FAIRCHILD MYSTERY

Faith Fairchild is on a catering job when a mystery boils over in Page's entertaining *The Body in the Ivy*. (Copyright © 2006 by Katherine Hall Page. All rights reserved. Reprinted by permission of Harper-Collins Publishers Inc.)

DeRonne explained in *Booklist*. In the end, the girls "solve the mystery, and they patch up a few relationships along the way," DeRonne concluded.

Page is also the author of a stand-alone young-adult novel titled *Club Meds,* which centers on a group of students with medical issues. Jack Sutton, who has ADHD, takes Ritalin for his condition, but he is forced to give twenty of his tablets each week to the school bully, Chuck Williams. With the help of his friend Mary, who also has ADHD and who chips in some of her pills to give to Chuck, Jack eventually finds the courage to faces down the bully. Jennifer Mattson wrote in *Booklist* that *Club Meds* "casts ADHD sufferers as clever avengers, and does so in a speedy narrative that won't overload their circuits." A *Publishers Weekly* contributor wrote: "Page has a finger on the pulse of high school dynamics, and she elucidates the social hierarchy unflinchingly."

Despite her successes with young-adult fare, Page concentrates most of her literary efforts on her popular mystery series featuring amateur sleuth Faith Fairchild. As the author stated on her home page, "One of the joys of writing a series is the ability to work with a kind of ensemble troupe, bringing characters back, creating new ones, but the major players are fixed, although their parts can change. Readers tell me that Faith has grown, matured as the series has progressed." Page added, "When people write to me about her, they write as if she were someone they knew, an actual person."

If you enjoy the works of Katherine Hall Page, you may also want to check out the following books:

A Quiche before Dying, 1993, and other "Jane Jeffry" novels by Jill Churchill.
Valerie Wolzien's "Susan Henshaw" series, including *Death at a Discount,* 2000.
The works in Carolyn G. Hart's "Death on Demand" series, including *Dead Days of Summer,* 2006.

On her home page, Page had this to say about her "Faith Fairchild" novels: "When I think about the series, I imagine Faith standing by a pond, its surface a mirror perhaps reflecting some white birches or catching the flight of a heron. Everything looks quite perfect and serene, but if she takes a stick and pokes it beneath the surface, who knows what lies below—what secrets will emerge from the murky depths? The difference between what seems and what is, has been a theme throughout all the books. It's the tension between appearance and reality that taps into our greatest fears." The contributor for the Tufts University Web site also noted of Page's fictional creation: "Fairchild is a complex woman. She can be judgmental and overzealous to the point of endangering both herself and others. But she can also be virtuous, altruistic, and fearless when it comes to seeking the truth. Simply put, Faith Fairchild represents the imperfections within every individual, the ying and yang that makes every human being, well, human."

■ Biographical and Critical Sources

PERIODICALS

Booklist, March 15, 1996, Stuart Miller, review of *The Body in the Bog,* p. 1243; December 1, 1996, review of *Christie and Company,* p. 665; May 1, 1997, Susan DeRonne, review of *Christie and Company Down East,* p. 1498; October 15, 1997, GraceAnne A. DeCandido, review of *The Body in the Fjord,* p. 392; November 15, 1998, Emily Melton, review of *The Body in the Bookcase,* p. 572; March 15, 2003, GraceAnne A. DeCandido, review of *The Body in the Lighthouse,* p. 1280; May 1, 2004, GraceAnne A. DeCandido, review of *The Body in the Attic,* p. 1515; May 1, 2005, GraceAnne A. DeCandido, review of *The Body in the Snowdrift,* p. 66; August 1, 2006, Jennifer Mattson, review of *Club Meds,* p. 66; October 15, 2006, Connie Fletcher, review of *The Body in the Ivy,* p. 33; April 1, 2008, Connie Fletcher, review of *The Body in the Gallery,* p. 29.

Kirkus Reviews, August 15, 2006, review of *The Body in the Ivy,* p. 813; March 1, 2008, review of *The Body in the Gallery.*

Library Journal, November 1, 1997, Rex E. Klett, review of *The Body in the Fjord,* p. 120; November 1, 1998, Rex E. Klett, review of *The Body in the Bookcase,* p. 129; January, 2002, Rex E. Klett, review of *The Body in the Bonfire,* p. 158; May 1, 2005, Rex E. Klett, review of *The Body in the Snowdrift,* p. 66; October 1, 2006, Jo Ann Vicarel, review of *The Body in the Ivy,* p. 52.

Mystery News, November-December, 1997, review of *The Body in the Fjord;* June-July 2005, review of *The Body in the Snowdrift;* October-November 2006, review of *The Body in the Ivy;* April-May, 2008, Lynn Kaczmarek, "Katherine Hall Page: The Body in the . . ."; June-July 2008, review of *The Body in the Gallery.*

New York Times Book Review, December 27, 1998, Marilyn Stasio, review of *The Body in the Bookcase,* p. 17; January 9, 2000, Marilyn Stasio, review of *The Body in the Big Apple,* p. 24; April 24, 2005, Marilyn Stasio, review of *The Body in the Snowdrift,* p. 21.

Publishers Weekly, January 19, 1990, review of *The Body in the Belfry,* p. 100; November 2, 1990, review of *The Body in the Kelp,* p. 66; October 11, 1991, review of *The Body in the Bouillon,* p. 52; July 13, 1992, review of *The Body in the Vestibule,* p. 48; October 11, 1993, review of *The Body in the Cast,* p. 72; September 19, 1994, review of *The Body in the Basement,* p. 54; March 11, 1996, review of *The Body in the Bog,* p. 46; April 15, 1996, review of *Christie and Company,* p. 69; October 6, 1997, review of *The Body in the Fjord,* p. 77; October 5, 1998, review of *The Body in the Bookcase,* p. 84; October 25, 1999, review of *The Body in the Big Apple,* p. 54; March 17, 2003, review of *The Body in the Lighthouse,* p. 57; April 26, 2004, review of *The Body in the Attic,* p. 45; April 18, 2005, review of *The Body in the Snowdrift,* p. 47; August 28, 2006, review of *Club Meds,* p. 56; September 4, 2006, review of *The Body in the Ivy,* p. 42; March 3, 2008, review of *The Body in the Gallery,* p. 32.

School Library Journal, August, 2006, Janet Hilbun, review of *Club Meds,* p. 127.

ONLINE

Cozy Library Web site, http://www.cozylibrary. com/(April 15, 2009), "Katherine Hall Page."

HarperCollins Web site, http://www.harpercollins. com/ (July 15, 2009) "Katherine Hall Page."

Katherine Hall Page Home Page, http://www. katherine-hall-page.org (June 6, 2007).

Tufts University Web site, http://www.tufts.edu/ (April 15, 2009), "Katherine Hall Page."*

(Photograph courtesy of Ulf Andersen/Getty Images.)

Annie Proulx

■ Personal

Surname is pronounced "Pru"; born Edna Annie Proulx, August 22, 1935, in Norwich, CT; daughter of George Napolean and Lois Nelly Proulx; married and divorced three times, including James Hamilton Lang, 1969 (divorced 1990), children: Jon Lang, Gillis Lang, Morgan Lang, Muffy Clarkson. *Education:* Attended Colby College; University of Vermont, Burlington, B.A. (cum laude), 1969; Sir George Williams University (now Concordia University), M.A., 1973, enrolled in Ph.D. program until 1975. *Hobbies and other interests:* Fishing, canoeing, skiing, bicycling, reading.

■ Addresses

Home—WY. *Agent*—Liz Darhansoff, Darhansoff, Verrill, Felman Literary Agents, 236 W. 26th St., New York, NY 10001.

■ Career

Writer, 1975—. Founder and editor of rural Vermont newspaper *Behind the Times,* 1984-86.

■ Member

PEN, Phi Beta Kappa, Phi Alpha Theta.

■ Awards, Honors

Kress fellow, Harvard University, 1974; Gardens Writers of America Award, 1986; Vermont Council on the Arts fellowship, 1989; National Endowment for the Arts grant, 1991; Guggenheim fellow, 1992; PEN/Faulkner Award for Fiction, 1993, for *Postcards;* National Book Critics Circle Award nomination for Best Fiction, National Book Award for Fiction, *Chicago Tribune* Heartland Prize for Fiction, and *Irish Times* International Fiction Prize, all 1993, and Pulitzer Prize for Fiction, 1994, all for *The Shipping News;* honorary D.H.L., University of Maine, 1994; Dos Passos Prize for Literature, 1996, for *Accordion Crimes;* National Magazine Award, 1998, and O. Henry Prize, both for *Brokeback Mountain;* award for fiction, *New Yorker,* 2000, for *Close Range;* Best Foreign Language Novels of 2002/Best American Novel Award, Chinese Publishing Association and Peoples' Literature Publishing House, 2002, for *That Old Ace in the Hole;* Aga Khan Prize for Fiction, 2002, for short story "The Wamsutter Wolf."

■ Writings

(Under name E. Annie Proulx) *Heart Songs and Other Stories,* Scribner (New York, NY), 1988.

(Under name E. Annie Proulx) *Postcards* (novel), Scribner (New York, NY), 1992.

(Under name E. Annie Proulx) *The Shipping News* (novel), Scribner (New York, NY), 1993.

(Under name E. Annie Proulx) *Accordion Crimes* (novel), Scribner (New York, NY), 1996.

Brokeback Mountain (short story; also see below), Fourth Estate (London, England), 1998, Scribner (New York, NY), 2005.

Close Range: Wyoming Stories (includes "Brokeback Mountain"), watercolors by William Matthews, Scribner (New York, NY), 1999.

That Old Ace in the Hole (novel), Scribner (New York, NY), 2002.

Bad Dirt: Wyoming Stories 2, Scribner (New York, NY), 2004.

(With Larry McMurtry and Diana Ossana) *Brokeback Mountain: Story to Screenplay*, Scribner (New York, NY), 2006.

Fine Just the Way It Is: Wyoming Stories 3, Scribner (New York, NY), 2008.

OTHER

(Under name E. Annie Proulx; with Lew Nichols) *Sweet and Hard Cider: Making It, Using It, and Enjoying It*, Garden Way (Charlotte, VT), 1980, third edition, under name Annie Proulx, published as *Cider: Making, Using, and Enjoying Sweet and Hard Cider*, Storey Publications (North Adams, MA), 2003.

(Under name E. Annie Proulx) *"What'll You Take for It?": Back to Barter*, Garden Way (Charlotte, VT), 1981.

(Under name E. Annie Proulx; with Lew Nichols) *The Complete Dairy Foods Cookbook: How to Make Everything from Cheese to Custard in Your Kitchen*, Rodale Press (Emmaus, PA), 1982.

(Under name E. Annie Proulx) *The Gardener's Journal and Record Book*, Rodale Press (Emmaus, PA), 1983.

(Under name E. Annie Proulx) *Plan and Make Your Own Fences and Gates, Walkways, Walls, and Drives*, Rodale Press (Emmaus, PA), 1983.

(Under name E. Annie Proulx) *The Fine Art of Salad Gardening*, Rodale Press (Emmaus, PA), 1985.

(Under name E. Annie Proulx) *The Gourmet Gardener: Growing Choice Fruits and Vegetables with Spectacular Results*, illustrated by Robert Byrd, Fawcett Columbine (New York, NY), 1987.

Contributor of stories to anthologies, including *Fiction, Flyfishing, and the Search for Innocence*, Birch Brook Press, 1994; contributor of essay to Andrea Modica, *Treadwell: Photographs*, Chronicle Books (San Francisco, CA), 1996. Contributor of articles to periodicals, sometimes under the name E.A. Proulx,

including *African Arts, Equinox, New York Times, National Wildlife, Yankee, Down East, Country Journal, Outside, Chicago Tribune, Walking,* and *Horticulture;* contributor of short stories to *Ploughshares, Gray's Sporting Journal, Seventeen, Esquire,* and *Harrowsmith.*

■ Adaptations

The Shipping News was adapted for film in 2001 and released by Miramax. Larry McMurtry and Dianna Ossana adapted *Brokeback Mountain* for a film directed by Ang Lee, released 2005.

■ Sidelights

"Annie Proulx is a master of the art of subtle accretion," wrote reviewer Sven Birkerts in *Book.* "The moments of her novel, the mostly unremarkable encounters of her characters, silt up to a thickness that starts to feel very much like the world itself. The prose may be slow and demand care from the reader, but Proulx repays our attention with a thousand shocks of charged recognition." Though Birkerts was reviewing Annie Proulx's fourth novel, *That Old Ace in the Hole,* he might have been describing her entire body of work. "Place and history are central to the fiction I write, both in the broad, general sense and in detailed particulars," Proulx explained in an interview with Matthew Testa for *Planet Jackson Hole.* "Rural North America, regional cultures, the images of an ideal and seemingly attainable world the characters cherish in their long views despite the rigid and difficult circumstances of their place and time interest me and are what I write about. I watch for the historical skew between what people have hoped for and who they thought they were and what befell them."

In both short fiction and novels that show how human resilience is shaped and honed in harsh, rusticated, sometimes merciless, yet ultimately beautiful geographic outposts, Proulx captures a unique facet of the mythic American character. It is a facet that she has embodied in her own life as a writer, slowly establishing herself as a unique literary stylist and a consummate storyteller. In the late 1980s, while writing under the name E. Annie Proulx, her writing career finally blossomed, earning her much critical and public acclaim for her fiction. Her 1992 novel, *Postcards,* won the PEN/ Faulkner Award for Fiction, while *The Shipping News,* published a year later, received numerous

Cover of Annie Proulx's National Book Award-winning novel, *The Shipping News.* (Cover etching by David Blackwood. Reproduced by permission of Scribner, an imprint of Simon & Schuster Macmillan, and David Blackwood, Inc.)

honors, including the National Book Award and a Pulitzer prize. Proulx is also the author of the short story *Brokeback Mountain.* Originally published in London, England, in 1998, the story, which is about two homosexual cowboys in 1960s Wyoming, was adapted for film and released to some measure of controversy in 2005.

Moving as a Way of Life

Born Edna Annie Proulx in Connecticut in 1935, Proulx was the first of five daughters of George Napoleon and Lois "Nellie" Proulx. Her ancestors had immigrated to North American in the seventeenth century, her mother's family from England and her father's from France. It was her mother, an artist and amateur naturalist, who taught Proulx

how to observe life from an imaginative perspective. "From the time I was extremely small, I was told, 'Look at that,'" the author recalled to *New York Times* interviewer Sara Rimer. "Most often it was anthills. My mother would say, 'Look at that one carrying a stick.' All these guys had characters. She would give them voices. We'd be watching them, and pointing out the various ones. There was Charlie, there was Mr. Jones. She had an animistic universe in her mind."

The Proulx family moved several times in her youth, to various New England states and to North Carolina. Proulx herself has subsequently lived in numerous locations, including Montreal, Vermont, New Hampshire, Newfoundland, and Wyoming. Proulx attended Colby College, and then studied history at the University of Vermont and Sir George Williams University (now Concordia University), where she earned her M.A. in 1973.

After completing most of the work for a doctorate, she left the university to begin work as a freelance writer, "a classic example of shifting from the frying pan to the fire," as she once explained. Speaking with Katie Bolick for *Atlantic Unbound*, Proulx discussed the dramatic shift: "In the 1970s, when I left graduate school and gave up the Ph.D., I went off to live in the woods with a friend. I was living in very remote, rural, difficult situations, and the question of how to make a living miles and miles from the nearest town came up. Writing seemed like a likely enough thing." Having already sold a number of stories, Proulx decided to pen articles about her lifestyle. "What interested me at this time was the back-to-the-land movement—communes, gardening, architecture, the difficulty of maintaining a long, dirt-road driveway," she remarked to Bolick. "Not only could I solve some of those problems in real life and observe what people were doing to make things work in rural situations, I could write about them and make some money. So I did. And I made a damned good living for a number of years doing this."

While living in northern Vermont, Proulx wrote article-length and book-length works on numerous aspects of rural living, from cider making, barter, and gardening to construction projects. In between, she penned short stories, at the rate of about two per year. Married and divorced three times, Proulx managed to support her children on this freelancing work. The short fiction she sold in the 1980s was mostly published in hunting and fishing magazines. As the readers of those magazines were largely male, she disguised her gender by writing under the byline of E.A. Proulx. "But gradually this kind of thing became more and more boring, and my interests changed," she explained to Bolick. "I began to move towards fiction for intellectual stimulation."

From Gardens to the Literary World

Proulx related her experiences moving from writing nonfiction to producing the nine tales collected in *Heart Songs and Other Stories,* telling John Blades of the *Chicago Tribune:* "After 19 years of writing tedious nonfiction, all these stories were just bottled up inside me, waiting to get out. Now writing fiction is sheer play." Assessing the volume for the *Los Angeles Times,* Elaine Kendall described *Heart Songs* as "hard stories set in a bleak climate; a closed, narrow world hostile to strangers and rough on its own." Taking place in northern New England, the stories in *Heart Songs* feature characters that Kenneth Rosen, writing in the *New York Times Book Review,* called "shy, battered, depleted." As they would with her subsequent fiction, some critics remarked upon the strange names of Proulx's characters and what reviewer Kendall called "a terse quirky humor" that is displayed in several stories. Of Proulx's tales, Rosen concluded: "Their sometimes enigmatic, often lyrical images seem to complement New England's lavish but barren beauty."

Each chapter of Proulx's first novel, *Postcards,* begins with a postcard connected in some way to the character Loyal Blood or to the parents and siblings Blood left behind after the ambiguous death of his girlfriend. The Blood family has worked their farm in New England for generations, but with Loyal's departure a decline begins, and through the descriptions of his aimless wanderings over the next thirty years, *Postcards* documents the slow death of the small American family farm.

Reviewers praised *Postcards* for its commentary on the American condition, but reserved their most lavish accolades for Proulx's abilities as a storyteller. As Frederick Busch stated in the *Chicago Tribune Book World,* "What makes this rich, dark and brilliant feast of a book is its furious action, its searing contemplations, its language born of the fury and the searching and the author's powerful sense of the gothic soul of New England." David Bradley, writing in the *New York Times Book Review,* concluded that "Story makes this novel compelling; technique

Kevin Spacey and Dame Judy Dench starred in the 2001 film adaptation of Proulx's award-winning novel *The Shipping News.* (Photograph courtesy of Miramax/Columbia/The Kobal Collection/Gregory Doane/The Picture Desk, Inc.)

makes it beautiful. What makes *Postcards* significant is that Ms. Proulx uses both story and technique to make real the history of post-World War II America."

Finds Her Way into the American Canon of Novels

The thread that connects Proulx's second novel, *The Shipping News,* to her earlier fiction is its setting in a hostile climate. Newfoundland, a remote Canadian province known for its sudden storms and icy seas, provides the harsh backdrop to the story of Quoyle, a huge, hapless journalist living in upstate New York. His unfaithful wife dies in a car wreck, leaving him with their two daughters and an overwhelming grief. When Quoyle's aunt arrives she easily convinces him to pack up his family and travel to Newfoundland to reclaim the family land and start over. According to Phoebe-Lou Adams writing for the *Atlantic:* "Proulx blends Newfoundland argot, savage history, impressively diverse characters, fine descriptions of weather and scenery, and comic horseplay without ever lessening the reader's interest in Quoyle's progress."

The Shipping News received an outpouring of critical acclaim upon its release. Howard Norman in the *New York Times Book Review* acknowledged "Proulx's surreal humor and her zest for the strange foibles of humanity." Emphasizing the effect of the watery setting of *The Shipping News* on the reader, Stephen Jones asserted in the *Chicago Tribune Book World:* "In spite of Proulx's invitations to dream in the coves, her plot rushes out of a confluence between the force of the characters and their environment to buoy you on. The result is that rare creation, a lyric page turner."

Proulx told Nicci Gerrard of the London *Observer:* "Eight years ago, I was looking for canoeing waters and I unfolded an old map of Newfoundland. Each place-name had a story—Dead Man's Cove, Seldom Come Bay and Bay of Despair, Exploits River, Plunder Beach. I knew I had to go there, and within 10 minutes of arriving, I'd fallen in love. I am pulled by the harshness of the weather, the strength of the landscape which is dark and stormy and rough, . . . the sense of a land holding its own against people."

Following on the commercial and critical success of *The Shipping News,* Proulx produced *Accordion Crimes.* A novel in the picaresque tradition, this work follows an accordion as it moves from owner to owner during the span of a century. Proulx uses this technique as a forum in which to discuss the immigrant experience in America, with the novel's

Cover of Proulx's short-story collection *Close Range,* in which she shares her love of Wyoming and western life. (Cover painting by William Matthew. Reproduced by permission of Scribner, an imprint of Simon & Schuster Macmillan.)

nine sections each set among a different ethnic group: a German settlement in Iowa; a Louisiana Cajun family; and a Mexican immigrant in Texas, among others. The accordion's change-of-ownership is initiated in each instance by a disaster of some sort; many of these, in typical Proulx fashion, take the form of grisly deaths related in parentheses by the author. "Instead of the river of time, you get a lawn sprinkler effect, a kind of jittery, jammed, off-balance feeling," Proulx told Sybil Steinberg in a interview for *Publishers Weekly.*

While not greeted with the kind of uniform praise as its immediate predecessor, *Accordion Crimes* nonetheless elicited many warm reviews from critics. As Chicago's *Tribune Books* reviewer Bharati Mukherjee remarked, "With Proulx as biographer, the accordion's life story becomes more than an occasion for dazzling displays of writing. . . . Proulx proves her thesis with bleak persistence: America hates its non-Anglo immigrants." Writing in the *Bloomsbury Review,* Steven C. Ballinger praised Proulx's storytelling skill: "She can pick the telling characteristic the way a watercolorist's stroke sets the scene. When she sets a dialect in motion through a character, it is absolute and sure." Some reviewers felt that Proulx's technique results in less-than-fully developed characters. *New York Times* critic Christopher Lehmann-Haupt, for instance, noted that "the moment you begin to identify with any of the novel's characters, the narrative pushes you away by conveying in various ways that they aren't worth bothering with." And *Newsweek* reviewer Malcolm Jones, Jr., called *Accordion Crimes* "a book with no unifying narrative drive. The chapters are meant to work as separate stories, but that's all they are, a collection of stories." Still, explained Lehmann-Haupt, "Such is the energy of Ms. Proulx's prose, the authenticity of her dialogue and the brilliance of her invention that you can't help being caught up by some of her set pieces." Commenting on her use of creative devices in this book, Proulx told Steinberg: "Everything that happens to characters comes welling out of the place. Even their definition of themselves, and a lot of this book is about the definition of self."

Proulx created a paean to Texas in her novel *That Old Ace in the Hole.* Here the main character, the hapless Bob Dollar, travels to the Texas panhandle to find land for his employer, Global Pork Rind, to purchase and convert to a hog farm. In the desolation of the city of Woolybucket, Dollar learns lessons about life and meets the small town's eccentric residents, including LaVon Fronk and Freda Beautyrooms. He also sees the environmental devastation employers such as his bring to the land, killing off family farms to build gigantic pig-breeding factories. "Proulx's laudable outrage over environmental abuses overshadows literary nuance, yet, as always, she revels in odd twists of fate and characters as quirky as their names," Donna Seaman noted in her *Booklist* review of *That Old Ace in the Hole.* Higher praise came from a *Publishers Weekly* contributor who concluded: "Nobody captures Americana like Proulx, and the lure of her idiosyncratic characters should spark sales. Her strong stand against rapacious land corporations will attract readers who admire her outspoken opinions."

Focus Turns to Short Fiction

While Proulx's more-recent work has largely been focused on short fiction, she deals with many of the same themes. Writing in the *Dictionary of Literary Biography,* Denis M. Hennessy commented that

"Proulx's novels . . . have brought her the popularity and success that allow her to write full-time; yet, her short stories are the works that give the swift and stunning insights into human behavior she desires most." In her interview with Bolick, Proulx discussed her shift from writing novels to penning short fiction as "intensely pleasurable," adding: "There's a pleasing rhythm in the writing of short stories, and the challenge is greater; I find them harder than novels to write, not only because of the conciseness and the fact that every single word, every piece of punctuation, has to drive the story forward, but also because writing stories with both depth and surface is a considerable challenge."

In the fiction collection *Close Range: Wyoming Stories* Proulx presents eleven tales that, as Dean Bakopoulos noted in the *Progressive,* focus on "the mythic legends of drunken cowboys, rodeo heroes, betrayed lovers, and aging ranchers, while exploring all the loneliness, blood, and dirt of the Western landscape." Bakopoulos also commented that, as a whole, *Close Range* "is powerful fiction, and somehow Proulx manages to give each story the plot, depth of character, sense of setting, and thematic weight of an entire novel." A *Publishers Weekly* reviewer, noting that the stories in *Close Range* run the gamut from "bleakly humorous" to "poignant," commented that Proulx's "ability to merge the matter-of-fact and the macabre, and her summary of life's pain in a terse closing sentence, will elicit gasps of pain and understanding. In the close range of a distinctive landscape, Proulx encapsulates the wide range of human experience: loss, longing and the Spartan determination to go on from day to day."

As Charlotte L. Glover, noted in *Library Journal,* "Proving that the Pulitzer Prize for *The Shipping News* was no fluke, Proulx once again demonstrates her creative mastery of the English language." Particularly of note, Glover added, is "Brokeback Mountain," which received a *New Yorker* award for fiction and was adapted for film in 2005. The story focuses on two ranch hands who have an erotic relationship, go on to have traditional family lives, and then are drawn together once again. Speaking with *Los Angeles Times* contributor Susan Salter Reynolds, Proulx remarked that *Close Range* constitutes "a backhand swipe at the mythology of the West— the old beliefs that aren't really true, like the idea that there are no homosexuals in Wyoming. Everyone here is playing some role: the brave pioneer woman, the cowboy."

Bad Dirt: Wyoming Stories 2 is predominantly set in fictional Elk Tooth, Wyoming, where eighty people live in a three-bar town. The characters that populate

Jake Gyllenhall and Heath Ledger starred in the 2005 film *Brokeback Mountain*, which is based on a novel by Proulx.
(Photograph courtesy of Focus Features/The Kobal Collection/The Picture Desk, Inc.)

these stories have strange names and stranger quirks. Proulx seems to indicate that it takes a character to live with the isolation and poverty characteristically found in the country. While reviewers did find fault with the collection, most concluded that it still stands as a worthy addition to Proulx's oeuvre. "The collection trips up . . . with the inclusion of a handful of stories that veer into magical realism," contended *New Statesman* contributor William Skidelsky, the critic also adding that Proulx's "trademark skills are on display in these tales; they include a talent for metaphor, a wry sense of humour and an ability to sum up a whole life in a sentence." An *Economist* critic echoed this sentiment in a review of *Bad Dirt*, noting Proulx's "masterful ability to condense a character's life into punchy sentences that underpin vivid images."

Proulx's third volume of Wyoming tales, *Fine the Way It Is: Wyoming Stories 3,* includes the reminiscences of a crusty ranch hand late in his life ("Family Man"), the hard times of a returning female Iraq war veteran who lost an arm ("Tits-Up in a Ditch")

and other "harrowing, sometimes darkly funny accounts" of life in Wyoming, as *Entertainment Weekly* contributor Jennifer Reese noted. For Reese, *Fine the Way It Is* is "unsentimental and affecting," while a *Publishers Weekly* reviewer termed the collection an "astonishing series of hardscrabble lives lived in the sparse, inhospitable West, where one mistake can put you on a long-winding trail to disaster." In the words of *Booklist* reviewer Brad Hooper, *Fine Just the Way It Is* "takes giant steps toward securing Proulx's position as one of the most inventive yet, at the same time, traditional story writers working today."

Proulx mixes a powerful lyrical style with vast, exacting knowledge about her subjects—knowledge gained through careful research and keen observation—to create engaging studies of human lives as they are shaped by historical, economic, and ecological circumstances. Discussing her work, Proulx told Gerrard: "I came to writing late, and I'm racing against the clock to get everything down. My head is jammed with stories; they are pushing to get out." After living for many years in Vermont,

Proulx now resides in Wyoming where, as she told Steinberg in *Publishers Weekly*, there is "room to walk. There's something about being able to shoot your eyes very far ahead. In northern New England, the trees got in the way."

If you enjoy the works of Annie Proulx, you may also want to check out the following books:

Susan Minot, *Monkeys*, 1986.
Carol Shields, *The Stone Diaries*, 1994.
Alice Munro, *Hateship, Friendship, Courtship, Loveship, Marriage*, 2001.

In a *Publishers Weekly* interview with Louisa Ermelino, Proulx remarked that what she likes best about the writing process is "'the architecture of writing, the faint ideas in your head that become tangible on the page and then something gets off the page and walks around on its own legs.'" As for the fame that writing has brought her, Proulx told Ermelino: "'It's distracting and incompatible with the writing. You can't get anything done. Everyone is pulling at you. I think most writers are happiest left alone under the shady tree.'"

■ **Biographical and Critical Sources**

BOOKS

Contemporary Literary Criticism, Gale (Detroit, MI), Volume 81, 1994, Volume 158, 2002, Volume 250, 2008.
Dictionary of Literary Biography, Volume 335: *American Short-Story Writers since World War II, Fifth Series*, Gale (Detroit, MI), 2007.

Annie Proulx with fellow award-winning writer A.R. Ammons at the National Book Awards, 1993. (Photograph courtesy of AP Images.)

PERIODICALS

Atlantic Monthly, April, 1993, Phoebe-Lou Adams, review of *The Shipping News,* pp. 131-132; December, 2000, review of *That Old Ace in the Hole,* p. 148.

Book, January-February, 2003, Sven Birkerts, review of *That Old Ace in the Hole,* p. 64.

Booklist, March 15, 1999, Donna Seaman, review of *Close Range: Wyoming Stories,* p. 1261; October 1, 2002, Donna Seaman, review of *That Old Ace in the Hole,* p. 276; May 1, 2008, Brad Hooper, review of *Fine Just the Way It Is: Wyoming Stories 3,* p. 5.

Bloomsbury Review, September-October, 1996, Steven C. Ballinger, review of *Accordion Crimes,* p. 18.

Chicago Tribune, March 29, 1993, John Blades, interview with Proulx, sec. 5, p. 3.

Commonweal, December 1, 1995, review of *Accordion Crimes,* p. 24.

Critique, spring, 1999, review of *Close Range,* p. 239.

Economist, January 8, 2005, review of *Bad Dirt: Wyoming Stories 2,* p. 76.

English Journal, January, 1996, review of *Accordion Crimes,* p. 94.

Entertainment Weekly, January 3, 2003, review of *That Old Ace in the Hole,* p. 68; September 19, 2009, Jennifer Reese, review of *Fine Just the Way It Is,* p. 76.

Kirkus Reviews, October 1, 2002, review of *That Old Ace in the Hole,* p. 1423; May 15, 2008, review of *Fine Just the Way It Is.*

Library Journal, May 1, 1999, Charlotte L. Glover, review of *Close Range,* p. 115.

Los Angeles Times, December 30, 1988, Elaine Kendall, review of *Heart Songs and Other Stories;* January 20, 1992, Carolyn See, review of *Postcards,* p. E2; March 14, 2006. "Proulx Pens Tirade over 'Crash' Oscar," p. E3; October 18, 2008, Susan Salter Reynolds, "Writer's No Longer at Home on Range," p. A1.

Nation, June 24, 1996, review of *Accordion Crimes,* p. 29.

New Republic, May 30, 1994, review of *The Shipping News,* p. 35.

New Statesman, January 10, 2005, William Skidelsky, review of *Bad Dirt,* p. 56.

New Statesman and Society, December 3, 1993, review of *The Shipping News,* p. 39.

Newsweek, June 10, 1996, Malcolm Jones, Jr., review of *Accordion Crimes,* p. 88.

New York Times, April 21, 1993, review of *The Shipping News,* p. C15; June 23, 1994, Sara Rimer, "At Home With: E. Annie Proulx; At Midlife a Novelist Is Born"; June 17, 1996, Christopher Lehmann-Haupt, review of *Accordion Crimes,* p. C14; May 10, 1999, Annie Proulx, "Writers on Writing: Inspiration? Head down the Back Road, and Stop for the Yard Sales."

New York Times Book Review, January 29, 1989, Kenneth Rosen, review of *Heart Songs and Other Stories,* p. 30; March 22, 1992, David Bradley, review of *Postcards,* p. 7; April 4, 1993, review of *The Shipping News,* p. 13; June 23, 1996, review of *Accordion Crimes,* p. 12; September 7, 2008, Ron Carlson, review of *Fine Just the Way It Is.*

Observer (London, England), November 14, 1993, Nicci Gerrard, review of *The Shipping News,* p. 18.

Progressive, September, 1999, Dean Bakopoulos, review of *Close Range,* p. 43.

Publishers Weekly, April 15, 1996, review of *Accordion Crimes,* p. 48; June 3, 1996, Sybil Steinberg, "E. Annie Proulx: An American Odyssey," p. 57; March 29, 1999, review of *Close Range,* p. 91; October 14, 2002, review of *That Old Ace in the Hole,* p. 63; May 26, 2008, review of *Fine Just the Way It Is,* p. 35; July 7, 2008, Louisa Ermelino, "Home on the Range," p. 29.

Spectator, December 18, 2004, Digby Durrant, review of *Bad Dirt,* p. 92; August 30, 2008, Philip Hensher, review of *Fine Just the Way It Is,* p. 27.

Time, June 24, 1996, review of *Accordion Crimes,* p. 82; May 17, 1999, John Skow, review of *Close Range,* p. 88; December 23, 2002, Richard Lacayo, review of *That Old Ace in the Hole.*

Times Literary Supplement, October 23, 1998, Lucy Atkins, review of *Brokeback Mountain,* p. 24.

Tribune Books (Chicago, IL), December 11, 1988, review of *Heart Songs and Other Stories,* p. 1; January 12, 1992, Frederick Busch, review of *Postcards,* pp. 1, 4; March 21, 1993, Stephen Jones, review of *The Shipping News,* pp. 1, 9; June 9, 1996, Bharati Mukherjee, review of *Accordion Crimes,* p. 1.

Voice Literary Supplement, April, 1993, review of *The Shipping News,* p. 29.

Wall Street Journal, June 14, 1996, review of *Accordion Crimes,* p. A12.

Women's Review of Books, September, 1996, review of *Accordion Crimes,* p. 11.

Yale Review, October, 1993, review of *The Shipping News,* pp. 133-135.

ONLINE

Atlantic Unbound, http://www.theatlantic.com/unbound/ (November 12, 1997), Katie Bolick, "Imagination Is Everything: A Conversation with E. Annie Proulx."

BookPage Web site, http://www.bookpage.com/ (December 1, 2002), Alden Mudge, "An Abiding Sense of Place."

High Country News Online, http://www.hcn.org/ (April 13, 2009), Emma Brown, "The Desert That Breaks Annie Proulx's Heart."

Planet Jackson Hole Web site, http://www.planetjh.com/ (December 7, 2005), Matthew Testa, "At Close Range with Annie Proulx."*

Alastair Reynolds

(Photograph by Josette Sanchez. Courtesy of Orion Publishing Group, Ltd.)

■ Personal

Born 1966, in Barry, Wales; married; wife's name Josette. *Education:* B.S.; St. Andrews University, Ph.D. (astronomy); post-doctoral studies at Utrecht University, 1994-96. *Hobbies and other interests:* Horse riding, birds, long walks in the woods, good curries, and old films.

■ Addresses

Home—Glamorgan, South Wales. *Agent*—Robert Kirby, United Agents, 130 Shaftesbury Ave., London W1S SEU, England. *E-mail*—dendrocopus@yahoo.co.uk.

■ Career

European Space Agency, Leiden, Netherlands, astrophysicist, 1991-94, contractor, 1996-2004; full-time writer, 2004—.

■ Awards, Honors

British Science Fiction Award nomination, and Arthur C. Clarke Award nomination, both for *Revela-tion Space;* British Science Fiction Award, 2001, for *Chasm City;* works shortlisted for British Science Fiction Award and Arthur C. Clarke Award.

■ Writings

NOVELS; EXCEPT AS NOTED

Century Rain, Gollancz (London, England), 2004, Ace Books (New York, NY), 2005.

Diamond Dogs, Turquoise Days (novellas), Gollancz (London, England), 2004, Berkley (New York, NY), 2005.

Pushing Ice, Gollancz (London, England), 2005, Ace Books (New York, NY), 2006.

Zima Blue and Other Stories, Night Shade Books (San Francisco, CA), 2006.

The Six Directions of Space (novella), Subterranean Press (Burton MI), 2008.

House of Suns, Gollancz (London, England), 2008, Ace Books (New York, NY), 2009.

Terminal World, Gollancz (London, England), 2009.

Thousandth Night; and, Minla's Flowers (novellas), Subterranean Press (Burton, MI), 2009.

"REVELATION SPACE" SERIES; SCIENCE FICTION

Revelation Space, Ace Books (New York, NY), 2001.

Chasm City, Gollancz (London, England), 2001, Ace Books (New York, NY), 2002.

Redemption Ark, Gollancz (London, England), 2002, Ace Books (New York, NY), 2003.

Absolution Gap, Gollancz (London, England), 2003, Ace Books (New York, NY), 2004.

Galactic North (short stories), Gollancz (London, England), 2006, Ace Books (New York, NY), 2007.

The Prefect, Gollancz (London, England), 2007, Ace Books (New York, NY), 2008.

OTHER

Contributor of short stories to periodicals, including *Interzone, Asimov's Science Fiction,* and *Spectrum.* Short fiction included in anthologies *In Dreams,* edited by Paul J. McAuley and Kim Newsman, Gollancz (London, England), 1992; *The Mammoth Book of Best New Science Fiction 11th Annual Collection,* Mammoth (London, England), 1997, and *Years' Best Science Fiction,* annual anthologies, 1998, 2000-02, all edited by Garner Dozois; *The Ant Men of Tibet and Other Stories,* Interzone, 2001; *Mars Probes,* edited by Peter Crowther, Daw Books (New York, NY), 2002; and *Infinities,* edited by Peter Crowther, Orion Books, 2002, among others. Also author of numerous articles on astrophysics published in professional journals.

Author's work has been translated into several languages, including Japanese, German, Czech, and Italian.

■ **Sidelights**

Alastair Reynolds is a Welsh author of highly regarded science-fiction novels and stories, including the works in his "Revelation Space" series, which draws from his experiences as a scientist with the European Space Agency. Reynolds is part of a generation of writers that create "hard" science fiction: stories focusing on technical detail and grounded in accuracy in terms of scientific information. In the words of *Andromeda Speedways Inflight Magazine* contributor Simon Petrie, Reynolds "is a prolific craftsman of stories which are probably best described as a cross between hard SF and space opera. His books have a tendency towards the hard SF rigour that follows from a career as an astrophysics researcher, while tending also to include the grandiose universe-building and intricate plotting which are the preserve of space opera. Most of his books have dealt with imagined events

over the next few thousands of years of human history." According to Ray Olson, writing in *Booklist,* Reynolds is "one of the best contemporary space-opera writers."

After working for several years as an astrophysicist while writing on the side, Reynolds committed himself full-time to writing in 2004, having already established a reputation for quality work. Speaking with Ernest G. Saylor and Joseph W. Dickerson on the *Aberrant Dreams* Web site, Reynolds stated: "For me, the whole thrust of my writing science fiction is not necessarily to throw up a mirror to the present. A lot of science fiction is couched in metaphoric terms; it's really about the present, rather that the future. For me, there's nothing inherently ignoble in speculating about the future, and in order to do

Cover of Alastair Reynolds' *Revelation Space,* **which introduces his futuristic brand of space opera.** (Cover art by Chris Moore. All rights reserved. Used by permission of Penguin Group (USA) Inc.)

that, you have to think about scientific progress and technology. I see science fiction, taken as a whole, as a collective thought experiment, where we're looking into the future and mapping not a future, but the space of all possible futures."

From Scientist to Science Fiction

Reynolds was born in Barry, in southern Wales, in 1966. His childhood environment was an influential factor in his choice of vocation; as Reynolds noted on his home page, "One third of the world's coal was exported out of Barry before the war, requiring a massive and fascinating infrastructure of docks, cranes, . . . and railway yards." Though derelict, much of this infrastructure was still in place when Reynolds was growing up, and this piqued his interest in industrial archaeology. He was introduced to science fiction at the age of eight, through *Speed & Power* magazine. "It was for small boys, and at the back it would reproduce a classic story by Arthur C Clarke," he recalled to Stuart Jeffries in the London *Guardian.* "The stories were so cleverly constructed and so simple that I loved them. I still do. What Clarke did was to write stories that treated human ignorance as the adversary. There was a marvellous purity in that, and I increasingly want to emulate what he achieved."

Reynolds spent part of his youth in Cornwall, and then earned an undergraduate degree in Newcastle and a doctorate in astronomy at St. Andrews University. Then he left for Europe where he worked for the European Space Agency for sixteen years. He always had the desire to write, however, and write more than just the astronomy articles he authored for professional journals. Short stories came first, and then, as these gained a wider readership, Reynolds turned to novels. Eventually, he left the agency to write full time, as he found it increasingly difficult to concentrate on his work. "There was always that tension but as a scientist I just had to knuckle down and do the job," he told *Wales on Sunday* contributor Catherine Jones. "Generally speaking, it was enough of a challenge finding the problem so there wasn't time to daydream." Reynolds added, "In the end I found I was struggling to perform at my best in my job and I would rather quit."

The career shift was a fortuitous one for Reynolds. "With a Ph.D. in astronomy and years working as an astrophysicist," Nick Gevers remarked on *SciFi. com.* "Reynolds was, from the start of his writing career, ideally equipped to become one of the leading authors of the British New Space Opera."

Cover of Reynolds' *Galactic North,* which collects the stories and novellas set in his fictional "Revelation Space" universe. (Cover art by Chris Moore. Used by permission of Penguin Group (USA) Inc.)

"Revelation Space" Series

Reynolds' first four novels introduce his "Revelation Space" series. According to Gevers, "These books paint a dark-yet-adventuresome portrait of scattered human colony worlds centuries from now, wracked by civil wars and nanotech plagues, split along fascinating ideological fault lines and menaced by the Inhibitors, guardians left behind by aliens billions of years ago to suppress any further emergence of spacefaring intelligent life in our galaxy." As Reynolds explained to Jeffries, "For me, space flight is all about the biological imperative. We won't do it because we've trashed the planet, but because we can. And that's surely optimistic. In the 'Revelation Space' stories, humanity is fragile and on the brink of extinction but it's an optimistic outlook—we're still out there, in the distant future, struggling to survive and make ourselves better."

In the first book, *Revelation Space,* Reynolds sets the stage for adventure 500 years in the future. Archaeologist Dan Sylvest is researching what destroyed the ancient Amarantin civilization on a distant planet. Meanwhile, he is being sought out as the only person who can cure the captain of the huge spaceship *Nostalgia for Infinity.* Meanwhile, assassin Ana Khouri, who has been hired to kill Sylvest, has managed to get on board the ship. Writing for the *SFSignal* Web site, a reviewer observed that *Revelation Space* "included lots of cool plot twists, surprises, and revelations." A *Publishers Weekly* contributor wrote that, "clearly intoxicated by cutting-edge scientific research—in bioengineering, space physics, cybernetics—Reynolds spins [a] ravishingly inventive tale of intrigue" in *Revelation Space.* According to London *Guardian* reviewer Jon Courtenay Grimwood, based on his fiction debut, "Reynolds is a name to watch."

Chasm City also takes place in the "Revelation Space" world and focuses on a city caught in the grasp of a virus that attacks both people and machines. Security expert Tanner Mirabel has traveled to the planet of Yellowstone to track the murderers of his late employers. After awakening at the end of the voyage—suffering from the temporary amnesia common following suspended animation used for long-distance space travel—Mirabel also discovers that he has a virus that is causing him to imagine the previous life of the historic figure Sky Haussman, complete with revelations about Haussman's dark side. Writing in the *Science Fiction Chronicle,* Don D'Ammassa commented that *Chasm City* "is one of the strangest metropolises you'll every visit, fictionally or otherwise, and its inhabitants are nearly as bizarre." The critic also wrote that "Haussman's story moves with a relentless sense of dread toward a series of startling revelations," and Ray Olson, writing in *Booklist,* called *Chasm City* an "intoxicating draught of cutting-edge biology." A *Publishers Weekly* contributor called the novel a "worthy follow-up" to *Revelation Space* and "an especially intelligent far-future foray."

A sequel to *Revelation Space, Redemption Ark* covers the return of the exploration ship, its dead occupants, and the investigators' efforts to discover what killed them. Only a few people know what the crew's mission was, and the investigation is complicated by the sentient weapons on the *Nostalgia for Infinity* that may threaten the existence of all life. "Told with skill and an attention to detail," ac-

cording to *Library Journal* contributor Jackie Cassada, "this space opera series belongs in most sf collections." In a review for the London *Guardian,* M. John Harrison felt that while *Revelation Ark* could do with more "humanity," it takes readers on "a turbulent, wildly entertaining ride, a kind of intellectual X-Games in which, strapped to a skateboard, you aim yourself voluntarily, feet-first, at the nearest star." In *Booklist* Roland Green concluded that "skilled narrative technique and well-developed characters make this a novel most readers will find absorbing."

The fourth book in Reynold's "Revelation Space" series, *Absolution Gap,* finds the sentient weapons known as the Inhibitors out to destroy the human race. A space abnormality known as the "Absolution Gap," which involves a planet that can disappear, is discovered and may offer the only hope to defeat the Inhibitors. Although stating that the plot moves slowly, Don D'Ammassa added in *Science Fiction Chronicle* that *Absolution Gap* "is as inventive as its predecessors, with interesting characters, well realized exotic settings, and a nicely developed sense of wonder." A *Publishers Weekly* contributor judged the series "a landmark in hard SF space opera."

The Prefect, is "a tale of one man's search for truth, however unpleasant or demanding it may be," as *Library Journal* contributor Jackie Cassada described the work. Here Tom Dreyfus is the prefect, or law enforcer, in the scattering of space nodes (living habitats) called the Glitter Band that circle Yellowstone. A sudden attack on the Glitter Band leaves 1,000 colonists dead, and now Dreyfus must get to the bottom of this violence before the colony's utopian way of life is destroyed. A *Publishers Weekly* reviewer termed *The Prefect* "a fascinating hybrid of space opera, police procedural and character study," while *Booklist* contributor Regina Schroeder praised the "magnificently imagined world" Reynolds brings to life in his fiction.

Tales of Deep Space and Far Future Time

Reynolds left the "Revelation Space" series to write *Diamond Dogs, Turquoise Days,* which contains two novellas. In "Diamond Dogs," Reynolds takes the reader to a world that is threatened with destruction from an alien artifact. Called the Blood Spire, it is a building with a maze of rooms that can only be opened by solving a complex mathematical problem; a wrong answer is lethal. The novella follows a group of mercenaries as they try to unravel the building's secrets. Writing in *MBR Bookwatch,* Harriet Klausner noted that Reynolds' "exhilarating . . . outer space caper feels more like a gothic

Best Science Fiction Novel of the Year—*Chronicle*

alastair reynolds

REDEMPTION ARK

"Reynolds confirms his place among the leaders of the hard-science space-opera renaissance."
—*Publishers Weekly* (starred review)

A sequel to *Revelation Space*, Reynolds' *Redemption Ark* is set amid a war between two competing tribes during the late twenty-sixth century. (Cover art by Chris Moore. All rights reserved. Used by permission of Penguin Group (USA) Inc.)

planetary noir with fabulous amoral mercenary antiheroes." A companion novella, "Turquoise Days," takes place in an aquatic world where semi-sentient beings rule. An evil starship crew is looking to use the Jugglers, microscopic life forms living in the seas of the planet Turquoise that can affect consciousness, to create an army of religious fanatics. D'Ammassa asserted in a review of *Diamond Dogs, Turquoise Days* that "both [novellas] are excellent adventures."

Century Rain, a stand-alone novel, was described by *Entertainment Weekly* critic Noah Robischon as a blend of "1950s pulp detective novel with a 24th-century Martian space war." Here a Parisian investigator in the distant future collides with a wormhole leading back to Earth circa the 1950s. Knowledge

from that time is vital to saving the future Earth. In *Booklist* Schroeder observed that "Reynolds blends noirish sleuthing and hard sf remarkably well," and a *Publishers Weekly* reviewer wrote that in *Century Rain* he "creates yet another quirky, noirish vision of humanity's future."

With *Pushing Ice* Reynolds "has chosen a classic space-opera plot," according to *Washington Post* contributor Sara Sklaroff. Set in 2057, the novel's action begins on a nuclear-powered mining space ship working on one of the moons of Saturn. As it turns out, however, the "moon" is actually a machine built by aliens, and as it begins to speed out of Earth's solar system, it takes the crew of the mining ship along with it. The crew, never to return to Earth, must now learn to cope in startlingly new environments and they work to establish a new society over several decades. Readers and reviewers responded positively to *Pushing Ice*, Sklaroff noting that "Reynolds crafts a devastating sense of isolation." A reviewer for *California Bookwatch* commended the "swift action and intrigue" in the novel, while *SFRevu.com* contributor John Berlyne concluded that the novel "is a marvelously satisfying unpredictable work—truly a voyage into the unknown."

Reynolds, writing on his home page, described his novel *House of Suns* as a "far-future galaxy-spanning space opera." "Six million years ago," Reynolds further explained, "at the very dawn of the starfaring era, Abigail Gentian fractured herself into a thousand male and female clones: the shatterlings." These shatterlings have seen the rise and fall of human empires for millions of years; every 200,000 years they rendezvous to share memories and exchange information. But now, at the thirty-second Gentian reunion, things go badly awry. Campion and Purslane, two of the shatterlings, bring along a strange robot, and then the clan discovers that serious enemies that are trying to destroy their line. For *Strange Horizons* reviewer Dan Hartland, *House of Suns* is a "novel of exploration—of discovery and inquiry." Petrie likewise dubbed the novel "a sweeping, audacious slice of galactic-scale intrigue and subterfuge," while Paul Kincaid, writing for the *SF Site* online deemed it "a tale of family intrigue and betrayal." Kincaid further noted: "There's enough here that is big, brash and bold to keep any space opera fan well satisfied."

In 2009 Reynolds released *Terminal World*, another science-fiction novel. Speaking with Gary Reynolds for *Concept Sci-fi* online, Reynolds described the work as "a kind of steampunk-tinged planetary romance, set in the distant future, about the last human city, a vast vertical structure called Spearpoint. The protagonist, a kind of doctor, is forced into exile, has various adventures, but must eventually return after the city suffers a terrible catastrophe. *Terminal World* is . . . probably the least Hard-SF thing I've done."

Reynolds is also the author of numerous short stories, ten of which were gathered for *Zima Blue and Other Stories*, a "solid collection," according to a *Publishers Weekly* reviewer. Reviewing the same work in *Booklist*, Schroeder noted that "Reynolds does short stories with particular flair, and this collection contains some spectacular sf storytelling." Reynolds has also written several other novella-length works, including *The Six Directions of Space*, which Schroeder termed an "impressive new space opera . . . about the Mongol Empire 999 years after the death of its founder."

If you enjoy the works of Alastair Reynolds, you may also want to check out the following books:

Vernor Vinge, *A Fire upon the Deep*, 1992.
Kevin J. Anderson's "Saga of the Seven Suns" series, including *Hidden Empire*, 2002.
Dan Simmons, *Ilium*, 2003.

Cover of *Absolution Gap*, a novel by Reynolds featuring cover art by Chris Moore. (Cover art by Chris Moore. All rights reserved. Used by permission of Penguin Group (USA) Inc.)

Though his writing has evolved over the years, Reynolds is still considered a "hard science fiction" author, a label with which he has become comfortable. In his interview for *Aberrant Dreams*, he remarked to Saylor and Dickerson: "I'm okay about being called a hard science fiction writer, but what I object to is the notion that because I am writing hard SF, I can't possibly have any wider interest in the literary world or any wider literary aspirations." He further explained, "If you are scientifically numerate—if you can put scientific ideas together in an imaginative way, and you can structure stories around them—then you have this enormously beneficial aspect to your writing. But, at the same time, it is assumed that you have a passing interest in characterization, that you are not particularly interested in prose, etc. I find I'm just as interested in prose, metaphor, character, and plot as I am in making sure that the planet goes around the right orbit."

According to Reynolds, his future writing will almost certainly incorporate some hard science fiction. "I really don't think I'm capable of doing it any other way," he told Roger Deforest for the *Hard Science Fiction* Web site. "No matter where I start with a story, they always bend into hard SF by the time I'm done with them." Still, it is Reynolds' focus on humanity, rather than technology, that sets his works apart; Jeffries remarked that the appeal of his novels is the "different human factions who use technology to transcend their biological limitations—and the political ramifications." As Reynolds told Deforest, "It's not . . . that I'm not inspired by technology so much as I'm wary of fetishizing it, which seems to be the case in so much hard SF. . . . I'm a big fan of technology in real life, certainly. I think the human condition will indeed always be more interesting than any mere gadgetry, but I'm more than willing to concede that technology may change us in profound ways—perhaps to the point where it wouldn't even make sense to think of us as human any more."

■ Biographical and Critical Sources

PERIODICALS

Booklist, April 1, 2002, John Mort, review of *Chasm City*, p. 1313; April 15, 2002, Ray Olson, review of *Chasm City*, p. 1387; June 1, 2003, Roland Green, review of *Redemption Ark*, p. 1755; June 1, 2005, Regina Schroeder, review of *Century Rain*, p. 1769; December 15, 2006, Regina Schroeder, review of *Zima Blue and Other Stories*, p. 31; June 1, 2008, Regina Schroeder, review of *The Prefect*, p. 58; December 15, 2008, Regina Schroeder, review of *The Six Directions of Space*, p. 30.

California Bookwatch, December, 2006, review of *Pushing Ice*.

Entertainment Weekly, July 8, 2005, Noah Robischon, review of *Century Rain*, p. 73.

Guardian (London, England), October 14, 2000, Jon Courtenay Grimwood, review of *Revelation Space*, p. 10; August 10, 2002, M. John Harrison, review of *Redemption Ark*, p. 21; December 20, 2003, review of *Absolution Gap*, p. 28; May 10, 2008, Eric Brown, review of *House of Sons*, p. 16; July 13, 2009, Stuart Jeffries, "'I've Been Called the High Priest of Gothic Miserablism,'" p. 10.

Kirkus Reviews, December 1, 2004, review of *Diamond Dogs, Turquoise Days*, p. 1126.

Library Bookwatch, February, 2005, review of *Diamond Dogs, Turquoise Days*.

Library Journal, April 15, 2002, Jackie Cassada, review of *Chasm City*, p. 128; May 15, 2003, Jackie Cassada, review of *Redemption Ark*, p. 131; January 1, 2005, Jackie Cassada, review of *Diamond Dogs, Turquoise Days*, p. 103; June 15, 2008, Jackie Cassada, review of *The Prefect*, p. 59.

MBR Bookwatch, January, 2005, Harriet Klausner, review of *Diamond Dogs, Turquoise Days*.

Publishers Weekly, May 28, 2001, review of *Revelation Space*, p. 55; March 11, 2002, review of *Chasm City*, p. 56; May 31, 2004, review of *Absolution Gap*, p. 56; November 29, 2004, review of *Diamond Dogs, Turquoise Days*, p. 27; May 9, 2005, review of *Century Rain*, p. 51; October 30, 2006, review of *Zima Blue and Other Stories*, p. 42; April 21, 2008, review of *The Prefect*, p. 40.

Science Fiction Chronicle, September, 2001, Don D'Ammassa, review of *Revelation Space*, p. 40; September, 2001, Don D'Ammassa, review of *Chasm City*, p. 41; May, 2003, Don D'Ammassa, review of *Absolution Gap*, p. 40; April, 2004, Don D'Ammassa, review of *Diamond Dogs, Turquoise Days*, p. 34.

Times (London, England), May 1, 2008, Lisa Tuttle, review of *House of Suns*.

Wales on Sunday, July 12, 2009, Catherine Jones, "The Appliance of the Appliance of Science," p. 30.

Washington Post, July 30, 2006, Sara Sklaroff, review of *Pushing Ice*, p. T8.

ONLINE

Aberrant Dreams Web site, http://www.hd-image.com/ (September 3, 2005), Ernest G. Saylor and Joseph W. Dickerson, interview with Reynolds.

Alastair Reynolds Home Page, http://www.alastairreynolds.com (April 13, 2009).

American Book Center Web site, http://www.abc.nl/ (March 8, 2005), interview with Reynolds.

Andromeda Speedways Inflight Magazine Online, http://www.asim.m6.net/ (June 18, 2008), Simon Petrie, review of *House of Suns*.

BBC News Online, http://news.bbc.co.uk/ (April 20, 2007), Darren Waters, "Science Fiction Thrives in Hi-Tech World."

Concatenation.org, http://www.concatenation.org/ (April 13, 2009), Tony Chester, review of *House of Suns*.

Concept Sci-fi Web site, http://www.conceptscifi.com/ (January 1, 2009), Gary Reynolds, interview with Reynolds.

Hard Science Fiction Web site, http://www.hardsciencefiction.rogerdeforest.com/ (June 29, 2006), Roger Deforest, "The Wonderful, Rational World of Alastair Reynolds."

Infinity Plus Web site, http://www.infinityplus.co.uk/ (April, 2001), Nick Gevers, "Deep Space, Deeper Revelations: An Interview with Alastair Reynolds."

SciFi.com, http://www.scifi.com/ (December, 2004), Nick Gevers, "Alastair Reynolds, Builder of the British New Space Opera, Is Busy Creating the Future One World at a Time."

SFReviews.com, http://www.sfreviews.com/ (March 8, 2005), reviews of *Redemption Ark* and *Revelation Space*.

SFRevu.com, http://www.sfrevu.com/ (April 13, 2009), John Berlyne, review of *Pushing Ice*.

SF Signal Web site, http://www.sfsignal.com/ (March 8, 2005), reviews of *Absolution Gap* and *Revelation Space*.

SF Site, http://www.sfsite.com/ (April 13, 2009), Paul Kincaid, review of *House of Suns*; Greg L. Johnson, review of *Zima Blue and Other Stories*, *Galactic North*, and *The Prefect*; Rich Horton, review of *Century Rain* and *Pushing Ice*.

Strange Horizons Web site, http://www.strangehorizons.com/ (May 12, 2008), Dan Hartland, review of *House of Suns*.

Zone Web site, http://www.zone-sf.com/ (March 8, 2005), Duncan Lawrie, interview with Reynolds.*

(Photograph by Bryan Bedder/Getty Images.)

Tim Sale

■ Personal

Born May 1, 1956, in Ithaca, NY; father a professor. *Education:* Studied art at University of Washington for two years; attended John Buscema Workshop and School of Visual Arts.

■ Addresses

Home—Southern CA.

■ Career

Artist and illustrator. Comic book penciller, inker, letterer, and cover artist; art consultant to *Heroes,* National Broadcasting Company (NBC), 2006—. Also worked variously at a fast food restaurant and a grocery store; Grey Archer Press, Seattle, WA, former illustrator.

■ Awards, Honors

Eisner Award for best limited series (with Jeph Loeb), 1998, for *Batman: The Long Halloween,* for best short story (with Matt Wagner), 1999, for "Devil's Advocate" in *Grendel: Black, White, and Red,* for best graphic album reprint (with Loeb), 1999, for *Batman: The Long Halloween,* for best penciller/inker, 1999, for both *Superman for All Seasons* and *Grendel Black, White, and Red,* and for best graphic album reprint (with Loeb), 2002, for *Batman: Dark Victory.*

■ Writings

(With Richard Starkings and John Roshell; and illustrator), *Tim Sale: Black and White,* Active Images (Los Angeles, CA), 2004, revised and expanded as *Drawing Heroes in the Backyard: Tim Sale Black and White,* Image Comics (Berkeley, CA), 2008.

Also contributor of stories to comic books, including *JSA: All Stars,* Issue 2, DC Comics (New York, NY), 2003, *Solo,* Issue 1, DC Comics, 2004, and *Tales of The Batman: Tim Sale,* DC Comics, 2009.

SKETCHBOOKS

Yeah, Baby, Active Images (Los Angeles, CA), 2005.
Pin-ups, Active Images (Los Angeles, CA), 2006.
Blues, Active Images (Los Angeles, CA), 2007.
Heroes, Villains, Babes, Active Images (Los Angeles, CA), 2008.

ILLUSTRATOR; COMIC BOOKS AND GRAPHIC NOVELS

Phil Foglio and Robert Asprin, *Myth Adventures,* (eight issues), Starblaze Graphics, 1984–1986.

Lynn Abbey and Robert Asprin, *Thieves' World* (six issues), Starblaze Graphics, 1985–1987.

Steven T. Seagle, *The Amazon* (three issues), Comico, 1985.

Matt Wagner, *Grendel* (eleven issues), Comico, 1988–1990.

Jeph Loeb, *Challengers of the Unknown* (eight issues), DC Comics (New York, NY), 1991, published in graphic-novel format as *Challengers of the Unknown Must Die*, 2004.

Sarah E. Byam, *Billi 99* (four issues), Dark Horse Comics (Milwaukie, OR), 1991, published in graphic-novel format, 2002.

James Robinson, *Batman: Legends of the Dark Knight* (three issues), DC Comics (New York, NY), 1992.

Jeph Loeb, *Batman: Haunted Knight: The Legends of the Dark Knight Halloween Special* (contains "Choices"), DC Comics (New York, NY), 1993.

Jeph Loeb, *Batman: Haunted Knight: The Legends of the Dark Knight Halloween Special* (contains "Madness"), DC Comics (New York, NY), 1994.

Brandon Choi and Jim Lee, *Deathblow* (thirteen issues), Image Comics, 1994–1995, selections published in graphic-novel format as *Deathblow: Sinners and Saints*, DC Comics (New York, NY), 1999.

Jeph Loeb, *Batman: Haunted Knight: The Legends of the Dark Knight Halloween Special* (contains "Ghosts"), DC Comics (New York, NY), 1995.

(With others) Jeph Loeb, Scot Lobdell, Howard Mackie, and Mark Waid, *X-Men: Dawn of the Age of Apocalypse*, Marvel (New York, NY), 1995.

Jeph Loeb, *Wolverine/Gambit: Victims*, (four issues), Marvel (New York, NY), 1995, published in graphic-novel format, 2002.

Jeph Loeb, *Batman: The Long Halloween* (thirteen issues), DC Comics (New York, NY), 1996–1997, published in graphic-novel format, 1998, published as *Absolute Batman: The Long Halloween*, 2007.

Matt Wagner, *Grendel: Black, White, and Red*, Dark Horse Comics (Milwaukie, OR), 1998.

Jeph Loeb, *Superman for All Seasons* (four issues), DC Comics (New York, NY), 1998, published in graphic-novel format, 1999.

Jeph Loeb, *Batman: Dark Victory* (thirteen issues), DC Comics (New York, NY), 1999–2000, published in graphic-novel format, 2000.

Jeph Loeb, *Daredevil: Yellow* (six issues), Marvel Comics (New York, NY), 2001–2002, published in graphic-novel format, 2002.

Jeph Loeb, *Spider-man: Blue* (six issues), Marvel Comics (New York, NY), 2002–2003, published in graphic-novel format, 2004.

Jeph Loeb, *Hulk: Gray* (six issues), Marvel Comics (New York, NY), 2003–2004, published in graphic-novel format, 2005.

Jeph Loeb, *Catwoman: When in Rome* (six issues), DC Comics (New York, NY), 2004–2005, published in graphic-novel format, 2005.

(With others) Jeph Loeb, Geoff Johns, Joe Kelly, Duncan Rouleau, and Marv Wolfman, *Superman: Infinite Crisis*, DC Comics (New York, NY), 2006.

Darwyn Cooke, *Superman Confidential: Kryptonite* (six issues), DC Comics (New York, NY), 2007–2008, published in graphic-novel format, 2008.

Also illustrator of comic-book series and miniseries, including *Action Comics*, *The Adventures of Superman*, *Batman: Shadow of the Bat*, *Black Hood*, *Buffy the Vampire Slayer: Tales of the Slayer*, *Conan vs. Rune*, *Dream Team*, *Excalibur*, *Grendel: Devil Child*, *Heartthrobs*, *JSA: All-Stars*, *The Matrix Comics*, *Robert E. Howard's Myth Maker*, *Solo*, *Superman*, *Total Eclipse*, *The Uncanny X-Men*, *Vampirella Monthly*, *Within Our Reach*, and *X-Men Unlimited*.

Illustrator of covers for comic-book series and miniseries, including *Batgirl*, *Batman: Turning Points*, *Detective Comics*, *Elephantmen*, *The Foot Soldiers*, *Harley Quinn*, *Kaboom*, *Living in Infamy*, *Madman Adventures*, *Queen & Country*, *Rest*, *Superboy*, and *X-Men Firsts*.

■ Sidelights

One of the comic-book industry's most renowned artists, Tim Sale has garnered praise for his stylish, expressive, and detailed illustrations. Best known for his collaborations with writer Jeph Loeb, including *Superman for All Seasons*, *Daredevil: Yellow*, and the Eisner Award-winning *Batman: The Long Halloween*, Sale has "made a name for himself by revisiting the early careers of some of comicdom's best-loved figures," according to *Comic Book Resources* contributor Russell Lissau. Additionally, Sale contributes art to the hit television series *Heroes*, which has introduced his work to a wider audience.

What is perhaps most extraordinary about Sale's success as an artist is that he works exclusively in black and white, a style necessitated by the fact that he is partially colorblind. "It isn't that I don't see color," he explained to Molly Mullen in the *Seattle Post-Intelligencer*. "I do see color . . . I [just] can't create with color; I can't play off foreground, middle ground, background. I don't have that ability." Sale's condition certainly has not hindered his career; as Owen Vaughn noted in the London *Times Online*, the illustrator has "brought his distinctive style to all of the big superheroes: Batman, Superman, Spider-man, the Hulk and Daredevil." Vaughn also lauded Sale's work with Loeb, noting that their

Tim Sale brings to life one of America's favorite super heroes in 1998's *Superman for All Seasons*. (Illustration © 1998 by DC
Comics. All rights reserved. Reproduced by permission.)

collaboration has "produced a series of critically acclaimed and award-winning books that have recaptured the joy and spirit of early comics."

An Early Interest in Art

Born in Ithaca, New York, in 1956, Sale moved with his family to Seattle, Washington, at the age of six. To keep his son amused during the cross-country drive, his father bought Sale a number of comic books, including a copy of *Spider-man*. "I learned how to read from comic books," Sale recalled to Richard Starkings in the autobiographical work *Drawing Heroes in the Backyard: Tim Sale Black and White*. "The first word I could read was 'BOOM!'" Sale also displayed a talent for drawing as a youngster, telling Starkings: "I drew a lot, but not always or compulsively . . . but then every child I know draws or paints a lot. It's just that most people stop at some point, and I never did." He further reflected, "I just never thought I wasn't an artist. Certainly by high school, it was assumed that art was how I would make a living, assumed by me, by my friends, and I suppose by my family."

Sale's interests in comics and illustration dovetailed when he was thirteen years old, during a visit to London, England, where his father was on a teaching assignment. There Sale met a young comic-book enthusiast who introduced him to the Popular Book Centers, a chain of stores that sold used U.S. comics. Sale's collection grew quickly, and when he returned to the United States, he began drawing his own comics, tracing works by Barry Windsor-Smith and other artists. The budding illustrator received undying support from his parents, especially his mother, who had studied art in college. "The main thing was she took something that I was passionate about—comics, which most of the world treated like a joke—and took it seriously, showed me a way that it fit into a history of art that was taken seriously," Sale related to Starkings. "It was important to me as an artist, and was a touchstone in my relation with my mother."

It was also around this time that Sale first fell in love with Marvel Comics, the home of writer (and future editorial director) Stan Lee, as well as of artists John Romita and Steve Ditko. "Spidey was my favorite hero growing up," Sale remarked to Lissau, adding that he had a particular fondness for issues drawn by Romita. "The soap opera of Peter Parker's life, the pretty girls and all the beginning-to-notice-each-other, does-she-like-me stuff especially. And the run of villains in those issues is rivaled only by Batman's: Kraven, the Vulture, Rhino, the

Lizard. . . ." In addition, Sale read comics featuring the Fantastic Four, Daredevil, Silver Surfer, the Avengers, and Thor. As he told Lissau, "This period, the mid- to late '60s, is my favorite period, the period where the innovations created at the beginning of the '60s were maturing, and Stan was unbelievably writing 12 titles a month and relying on the best, most innovative artists in the business who were doing the work of their lives."

After graduating from high school, Sale attended the University of Washington to study art. It was during a painting class in college that he learned he was colorblind. "I distinctly remember doing a birthday card for my sister, a Robin Hood figure in the forest, and I thought I was making him brown or sepia," he recalled to Starkings. "Well, the paint had turned. The colored ink has gone bad. And Maggie asked why is he green, and I couldn't see it. I saw it as a tan, but it was a yellowish green." Sale now executes his black-and-white comic book drawings in a traditional style, using a brush, pen, marker, and ink; the illustrations are finished by a colorist. For his tonal work, he adds gradations of grays, using ink wash or charcoal.

Sale spent two years at the University of Washington before moving to New York City, where he was accepted into the John Buscema Workshop. He studied under Buscema, Romita, and Marie Severin but returned to Seattle after just nine months, frustrated by the criticism he received and suffering from a bout of homesickness. For the next few years, Sale worked at a variety of odd jobs and completed fantasy prints and cards for Grey Archer Press, a business started by his sister. His interest in comics was rekindled after he read an interview with John Byrne, an author and artist who helped popularize *The Uncanny X-Men*, as well as by his relationship with Rod Dyke, owner of a bookstore that specialized in comics. When Dyke hosted an event with Richard and Wendy Pini of *Elfquest* fame, Sale took the opportunity to show them his work; he was hired as an inker for *Myth Adventures*, a series by Robert Aspirin and Phil Foglio. Sale described *Myth Adventures* as "my first professional work" to Starkings; he earned 500 dollars for the job, as he told Starkings.

In 1985 Sale was hired as a penciller, inker, and letterer for *Thieves' World*, a comic-book series published by Starblaze Graphics. Though the series was not a financial success, the experience proved invaluable for the artist. As he told Starkings, "I knew I still wanted to do comics and I felt more confident about my storytelling abilities. There were always three or four plotlines in each issue, and I was helping pace it and tell the story." His growing portfolio eventually drew the attention of agent Mike Friedrich, who, Sale recalled, "helped me bridge the smaller black-and-white work I'd been doing to the more mainstream work that was to come." Sale went on to illustrate such works as Matt Wagner's *Grendel* and Steven T. Seagle's *The Amazon.*

Sale and Loeb

In the late 1980s Sale attended Comic-con, an international convention where he met, among others, DC Comics editor Barbara Randall. Joining DC, the artist was paired for the first time with Loeb, a writer who had just completed his debut comic-book series, *Challengers of the Unknown,* a revival of a DC series from the 1950s. First published in 1991 and reissued in 2004 as *Challengers of the Unknown Must Die,* the work centers on a quartet of superheroes in retirement after a tragic accident, with the remaining members having assumed aliases. The arrival of a former enemy, however, forces them back into action. The comic drew praise from *Booklist* contributor Gordon Flagg, who applauded "Loeb's capacity to effectively reimagine hoary concepts and

Sale's clean art and imaginative storytelling." Understanding Loeb's vision for the work was a process of give-and-take, Sale recalled to Starkings: "Jeph was always trying to push the excitement visually—the example he gave was that he's the kind of guy that wants to put a camera on a stick and throw it through the window for an effect. He wanted to bend the form, it was a [Jim] Steranko approach to the page. I was instinctively much less experimental, and also had more of a European-influenced decision-making process about where to put the camera—my instinct was always to pull back, Jeph's was to zoom in and be in your face."

The relationship between author and artist—both personal and professional—has grown considerably in the years since, Sale noted. "We both have strong personalities, we both tend to think we're always right and we both enjoy criticizing other things, both favorably and not," the artist told Whitney Matheson in a *Pop Candy* online interview. "So there's a fun in that repartee, with an underlying sense that we both share an awful lot of core values." Sale also remarked to Vaughan that Loeb "writes full scripts for me—so I get, 'here's the page, here's the panels, here's what goes on, here's the

Sale's artwork is a feature of *Catwoman: When in Rome*, a graphic novel featuring a text by Jeph Loeb.

dialogue,' and he allows me to break it down in different ways if I feel strongly about it. But he's also writing for me. I don't know how he writes for other people, but it's very clear when I read his scripts that he's writing for me and he can only do that because we've doing it for so long."

Shortly after completing *Challengers of the Unknown*, Sale teamed with James Robinson on *Batman: Legends of the Dark Knight,* his first work featuring the Caped Crusader. "I've found joy in every character I've drawn," he related to Vaughn. "I wouldn't take on a job unless I could, but the easiest one for me to go back to, that I never really tire of, is Batman." Sale continued, "I think of myself as an expressionistic artist, a cartoonist exaggerating for effect, and there's so much that's over the top about Batman, both visually and in the melodrama of the story. I'm just drawn to this tragic figure and I like depicting him on the page."

Sale has worked on numerous "Batman" stories during his career, and his efforts with Loeb have earned particular acclaim. In *Batman: The Long Halloween* the duo created a storyline featuring mob boss Carmine "The Roman" Falcone. Batman is caught up in solving the murders of mafia crime-family members who are killed on holiday during every month of the year by a mysterious figure dubbed "Holiday." The thirteen-issue work also featured a rogues' gallery of Batman's most formidable adversaries, including the Joker, the Penguin, Two-Face, and Poison Ivy. Sale remarked in his interview with Starkings that he enjoyed the challenge of drawing such familiar villains, noting that "what was really interesting to me is to try to make each character, each icon, my own." Reviewing *Absolute Batman: The Long Halloween*, Flagg complimented "Sale's expressive illustration, with its gauntly elegant figures and attractively designed compositions."

In *Catwoman: When in Rome* Sale and Loeb joined forces with colorist Dave Stewart on a work that concerns perhaps the most enigmatic character in the "Batman" universe. Accompanied by the Riddler, the wily cat burglar attempts to steal a valuable ring from the Vatican, only to find herself engaged in nightmarish confrontations with Cheetah, Mr. Freeze, the Scarecrow, and Batman himself. According to Flagg, Sale "reaches new heights of stylishness . . . , aided by bold, moody coloring by Dave Stewart." In his interview with Starkings, Sale observed that "the cementing of my working relationship with . . . Stewart is the most valuable thing" to come out of *Catwoman: When in Rome.* "He is an amazing artist and man, the best partner in the best way as far as artist/colorist goes. He's imaginative, thoughtful, technically masterful, fast, and happy to work with me."

Sale and Loeb tackled another iconic DC character in *Superman for All Seasons.* In this work, they return to Superman's roots, portraying a young Clark Kent coming to terms with his awesome powers and the responsibilities they entail. Clark's story is told through several narrators, including his father, Lois Lane, Lex Luthor, and Lana Lang. Sale remarked to Starkings that his illustrations for this series were inspired by the paintings of Norman Rockwell, the beloved American artist: "I was much more interested in the stuff on the stoop of the farmhouse and in the cornfields than Metropolis. We could have stayed in Kansas, and I would have been happy. I wanted the contrast, but it was much more fun drawing Kansas. It took a long time but that's where I could really get into the Rockwell of it all." Yannick Belzil, reviewing the work for *11th Hour* online, noted the painter's influence, commenting that Sale's "Clark Kent/Superman is as big as a brick house, with an honest, naive face. A tremendous nod goes to his renditions of backgrounds—Clark's Smallville might've come straight out of a Norman Rockwell painting, while Metropolis truly resembles the retro-futuristic 'City of Tomorrow' that it was meant to be."

Sale has also produced a number of highly regarded comics for Marvel, including collaborations with Loeb on several modern treatments of the early years of various superheroes. Known collectively as the "color" books, *Daredevil: Yellow, Spider-man: Blue,* and *Hulk: Gray* feature ink washes by Sale and are titled after a component of the costume that each super hero wears. "Marvel was interested in us working for them," the illustrator told Joe McCabe in a *Comics Journal* online interview. "The Loeb-Sale way of doing comics, and the imprint of the team, Marvel was interested in doing stories about that," Sale added. "They said, 'What do you want to do?' We said, 'We want to tell Year One-ish stories about these characters.'"

In *Daredevil: Yellow* Sale and Loeb revisit the origins of the blind, acrobatic crimefighter whose costume, now bright red, was primarily yellow. The wash technique, Sale recalled to Starkings, "was a different way of coming at the story. How do you apply the technique to the story and keep yourself interested? It was also a way of having more control; I was sort of painting without color." In *Spider-man: Blue,* Sale and Loeb reinvent a story from the 1960s, and looks at a tragic result of Peter Parker's heroism, as his girlfriend dies shortly after a battle. "The stories that we touched on in *Spider-man: Blue* were my favourite Spider-man stories of all time," Sale told Vaughn. "Those were the stories that got me into comics." *Hulk: Gray* offers a retelling of the creature's origin, exploring the immediate effects of Bruce Banner's transformation. "Sale's art blends

The New Year.

One where the promise I made to my parents...

LOEB SALE 1996

Loeb and Sales team up to create the comic-book series published in graphic-novel format as *Batman: The Long Halloween.* (Illustration by Tim Sale. © 1998 by DC Comics. All rights reserved. Reproduced by permission.)

caricature and realism, explosive action and ominous mood," a contributor in *Publishers Weekly* stated. "I continue to be amused by the act of drawing the Hulk and inspired by . . . the act of drawing Batman," Sale told Starkings. "Both can so easily be manipulated visually to be expressions of the emotion of each scene."

Joins the World of Television

In 2006 Sale was invited by *Heroes* creator Tim Kring, a friend of Loeb's, to contribute artwork to Kring's television series. Sale works on the paintings that are displayed in the studio of Isaac Mendez, a prophetic artist; he produces the black, white, and gray originals on paper, and these are then scanned into a computer and colored by Stewart. Those images are later enlarged and printed on canvas by members of the show's prop department. Sale also creates panels for the *9th Wonders* comic book that helps drive the plot. "In reading the script for the pilot, I distinctly remember feeling how much fun I was having, how much it was telling the kinds of stories that I enjoyed, and how cool a comic book it would make," he remarked in a *Newsarama.com* interview with Zack Smith. "I thought it was terrific. It's the nature of these things for there to be a lot of changes from script to film, but Tim's tone and interest and talent remained constant throughout."

After more than twenty years in the comic-book industry, Sale has achieved a rare measure of success. Still, he is not content to rest on his laurels. As he mentioned in his interview with Starkings, "I'm hopefully trying to grow and do things a little differently, more assuredly, but still looking to figure things out. I rarely look at my pencils and think that it looks assured. I'm more confident in my inking." He further noted, "I'm always trying to do something different, to change the technique a little bit, so that we have a different look to each book."

If you enjoy the works of Tim Sale, you may also want to check out the following:

The work of N.C. Wyeth, Beatrix Potter, and E.H. Shepard, who influenced Sale.
The fantasy art of Barry Windsor-Smith and the fashion illustrations of René Gruau.
The work of comic-book artists Neal Adams, John Romita, and Bruce Timm.

Asked about his plans for the future, Sale remarked that, while he is open to new ventures, comic books will always remain his first love. "I'd never leave comics altogether, no," he told Smith. "I love comics too much. And I would never want to only do one thing. That's part of my personality, I move on. It's why I can't do a regular comic book series. I get bored." Sale concluded, "There may be a point when I'm doing something else for a while, but I imagine if that happens, I'll always want to come back to comics at some point. I just dig the medium too much."

■ Biographical and Critical Sources

BOOKS

Sale, Tim, Richard Starkings, and John Roshell, *Tim Sale: Black and White*, Active Images (Los Angeles, CA), 2004, revised and expanded as *Drawing Heroes in the Backyard: Tim Sale Black and White*, Image Comics (Berkeley, CA), 2008.

PERIODICALS

Booklist, December 1, 2004, Gordon Flagg, review of *Challengers of the Unknown Must Die*, p. 643; December 15, 2005, Gordon Flagg, review of *Catwoman: When in Rome*, p. 32; July 1, 2007, Gordon Flagg, *Absolute Batman: The Long Halloween*, p. 46; November 15, 2008, Gordon Flagg, review of *Superman Confidential: Kryptonite*, p. 25.

New York Post, November 26, 2006, "Comic Hiro—How TV's Coolest Show Jumped off the Page," p. 1.

Publishers Weekly, May 19, 2003, review of *Billi 99*, p. 55; August 9, 2004, review of *Hulk: Gray*, p. 234.

School Library Journal, May, 2003, Jody Sharp, review of *Billi 99*, p. 181; July, 2004, Steve Weiner, "The Superhero Next Door," review of *Spider-man: Blue*, p. 21; May, 2006, Andrea Lipinski, review of *Catwoman: When in Rome*, p. 163.

Seattle Post-Intelligencer, July 19, 2008, Molly Mullen, "A Moment with Tim Sale, Comic Book Artist," p. C1.

Voice of Youth Advocates, October, 2008, Snow Wildsmith, review of *Drawing Heroes in the Backyard: Tim Sale Black and White*, p. 364.

Sale rounds out his pantheon of American comic-book super heroes by illustrating Loeb's *Spider-man: Blue.* (Illustration by Tim Sale © 2002 and 2008 by Marvel Characters, Inc. All rights reserved. Reproduced by permission.)

Sale's art brings to life Loeb's original story in *Challengers of the Unknown Must Die.* (Illustration by Tim Sale © 2004 by DC Comics. All rights reserved. Reproduced by permission.)

ONLINE

Comic Book Database, http://www.comicbookdb. com/ (June 1, 2009), "Tim Sale."

Comic Book Resources Web site, http://www. comicbookresources.com/ (May 20, 2002), Russell Lissau, "Feeling 'Blue': Talking with Tim Sale."

Comics Journal Online, http://www.tcj.com/ (July, 2008), Joe McCabe, "Yellow, Gray, Blue: The Tim Sale Interview."

11th Hour Web site, http://www.the11thhour.com/ (February, 2000), Yannick Belzil, reviews of *Batman: The Long Halloween* and *Superman for All Seasons.*

Newsarama.com, http://www.newsarama.com/ (November 14, 2006), Zack Smith, "Talking *Heroes* and Comics with Tim Sale."

Pop Candy Web log, http://blogs.usatoday.com/ popcandy/ (March 28, 2008), Whitney Matheson, "A Q&A with Tim Sale."

Times Online, http://entertainment.timesonline.co. uk/ (March 6, 2009), Owen Vaughn, "*Heroes* Artist Tim Sale on the True Colour of Batman and Spider-man."

Tim Sale Home Page, http://www.timsale1.com (June 1, 2009).*

Charles Stross

■ Personal

Born October 18, 1964, in Leeds, Yorkshire, England; married Feorag NicBhride, 2003. *Education:* College degree (pharmacy). *Hobbies and other interests:* Music.

■ Addresses

Home—Edinburgh, Scotland. *E-mail*—charles@pop3. demon.co.uk.

■ Career

Fiction writer and computer programmer. Datacash, senior programmer until 1999; FMA, Ltd. (Web site consultants), senior programmer. Also worked as a pharmacist.

■ Awards, Honors

Hugo Award nomination, 2002, for novelette "Lobsters," 2003, for novelette "Halo," 2004, for *Singularity Sky*, 2005, for *Iron Sunrise*, 2006, for *Accelerando*, 2007, for *Glasshouse*, 2008, for *Halting State*, and 2009, for *Saturn's Children;* British Science Fiction Award nomination, 2005, and Arthur C. Clarke Award nominee, 2006, both for *Accelerando;* Prometheus Award nomination, 2006, for *The Hidden Family;* Sidewise Award in long-form category, 2007, for *The Family Trade, The Hidden Family,* and *The Clan Corporate;* Locus Award for best novella, 2007, for *Missile Gap;* Prometheus Award, 2007, for *Glasshouse;* Edward E. Smith Memorial Award for Imaginative Fiction (Skylark Award), New England Science-Fiction Association, 2008.

■ Writings

"SINGULARITY SKY" NOVEL SERIES

Singularity Sky, Penguin Putnam (New York, NY), 2003.
Iron Sunrise, Ace Books (New York, NY), 2004.

"MERCHANT PRINCES" NOVEL SERIES

The Family Trade, Tor (New York, NY), 2004.
The Hidden Family, Tor (New York, NY), 2005.
The Clan Corporate, Tor (New York, NY), 2006.
The Merchant's War, Tor (New York, NY), 2007.
The Revolution Business, Tor (New York, NY), 2009.

NOVELS

The Atrocity Archives, introduction by Ken MacLeod, Golden Gryphon Press (Urbana, IL), 2004.

Accelerando, Ace Books (New York, NY), 2005.

Glasshouse, Ace Books (New York, NY), 2006.

The Jennifer Morgue, Golden Gryphon Press (Urbana, IL), 2006.

Missile Gap, Subterranean Press (Burton, MI), 2006.

On Her Majesty's Occult Service (includes *The Atrocity Archives* and *The Jennifer Morgue*), Science Fiction Book Club (Mechanicsburg, PA), 2007.

Halting State, Ace Books (New York, NY), 2007.

Saturn's Children: A Space Opera, Ace Books (New York, NY), 2008.

OTHER

Approaching Xanadu (chapbook), Back Brain Recluse (Sheffield, England), 1989.

The Web Architect's Handbook, Addison-Wesley (Reading, MA), 1996.

Toast and Other Rusted Futures (short stories), Cosmos/Wildside, 2002.

Festival of Fools (chapbook), Ace Books (New York, NY), 2003.

Wireless (short stories), Ace Books (New York, NY), 2009.

Author of novelettes, including "Lobsters" and "Halo." Author of nonfiction books, including *SCO OpenServer Operating System User's Guide.* Columnist for *Linux Format* and *Computer Shopper.* Contributor of short stories and articles to science-fiction magazines and computer journals, including *Asimov's, Interzone, New Worlds,* and *PC Plus;* contributor of stories and novelettes to numerous anthologies.

■ Sidelights

A prolific author of speculative and science-based fiction, Charles Stross is part of a generation of British writers that focuses on technical detail and accuracy in terms of scientific information. Among his best-known titles in the "hard" science-fiction genre are the novels *Accelerando* and *Glasshouse.* Writing on the Infinity Plus Web site, Lou Anders remarked that Stross imbues his works "with a startlingly sharp level of insight into current geo-political trends, and his words are informed by a deeply embedded knowledge of the current technological landscape. The result is . . . a brand new and unique speculative voice, charting new territories far in advance of any other writer of hard SF."

Stross also adopts the style of science fiction known as space opera in his "Singularity Sky" series as well as his novel *Saturn's Children: A Space Opera.* Additionally, Stross has written horror in the H.P. Lovecraft vein, blending humorous touches into *The Atrocity Archive* and *The Jennifer Morgue,* and turns to fantasy in his "Merchant Princes" novel series. A former computer maven and information technology specialist, Stross is an advocate of the "commons" concept for the Internet, which involves sharing intellectual property. To that end, he makes many of his works available online as electronic books or downloads. Stross boasts a wide readership that includes Nobel Laureate economist Paul Krugman, who mentioned his status as a fan of Stross's work on his blog *Conscience of a Liberal.*

Writing in the London *Guardian Online,* Damian G. Walter noted of Stross's work: "The rapid normalisation of the technologies which are changing

Cover of British writer Charles Stross's novel *Iron Sunrise,* featuring artwork by Danilo Ducak. (Cover art by Danilo Ducak. All rights reserved. Used by permission of Penguin Group (USA) Inc.)

people's lives is a recurrent theme in his fiction. Despite their hard-edged technological focus, Stross's worlds are often as quotidian as they are fantastic. . . . He has always made a point of working in as many of science fiction's diverse subgenres as possible, resisting the pressures . . . to repeat a formula." Stross explained to Walter, "'Many science fiction writers are literary autodidacts who focus on the genre primarily as a literature of ideas, rather than as a pure art form or a tool for the introspective examination of the human condition.'" Stross further commented, "'I'm not entirely at ease with that self-description.'"

A Dot-com Casualty

Stross was born in Leeds, England, in 1964, and earned a degree in pharmaceuticals before shifting his career to information technology in cyber banking. Meanwhile, he also began a career as a writer, publishing articles on role-playing games and computing. He published his first short story in 1987 and thereafter wrote thousands of words annually in the short-story genre while still working full time in information technology. When things became excessively stressful with his job at Datacash, an online credit card payment company, Stross quit and turned to freelance writing. After several years publishing short stories and nonfiction works, he released his first novel, *Singularity Sky,*.

Singularity Sky is set far in the future, after a technical and social evolution is triggered by the Eschaton, a godlike being. Now a repressive colony has come under attack by a technological plague. Although a rescue mission is sent from Earth to the colony, the motives of its leaders seem unclear. A contributor to *Publishers Weekly* described *Singularity Sky* as "an energetic and sometimes satiric mix of cutting-edge nanotechnology, old-fashioned space opera, and leftist political commentary." Rick Kleffel, writing for the *Agony Column* online, noted that, "as a reading experience it veers between hilariously absurd, surprisingly accessible and even touchingly poignant." Writing on the *SF Site*, Alma A. Hromic stated that *Singularity Sky* "is at once a story that's deceptively simple . . . and deeply complex in a sort of cerebrally witty way."

In the sequel, *Iron Sunrise,* the space colony of New Moscow sends out a slower-than-light counterstrike against its trade rival, New Dresden, just before being destroyed. The Earth Central Government knows that New Dresden was manipulated into the conflict; now it is having great difficulty obtaining access codes to stop the counterstrike from

In *Singularity Sky* Stross takes readers to a near future where artificial intelligence and travel at faster than light speed change everything. (Cover art by Danilo Ducak. All rights reserved. Used by permission of Penguin Group (USA) Inc.)

occurring. A contributor to *Publishers Weekly* mentioned that Stross "skillfully balances suspense and humor throughout" the novel. In a *Booklist* review, Hays noticed improvement over the first novel, particularly "better characterizations and entertaining technological inventiveness."

"Merchant Princes"

In the first book in Stross's "Merchant Princes" series, *The Family Trade,* investigative reporter Miriam Beckstein finds herself transported to the kingdom of Gruinmarkt through a locket her mother gave her. The kingdom, populated by mounted knights armed with automatic weapons, is at war with itself, each faction headed by six princes. Beckstein becomes involved in the feuding when she learns of her own personal connection to the situation. Roland Green, writing in *Booklist*, called *The Family Trade* "a solid page-turner and an uncommonly promising series launcher." Kleffel stated that "Stross has created a very satisfying character and set-up" using just "the right mixture to appeal to a wide variety of readers."

The Hidden Family, the second "Merchant Princes" novel, finds Miriam—now Countess Helge Thorold-Hjorth—a member of the "hidden family." Her mafia-like family, the Clan, however, begins to get suspicious at her business methods as she attempts to uncover who is trying to kill her. A contributor to *Publishers Weekly* wrote that "Stross continues to mix high and low tech in amusing and surprising ways," while Green concluded in *Booklist*: "Laugh your way to an ending that clearly promises further enjoyable volumes." Greg L. Johnson, writing on *SFSite.com*, called *The Hidden Family* a novel "for people who know, understand, and love science fiction."

In *The Clan Corporate* the ante is increased for Miriam. Now it appears that the Clan is holding her mother hostage in an attempt to get Miriam to arrange a political marriage. At the same time, Miriam's one-time boyfriend, now working for Homeland Security, has infiltrated her alternate world and finds that the Clan have laid a series of nuclear bombs in our own world. A *Publishers Weekly* contributor praised the series addition, noting that *The Clan Corporate* "gallops along to a cliffhanger ending that will leave readers eagerly awaiting future installments." Similarly, Green concluded that "readers [will be] hoping for more than the three volumes" Stross thus far provided.

The "Merchant Princes" saga continues in *The Merchants' War*, as the alternate world Miriam now occupies devolves into war after an attack at the announcement of her engagement to Prince Creon of Gruinmarkt. The prince survives the bombing attack following the engagement, and his followers rally against the Clan in this "fourth successive thriller in a fantastically thrilling series," as *Booklist* contributor Frieda Murray noted. Further praise came from a *Publishers Weekly* reviewer who concluded: "For sheer inventiveness and energy, this cliffhanger-riddled serial remains difficult to top." Stross has carried his series forward, producing a fifth installment, *The Revolution Business*.

Stand Alone Novels

Stross's novel *Accelerando* is taken from a number of previously published short stories. In it he covers three generations of the Macx family from the early twenty-first century to a world of transhumans of the outer solar system nearly half a century later. Hays wrote in *Booklist* that Stross's "brilliant and panoramic vision of uncontrollably accelerating technology vaults him into the front rank of [science-fiction] trailblazers," while in *Library Journal* Jackie Cassada mentioned that the author "fuses ideas and characters with cheerful abandon." A critic writing in *Kirkus Reviews* commented that "Stross spins this generational saga with great wit and energy," making *Accelerando* "cutting-edge science fiction."

Glasshouse is set in the same future as *Accelerando* but takes place after the war. Robin, a former soldier, has had his mind erased of wartime memories. Still pursued by his enemies, however, he volunteers to enter the Glasshouse, a reality simulation that mimics life on Earth from 1950 to 2050. While getting used to living as a woman in the Glasshouse, Robin's erased memory slowly starts to return and he finds himself surrounded by former spies and soldiers. In a *Booklist* review, Hays applauded the blending of "suspenseful action with inventive, futuristic technology" in *Glasshouse*. A *Publishers Weekly* contributor noted that the author's "wry SF thriller satisfies on all levels, with memorable characters and enough brain-twisting extrapolation for five novels." Writing in the *New York Times Book Review*, Dave Itzkoff commented, "Stross is peerless at dreaming up devices that could conceivably exist in 6, 60 or 600 years' time, but what concerns him more in *Glasshouse* is how such innovations might be abused."

Stross also takes readers on a sci-fi adventure in the novels *The Atrocity Archives* and *The Jennifer Morgue*. In the former, Bob Howard is an official hacker for a British agency tasked with fighting off alien invasions via space-time incursions. His agency, the Laundry, ultimately promotes Bob to field agent, whereupon he enters a time portal in Amsterdam to battle an enemy ready to invade planet Earth. With *The Atrocity Archives*, "Stross's genius lies in devoting fully as much time to the bureaucratic shenanigans of the Laundry as he does to its thaumaturgic mission," maintained *Washington Post* contributor Paul Di Filippo. Writing on the New England Science-Fiction Association Web site, Mark L. Olson called *The Atrocity Archives* "a good, solid piece of SF based on Lovecraftian horror. It's quite an accomplishment." Focusing on the lighter aspects of the same work, *SFSite.com* reviewer Rich Horton called it "a very breezy, fun, and imaginative novel."

"*Accelerando* is to cyberpunk what Napster was to the music industry: volatile, visionary, a bit flawed, and a lot of fun."
—*Entertainment Weekly*

Stross expanded a popular short story into his acclaimed science-fiction novel *Accelerando*. (Cover art by Digital Vision/Getty Images. All rights reserved. Used by permission of Penguin Group (USA) Inc.)

Howard goes into action again in *The Jennifer Morgue*. Here he and other members of the Laundry attempt to thwart the ambitions of a billionaire hoping to find a magical device that permits communication with the dead. Such an endeavor could raise the ire of the Great Old Ones and bring about universal destruction. *California Bookwatch* reviewer Diane C. Donovan found *The Jennifer Morgue* a "gripping saga," and a *Publishers Weekly* reviewer termed Stross's novel an "alternately chilling and hilarious sequel" to *The Atrocity Archives*.

In *Missile Gap* Stross posits an alternate history of the cold war of the mid-twentieth century. In the work, the United States and the Soviet Union

engage in battle, not on Earth, but on the upper skin of the planet, which has been peeled off and laid out flat on an enormous disc by an alien power. Writing in *Booklist*, Hays termed Stross's novel a "mind-bending, intriguing yarn." A *Publishers Weekly* reviewer further positively commented on the "clear, chilly and fashionably cynical style that lets Stross get away with premises that would be absurdly cheesy in anyone else's hands."

In *Halting State* Stross treats readers to a "brilliantly conceived techno-crime thriller," according to a *Publishers Weekly* reviewer. Set in 2012, the novel features a world in which China, Europe, and India are fighting for global economic prowess, while the United States has crumbled into economic ruins. Meanwhile, in Scotland, an unlikely team tries to get to the bottom of a massive theft scheme against the global Hayek Associates. A *Publishers Weekly* contributor found this "a deeply immersive story," while *Booklist* reviewer Hays observed that "Stross again displays his genius for envisioning a complex future society that appears all too inevitable." *Entertainment Weekly* contributor Adrienne Day also had a high assessment of *Halting State*, praising the book's "richly drawn characters, imaginative use of virtual and enhanced reality, and . . . genuine plot surprises."

In *Saturn's Children: A Space Opera* Stross produced an "erotic futuristic thriller," according to a *Publishers Weekly* contributor. The novel takes place in a far-future world inhabited by androids divided into an upper class, known as "aristos," and a lower class, most of whom are enslaved and function as sexual servants. A *Publishers Weekly* contributor acknowledged that the author "has a deep message of how android slavery recapitulates humanity's past mistakes," but felt that such a message was blurred by too much sex and action. Much higher praise came from Hays, who wrote in *Booklist* that "Stross takes a plot device common to mystery novels and turns it into one of the most stylishly imaginative robot tales ever penned." *Magazine of Fantasy and Science Fiction* reviewer Chris Moriarty also had praise for *Saturn's Children*, noting that it is, "first and foremost, a romp." Moriarty further commented: "Stross, being Stross, comes down pretty strongly on the side of flamboyant individuality—complete with his characteristic open source optimism about the ability of individuals to reboot their lives and reshape their destinies."

The depth and variety of Stross's writings can be traced, in part, to his tremendous curiosity. "I'm a bit of an information junkie: I read widely for sense-of-wonder, and don't confine myself to the SF field to get the kick," he told Anders in his Infinity Plus online interview. "If you follow coverage in non-technical science magazines like *New Scientist* or *Scientific American* you can pick up interesting leads on stuff that is attracting a current-day buzz; some of this stuff has implications far beyond what makes it into those magazines, implications that go all the way into paradigm-shift this-is-the-new-revolution territory."

Speaking to Anders, Stross speculated on the development of the science fiction genre in an age of vast technological change, stating, "SF writers tend to take what they see and project it on the future. That being the case, when new things come into view the future they project may show startling similarities and look different from whatever was in sight before." He added, "SF writers have been

If you enjoy the works of Charles Stross, you may also want to check out the following books:

Neal Stephenson, *Snow Crash*, 1992.
Eric Flint, *1632*, 2000.
Robert Charles Wilson, *Spin*, 2005.

outliving their prognostications for decades. That doesn't make things any less interesting, because the core study of any branch of fiction is people."

Cover of Stross's 2006 novel *The Hidden Family*, a "Merchant Princes" installment featuring artwork by **Paul Youll.** (Tor Books, 2006. Cover art by Paul Youll. Reproduced by permission.)

■ **Biographical and Critical Sources**

PERIODICALS

Booklist, August 1, 2003, Roland Green, review of *Singularity Sky,* p. 1969; July 1, 2004, Carl Hays, review of *Iron Sunrise,* p. 1829; November 15, 2004, Roland Green, review of *The Family Trade,* p. 572; June 1, 2005, Roland Green, review of *The Hidden Family,* p. 1769, and Carl Hays, review of *Accelerando,* p. 1911; May 1, 2006, Roland Green, review of *The Clan Corporate,* p. 77; June 1, 2006, Carl Hays, review of *Glasshouse,* p. 50; September 15, 2006, Carl Hays, review of *Missile Gap,* p. 35; September 15, 2007, Carl Hays, review of *Halting State,* p. 52; October 1, 2007, review of Frieda Murray, *The Merchants' War,* p. 41; July 1, 2008, Carl Hays, review of *Saturn's Children: A Space Opera,* p. 49.

California Bookwatch, November, 2006, review of *Glasshouse;* March, 2007, Diane C. Donovan, review of *The Jennifer Morgue.*

Entertainment Weekly, June 30, 2006, Neil Drumming, review of *Glasshouse,* p. 167; October 26, 2007, review of *Halting State,* p. 71.

Kirkus Reviews, June 1, 2005, review of *Accelerando,* p. 618; May 15, 2006, review of *Glasshouse,* p. 502.

Library Journal, July 1, 2003, Jackie Cassada, review of *Singularity Sky,* p. 132; May 15, 2004, Jackie Cassada, review of *The Atrocity Archives,* p. 119; July 1, 2004, Jackie Cassada, review of *Iron Sunrise,* p. 75; November 15, 2004, Jackie Cassada, review of *The Family Trade,* p. 54; July 1, 2005, Jackie Cassada, review of *Accelerando,* p. 73; June 15, 2006, Jackie Cassada, review of *Glasshouse,* p. 63.

Locus, September, 2002, Jonathan Strahan, review of *Toast and Other Rusted Futures,* pp. 29, 31.

Magazine of Science Fiction and Fantasy, January, 2009, Chris Moriarty, review of *Saturn's Children*, p. 47.

New York Times Book Review, July 9, 2006, Dave Itzkoff, review of *Glasshouse*, p. 20.

Publishers Weekly, July 7, 2003, review of *Singularity Sky*, p. 57; April 26, 2004, review of *The Atrocity Archives*, p. 46; June 28, 2004, review of *Iron Sunrise*, p. 35; November 8, 2004, review of *The Family Trade*, p. 40; April 25, 2005, review of *The Hidden Family*, p. 43; June 13, 2005, review of *Accelerando*, p. 37; March 20, 2006, review of *The Clan Corporate*, p. 41; April 24, 2006, review of *Toast and Other Rusted Futures*, p. 43; May 8, 2006, review of *Glasshouse*, p. 50; September 18, 2006, review of *Missile Gap*, p. 40; November 6, 2006, review of *The Jennifer Morgue*, p. 40; August 13, 2007, review of *Halting State*, p. 48; August 27, 2007, review of *The Merchant's War*, p. 65; May 12, 2008, review of *Saturn's Children*, p. 41.

Socialist Review, November, 2005, Martin Empson, interview with Stross.

Washington Post, July 11, 2004, Paul Di Filippo, review of *The Atrocity Archives*, p. T10.

ONLINE

Agony Column Web site, http://www.trashotron.com/agony/ (June 14, 2007), Rick Kleffel, reviews of *Singularity Sky*, *Accelerando*, *Missile Gap*, *Iron Sunrise*, *The Family Trade*, and *The Atrocity Archives*.

BBC News online, http://news.bbc.co.uk/ (July 10, 2007), "The Tech Lab: Charles Stross."

Charles Stross Home Page, http://www.antipope.org (April 13, 2009).

Charles Stross Web log, http://www.accelerando.org/ (April 13, 2009).

Conscience of a Liberal Web site, http://krugman.blogs.nytimes.com/ (January 27, 2009), Paul Krugman, "Charles Stross Seminar."

Guardian Online, http://www.guardian.co.uk/ (June 9, 2008), Damian G. Walter, "Tomorrow's Everyday."

Infinity Plus Web site, http://www.infinityplus.co.uk/ (January 8, 2003), Lou Anders, "New Directions: Decoding the Imagination of Charles Stross" (author interview).

Internet Review of Science Fiction, http://www.irosf.com/ (December 1, 2008), Robert Bee, review of *Saturn's Children*.

Locus Online, http://www.locusmag.com/ (April 13, 2009), "Charles Stross Interview Excerpts."

New England Science Fiction Association Web site, http://www.nesfa.org/ (April 13, 2009), Mark L. Olson, review of *The Atrocity Archives*.

New Scientist Online, http://www.newscientist.com/ (November 12, 2008), Jeff Hecht, review of *Saturn's Children*.

Salon.com, http://www.salon.com/ (June 6, 2005), Andrew Leonard, review of *The Hidden Family*.

SciFi.com, http://www.scifi.com/ (June 14, 2007), profile of Stross.

SFReviews.net, http://www.sfreviews.net/ (April 13, 2009), review of *Halting State*.

SFSite.com, http://www.sfsite.com/ (June 14, 2007), Stuart Carter, reviews of *The Jennifer Morgue* and *Missile Gap*; Greg L. Johnson, reviews of *The Hidden Family* and *Accelerando*; Rich Horton, review of *The Atrocity Archives*; Alma A. Hromic, review of *Singularity Sky*; (April 13, 2009), Rich Horton, review of *The Clan Corporate*; Peter D. Tillman, review of *Glasshouse*;

Strange Horizons Web site, http://www.strangehorizons.com/ (June 14, 2007), L. Timmel DuChamp, review of *Glasshouse*; (March 12, 2008), David V. Barrett, review of *Halting State*.

Whatever Web log, http://whatever.scalzi.com/ (September 2, 2007), John Scalzi, "A Month of Writers, Day Two: Charles Stross."

Zone Web site, http://www.zone-sf.com/ (April 13, 2009), Jonathan McCalmont, review of *The Family Trade*.*

Erich von Stroheim

(The Kobal Collection/The Picture Desk, Inc.)

■ Personal

Born Erich Oswald Stroheim, September 22, 1885, in Vienna, Austria; son of Benno (a hat merchant) and Johanna Stroheim; died of cancer May 12, 1957, in Maurepas, France; immigrated to United States, 1909, naturalized citizen, 1926; married Margaret Knox, February 19, 1913 (separated, 1914; died, 1915); married Mae Jones (a seamstress and dressmaker), 1916 (divorced, 1918); married Valerie Germonprez, October 15, 1920 (separated); partner of Denise Vernac, beginning 1939; children: (second marriage) Erich, Jr.; (third marriage) Josef. *Education:* Attended Grazer Handelsakademie (Graz, Austria), 1901-03.

■ Career

Film director, actor, and writer. Simpson-Crawford (department store), New York, NY, gift wrapper; Max Grab Fashion Company, traveling salesman; worked at West Point Inn, CA, 1912; also worked as travel agent and railway worker until 1914; actor, assistant, and military adviser to film director D.W. Griffith, 1914-15; assistant director, military adviser, and set designer to director John Emerson, 1915-17; film director, beginning 1918.

Actor in films, including: (uncredited) *The Birth of a Nation*, 1915; (as Lutz) *Old Heidelberg*, 1915; *Ghosts*, 1915; (as officer on horseback) *Captain Macklin*, 1915; *Farewell to Thee*, 1915; *The Failure*, 1915; (as Gangster) *His Picture in the Papers*, 1916; (as Accomplice) *The Flying Torpedo*, 1916; *Macbeth*, 1916; (as Pharisee and other roles) *Intolerance*, 1916; (as The Buzzard) *The Social Secretary*, 1916; *Less than the Dust*, 1916; *Sylvia of the Secret Service*, 1917; (as Lieutenant) *Panthea*, 1917; (as Russian officer) *In Again, Out Again*, 1917; (as Prussian officer) *For France*, 1917; *Draft 258*, 1917; (as Prince Badinoff's aide) *Reaching for the Moon*, 1917; (as Eric von Eberhard) *The Heart of Humanity*, 1918; (as German officer) *The Unbeliever*, 1918; (as Von Bickel) *The Hun Within*, 1918; (as Lieutenant von Steuben) *Blind Husbands*, 1919; (as Count Wladislas Serge Karamzin) *Foolish Wives*, 1922; (as celebrity) *Souls for Sale*, 1923; (as Prince Nicki von Wildeliebe-Rauffenburg) *The Wedding March*, 1928; (in title role) *The Great Gabbo*, 1929; (as Valdar/Schiller Blecher) *Three Faces East*, 1930; (as Victor Sangrito) *Friends and Lovers*, 1931; (as Artur von Furst) *The Lost Squadron*, 1932; (as Karl Salter) *As You Desire Me*, 1932; (as Hauptmann Oswald Von Traunsee) *Fugitive Road*, 1934; (as Wolters) *Crimson Romance*, 1934; (as Dr. Andre Crespi) *The Crime of Dr. Crespi*, 1936; (as Colonel Mathesius) *Mademoiselle Docteur*, 1937; (as Colonel Mathesius) *Under Secret Orders*, 1937; (as Tschou-Kin) *Les pirates du Rail*, 1937; *Marthe Richard*, 1937; (as Captain von Rauffenstein) *La Grande Illusion*, 1937; (as Denis) *L'affaire Lafarge*, 1937; (as Winckler) *L'alibi*, 1937; (as Marson) *Gibraltar*, 1938; (as Walter) *Les disparus de Saint-Agil*, 1938; (as Emile Lasser) *La revolte des vivants*, 1939; *Paris—New York*, 1939; (as Kohrlick) *Tempete*, 1939; (as

Pears) *Pieges,* 1939; *Le monde tremblera,* 1939; (as Hoffman) *Menaces,* 1939; (as Werner von Krale) *Macao, l'enfer du Jeu,* 1939; (as Andre Desormeaux) *I Was an Adventuress,* 1939; (as Eric) *Derriere la façade,* 1939; (as General Simovic) *Ultimatum,* 1940; (as Captain Stanley Wells) *Rappel Immediat,* 1940; (as Brenner) *So Ends Our Night,* United Artists, 1941; (as Dr. Otto Von Harden) *The North Star,* 1943; (as Field Marshal Erwin Rommel) *Five Graves to Cairo,* 1943; (as Deresco) *Storm over Lisbon,* 1944; (as Professor Franz Mueller) *The Lady and the Monster,* 1944; (as Carl Hoffmeyer) *Scotland Yard Investigator,* 1945; (in title role) *The Great Flamarion,* 1945; (as Edgar) *La danse de mort,* 1946; (as Eric von Berg) *On ne meurt pas comme ça,* 1946; (as Diijon) *The Mask of Diijon,* 1946; *La foire aux chimeres,* 1946; *La prigioniera dell'Isola,* 1947; *Le signal rouge,* 1948; *Portrait d'un assassin,* 1949; (as Werner Krali) *Mask of Korea,* 1950; (as Max Von Mayerling) *Sunset Boulevard,* 1950; (as Jacob ten Brinken) *Alraune,* 1952; (as Professeur Kieffer) *Minuit . . . quai de Bercy,* 1953; (as William O'Hara) *L'envers du paradis,* 1953; (as Conrad Nagel) *Alerte au sud,* 1953; *La madone des Sleepings,* 1955; (as Sacha Zavaroff) *Serie noire,* 1955; and (as Ludwig van Beethoven) *Napoleon,* 1955. Actor on stage, including in touring production of *Arsenic and Old Lace,* c. 1940s.

Director of films, including: (and art director and editor) *Blind Husbands* 1919; (and art director) *The Devil's Passkey,* 1920; (with Rupert Julian; and art director costume designer) *Merry-Go-Round,* 1922; (and art director and costume designer) *Foolish Wives,* 1922; (and producer, art director, and costume designer) *The Merry Widow,* 1925; (and art director and editor) *Greed,* 1925; *The Honeymoon,* 1928; (and art director, costume designer, and editor) *The Wedding March,* 1928; *The Great Gabbo,* 1929; (and art director, with others) *Queen Kelly,* 1929; and *Hello, Sister,* 1933. Other film work includes: costume designer, *Ghosts,* 1915; technical director, *Old Heidelberg,* 1915, and *Blind Man's Luck,* 1917; assistant director, *His Picture in the Papers,* 1916, *Macbeth,* 1916, *Intolerance,* 1916, *The Social Secretary,* 1916, *Less than the Dust,* 1916, *Sylvia of the Secret Service,* 1917, *Panthea,* 1917, (and art director) *In Again, Out Again,* 1917, and *The Heart of Humanity* 1918. Sometimes credited as Count von Stroheim, Erich O.H. von Stroheim, and Karl von Stroheim. *Military service:* Served in Austro-Hungarian Royal-Imperial Army, 1906-07; attained rank of corporal.

■ Awards, Honors

Academy Award nomination for Best Supporting Actor, 1950, for *Sunset Boulevard;* Certificate of Merit for Services to Film, British Academy of Film and Television Arts, 1954; awarded French Legion of Honor, 1957.

■ Writings

SCREENPLAYS

(And director) *Blind Husbands,* Universal, 1919.

(And director) *The Devil's Passkey,* Universal/Jewel, 1919.

(And director) *Foolish Wives,* Universal, 1921.

(And director) *Merry-Go-Round,* Metro-Goldwyn-Mayer, 1922.

(And director) *Greed* (based on the novel *McTeague* by Frank Norris; produced by Metro-Goldwyn-Mayer, 1924, restored version, Turner Classic Movies, 1999), Cinematheque Royale de Belgique, (Brussels, Belgium), 1958.

(And director) *The Merry Widow,* Metro-Goldwyn-Mayer, 1925.

(And director) *The Wedding March,* Paramount, 1927.

The Tempest, Metro-Goldwyn-Mayer, 1927.

(And director) *The Honeymoon,* Universal, 1928.

(And director) *Queen Kelly,* United Artists, 1928.

(And director) *Walking down Broadway,* Universal, 1933.

Fugitive Road, Universal, 1934.

Devil Doll, Metro-Goldwyn-Mayer, 1936.

San Francisco, Metro-Goldwyn-Mayer, 1936.

Between Two Women, Universal/Jewel, 1937.

Co-adaptor and contributor to dialogue, *La danse de mort,* 1947.

OTHER

Paprika (novel; based on the screenplay *Blind Husbands*), Macaulay (New York, NY), 1935.

Les feux de la Saint-Jean: Veronica, Givors (France), 1951.

Les feux de la Saint-Jean: Constanzia, Givors (France), 1952.

Poto-Poto, [Paris, France], 1956.

Author of short play *In the Morning,* 1912, published as *Brothers* in *Film History,* 1988. Contributor to periodicals, including *Positif* and *Film Weekly.*

Author's papers and photographs are housed at the Margaret Herrick Library, Academy of Motion Picture Arts and Sciences, Beverly Hills, CA.

■ Adaptations

The film *Between Two Women*, based on a story by von Stroheim, was released in 1937.

■ Sidelights

Considered among the greatest film directors of silent films, Erich von Stroheim has also earned a measure of notoriety: in addition to being praised for his role in Jean Renoir's *La Grande Illusion*, he also entertained filmgoers with the villainous, stereotypically Germanic persona that would prompt one journalist to dub him "The Man You Love to Hate." Von Stroheim's ability to recreate himself was his strength as well as his undoing; as Arthur Lennig noted in his biography *Stroheim*, the legendary actor and director's "sense of destiny . . . gave him the strength to persevere, for when happenstance and hunger brought him to the fledgling movie industry, he not only found his métier, but soon grew to master it. . . . Through the authority of his aristocratic stance, he was able to convince Hollywood, at least for a while, to come to his terms. Such an incredible presence was not fathered by a press agent; [Von Stroheim] . . . gave birth to himself."

Frequently cited as a protégé of noted filmmaker D.W. Griffith, von Stroheim adopted Griffith's quest for total realism and perfection in each of the films he would direct between 1919 and 1929. As his uncompromising demands on cast, crew, and especially budget-conscious studio producers became increasingly unreasonable, the director was dropped by studio after studio, and efforts at film direction in France were also hampered by von Stroheim's stubbornness. While many film historians list von Stroheim's 1924 film *Greed* among the greatest dramas of the silent era, the director himself has

Erich von Stroheim's first major film, *Greed*, ran nine hours in its uncut version and cemented his reputation as a controversial director. (Metro-Goldwyn-Mayer/The Kobal Collection/The Picture Desk, Inc.)

The 1937 film *Mademoiselle Docteur* **teamed a militaristic von Stroheim with fellow actor Clifford Evans.** (Hulton Archive/ Getty Images.)

a less-lofty claim to fame: as an actor and director of great potential whose personal demons ultimately destroyed his promising career.

Aspires to Life of Pomp and Affluence

Von Stroheim was born in Vienna, Austria, on September 22, 1885. His father, a seller of straw hats under the name Baeger & Stroheim, had a business in the city, and his family—practicing Jews in a predominately Catholic country—lived a middle-class life. The elder Stroheim was reportedly irresponsible with money, however, and the financial stresses in the family—Benno and Johanna Stroheim had two sons, Erich and Bruno—made home an unhappy place. However, the city of Vienna was

flush with the militaristic pomp and ceremony of the court of Emperor Franz Josef, and the arts flourished amid opulent Habsburg culture. Along with enjoying opera, theatre, and music, the aristocratic class also contemplated the psychoanalytic theories of Dr. Sigmund Freud, theories that forced an awareness of the darker side of man's nature. Von Stroheim was captivated by the energy generated by Viennese society; however, as a member of the mercantile class, he was also very aware of the large working class whose hard work propped up the indulgent self-reflection of Vienna's high society.

Physically unattractive, the young von Stroheim was also small for his age, a fact that made him less than adequate in a nation that valued strength and power. Although the actor/director would later boast that he attended cadet training school prior to serving five years as a second lieutenant in the Austrian Army, in fact he made a poor showing at business school, then attempted to join the military but was rejected in 1906 as weak and otherwise unfit. Through determination, he ultimately earned a year-long commission with the Royal and Imperial Training Regiment, which handled army supply and horse-drawn transport, but was discharged after five months due to his unsuitability for military service. A year later, in 1908, von Stroheim left the Jewish faith. He returned to the slowly failing family business and worked there until November of 1909 when he boarded the *Price Friedrich Wilhelm* bound for America.

A New Life in a New Country

Von Stroheim arrived at Ellis Island in November of 1909, and entered the country as Erich Oswald Hans Carl Maria von Stroheim, the son of an Austrian count who had recently graduated with honors from military school. Despite his exotic provenance, however, the twenty-four-year-old immigrant soon found himself working in the gift-wrapping department at a New York City department store. Several other menial jobs followed, but none allowed the young immigrant to gain a foothold into the society he aspired to. After a short stint as a traveling salesman for the Max Grab Fashion Company, von Stroheim ended up in California, and in 1912 he moved in with Margaret Knox, marrying the well-off woman early the following year. Knox encouraged von Stroheim to write, and he soon produced the short play *In the Morning*, a story that features what would become his characteristic themes: the corruption of the aristocracy and woman's innocence debased. Due to von Stroheim's volatile personality, his marriage to Knox ended within months.

The highly ornate 1925 silent film *The Merry Widow* featured costumes and sets designed by von Stroheim. (Hulton Archive/Getty Images.)

With monies gained from another female patron captivated by his fanciful life story, von Stroheim relocated to Hollywood. Here fact and fiction blur, and truths have remained hidden even from the actor/director's biographers. According to some sources, in the summer of 1914 von Stroheim was cast as an extra in D.W. Griffith's monumental epic *The Birth of a Nation*. Gaining Griffith's eye, he worked his way up to stunt man, and eventually served as assistant director. Other sources note the actor's presence, not in Griffith's work, but in minor roles in several small films shot in 1915, among them *Old Heidelberg, Captain Macklin*, and a film version of Heinrich Ibsen's play *Ghosts*.

In fact, during the production of *Old Heidelberg*, von Stroheim began a working association with its director, John Emerson, and he worked with Emerson as an assistant and technical advisor for the next two years. He also married again, this time briefly to dressmaker Mae Jones, with whom he had a son, Erich Jr., before divorcing in 1918. While assisting on Emerson's 1916 drama, *His Picture in the Papers*, von Stroheim also took advantage of an acting role to create the one-eyed, one-armed villain that cemented his reputation as "The Man You Love to Hate."

Meanwhile, Griffith was directing another of his masterpieces, *Intolerance*, and although von Stroheim has been credited with work on this film, evidence as to his contributions remains questionable and is likely minimal, according to biographer Lennig. Whether or not he actually worked with Griffith, von Stroheim was heavily influenced by the director's realistic approach, as well as by Griffith's consummate attention to detail. In films under von Stroheim's control shooting was often done on location rather than in the staged sets used in most films of the era. Knicknacks, graffiti, and the clutter of everyday living area are readily visible in a von Stroheim production, none of it sanitized.

From Actor to Director

Returning to Hollywood, von Stroheim assisted Emerson on several films for Triange/Fine Arts, maintaining later that he was relegated to assistant director or technical advisor due to his German heritage. Among these films was *Macbeth*, a 1916 production starring noted Shakespearean stage actor Sir Herbert Beerbohm Tree. Von Stroheim broke with Emerson long enough to assist director Allan Dwan on 1917's *Panthea*, a film notable for the first appearance of von Stroheim's "evil Hun" character

in the role of a Russian lieutenant. As anti-German sentiment grew throughout the United States due to World War II, he reprised this character in a string of films, including *For France, The Unbeliever,* and *The Hun Within*.

On the strength of the legend he himself had created, von Stroheim was also relied upon for his purported knowledge of military protocol, and in 1917 he won over his hero, Griffith, who hired him as a military advisor and minor actor on *Hearts of the World*. His first leading role—as a monocle-wearing, militaristic German lieutenant—came in 1918's *The Heart of Humanity*, a film designed to tap fans of Griffith's similarly titled epic. The film is famous for showing the amorality of von Stroheim's Hun character: as the lieutenant prepares to assault the film's heroine, he is annoyed by a screaming baby in her charge and callously tosses the sobbing infant out an open window.

With the end of the war in 1919, von Stroheim's stock character was no longer a box-office draw. The thirty-three-year-old former actor now turned to directing as a way to continue his film career. Determined to sell his original screenplay, *Blind Husbands*, to Carl Laemmle at Universal Studios, he was turned away several times before gaining the directorship by boldly showing up at the studio head's doorstep. The successful 1919 film showcases von Stroheim's directorial style: creating sophisticated films with a very European approach to romantic and sexual relationships. Other films exploring similar themes included *The Devil's Passkey* and *Foolish Wives*, the latter a film set in Monte Carlo that cost over a million dollars to film and ran over seven hours (twenty reels) in its uncut form.

Gains Reputation as Difficult Director

As a director, von Stroheim was dismissive of Hollywood's approach, which he viewed as compromising his creative vision and desire for perfection. As was the case with *Foolish Wives*, the director's many demands, his refusal to adhere to budgets, and his unwillingness to edit films to realistic running times put him in direct conflict with Universal Studios producer Irving Thalberg. Thalberg resorted to firing von Stroheim as the only way to edit *Foolish Wives* down to the standard, audience-friendly 10-to-12-reel length. On *Merry-Go-Round* the temperamental director lasted only five weeks before Thalberg fired him in order to rein in an overextended budget. As Thalberg realized, but von Stroheim refused to acknowledge, a film over budget was a film that lost money for the studio.

Widely reported by the Hollywood press, von Stroheim's temperamental nature caused him to be physically removed from the editing room on numerous occasions. This was most notably the case during the editing of his 1924 film, *Greed*. The film's original 42-reel, nine-hour version was shown once, on January 12, 1924. At this point a frustrated Thalberg had the film edited down to two hours and ordered that the deleted footage be burned. Ironically, despite the film's contentious origins, *Greed* still stands as one of the most outstanding silent films ever made.

Directs Silent-Film Masterpiece

Hailed as von Stroheim's crowning achievement as a director, *Greed* is based on Frank Norris's novel *McTeague*. The plot follows an oafish man from a mining town who aspires to become a dentist in San Francisco. He seduces and marries Trina, the girlfriend of his own friend, but retribution comes when Trina becomes unbearable to live with and McTeague is himself betrayed by a friend. von Stroheim's meticulous attention to detail is apparent throughout the film, and his fascination with the darker side of the human libido makes *Greed* unique among films of the silent era. With its focus on lust, avarice, and murder, the confrontative film threatened, shocked, and angered contemporary audiences and ultimately failed at the box office. Subsequent opinions have ranked the film far differently. As Peter Noble wrote in *Hollywood Scapegoat: The Biography of Erich von Stroheim*, for example, in *Greed* the director "revealed himself to be a veritable

In the 1943 film *Five Graves to Cairo* von Stroheim reprised his role as the "evil Hun." (Paramount/The Kobal Collection/The Picture Desk, Inc.)

master of the delineation of tragedy and realism as well of sophisticated romance."

Discussing the four-hour 1999 restoration of *Greed*—a fête accomplished by collecting still photographs taken from the footage famously burned by Thalberg and connecting these using interior titles that fill gaps in the action—Todd McCarthy wrote in *Variety* that the effort stands as an "enormously successful attempt to rehabilitate one of the two or three most celebrated and mourned mutilated masterpieces in cinema history." In contrast, William K. Everson argued in *Films in Review* that Universal's original release "was cut with respect and care and its editing is masterly" rather than "a job of slick condensation. . . . Critics are unanimous that *Greed* is a motion picture masterpiece, and this judgment is based upon the 'butchery' of this [original] cutter, not on Stroheim's original conception or on all the footage he shot."

Von Stroheim's directorial report card continued to chart both successes and failures. *The Merry Widow,* produced in 1925, was commercially successful, even though the director condemned it by turning his back on Universal—and nemesis Thalberg—and moving to Paramount. *The Wedding March* was also critically well received, but at its 1929 release it was credited to director Josef von Sternberg because the temperamental von Stroheim had refused to adhere to budgets and shooting schedules. His final directorial effort, *Queen Kelly,* was based on von Stroheim's

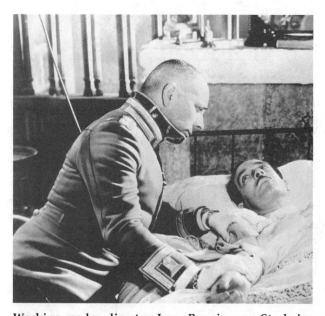

Working under director Jean Renoir, von Stroheim earned acclaim for his role in the 1937 film *La Grande Illusion.* (Realisations © Cinematographique/The Kobal Collection/The Picture Desk, Inc.)

original screenplay and starred Gloria Swanson as an orphan who becomes the romantic target of a queen's lover. After Swanson became dismayed over the increasingly dark storyline, von Stroheim was fired from the production.

Queen Kelly marked von Stroheim's last stint as director; although he was offered the director's spot in 1932's *Walking down Broadway,* that film ultimately became a casualty of an internal studio battle. In 1936 he abandoned his third wife, Valerie Germonprez, whom he had married in 1920, as well as sons Erich Jr. and Josef, to move to France and direct Jean Renoir's *La dame Blanche.* Here, too, production was halted, in this case due to the outbreak of World War II in September of 1939.

Acting Triumphs in Later Years

Dismayed, von Stroheim returned to the United States, where a succession of acting jobs would round out his film career. The title role in 1929's *The Great Gabbo* had marked von Stroheim's talking-picture debut, and characteristically, he had embellished the role with histrionics that played up his image as "The Man You Love to Hate." Now, with Americans once again united in their hatred for all things German, he was able to reprise his evil Hun in *Three Faces East.* In addition to touring in a production of *Arsenic and Old Lace,* von Stroheim earned international acclaim for his role as Captain von Rauffenstein in Renoir's 1937 war film *La Grande Illusion.* Working with director Billy Wilder, he also gained recognition for his role in 1943's *Five Graves to Cairo* and 1950's *Sunset Boulevard,* the latter which reunited von Stroheim and Swanson and also earned the former director an Academy Award nomination for his role as stoic butler Max Von Mayerling.

Apart from film work, von Stroheim also wrote two novels as well as articles and film reviews. Although he never divorced his third wife, he spent his final years with Denise Vernac, an actress whom he had hired as a secretary in 1938. Von Stroheim died on May 12, 1957 in Maurepas, France, two months after being named to the French Legion of Honor.

Considered one of the world's top six directors in 1925, von Stroheim found himself unemployed and desperate for work throughout much of his career. Audience response to the actor/director experienced similarly mercurial shifts as public tastes caught up with the director's sophisticated vision. Writing in *Photoplay* in 1921, a contributor concluded in a review of *Foolish Wives* that von Stroheim's films are

Von Stroheim and Gloria Swanson starred in the award-winning 1950 film *Sunset Boulevard*. (The Kobal Collection/The Picture Desk, Inc.)

If you enjoy the works of Erich von Stroheim, you may also want to check out the following films:

All Quiet on the Western Front, based on the novel by Erich Maria Remarque, 1930.
Paths of Glory, directed by Stanley Kubrick, 1957.
No Country for Old Men, written and directed by Joel and Ethan Coen, 2007.

"unfit for the family to see" as well as "an insult to American ideals and womanhood." By 1937, however, Herman G. Weinberg was writing in *Film Art* that, "Thanks to Stroheim[,] the women and young girls of America learned to prefer the slick, insolent archdukes whose kisses burned like the lash of a

whip, to . . . bucolic American heroes." In 1947, *Film Quarterly* correspondent Oswell Blakeston noted a further change in the perspective of film audiences, proclaiming of the director's body of work: "Stroheim taught the Americans how to make love."

■ **Biographical and Critical Sources**

BOOKS

International Dictionary of Films and Filmmakers, Volume 2, *Directors*, St. James Press (Detroit, MI), 1991.
Koszarski, Richard, *The Man You Loved to Hate: Erich von Stroheim and Hollywood*, Oxford University Press (New York, NY), 1983.

Koszarski, Richard, *Von: The Life and Films of Erich von Stroheim,* Limelight Editions (New York, NY), 2001.

Lennig, Arthur, *Stroheim,* University Press of Kentucky (Lexington, KY), 2000.

Noble, Peter, *Hollywood Scapegoat: The Biography of Erich von Stroheim,* Fortune Press (London, England), 1950.

Twentieth-Century Literary Criticism, Volume 71, Gale (Detroit, MI), 1997.

PERIODICALS

Atlantic Monthly, September, 1987, Nancy Caldwell Sorel, "Jean Renoir and Erich von Stroheim," p. 73.

Choice, June, 2001, A. Hirsch, "Ethics and Social Criticism in the Hollywood Films of Erich von Stroheim, Ernst Lubitsch, and Billy Wilder," p. 1802.

Cinématographiques (special Stroheim issue), numbers 48-50, 1966.

Film Art, spring, 1939, Herman G. Weinberg, "Erich von Stroheim."

Film Comment, May-June, 1974, Jonathan Rosenbaum, "Second Thoughts on Stroheim"; November, 1999, Richard Koszarski, "Reconstructing *Greed,*" p. 10.

Film Quarterly, spring, 1947, Oswald Blakeston, "Tribute to Stroheim."

Films in Review, August-September, 1957, William K. Everson "The Career of Erich von Stroheim," p. 313

Motion Picture Classic, January, 1920, "Erich von Stroheim and the Miracle," p. 35.

New Yorker, June 3, 1972, Penelope Gilliatt, "The Scabrous Poet from the Estate Belonging to No One."

Photoplay, December, 1919, Robert Yost, "Gosh, How They Hate Him!"; August, 1921, review of *Foolish Wives.*

Variety, September 13, 1999, Todd McCarthy, review of *Greed,* p. 44.

OTHER

The Man You Love to Hate (videocassette), 1994.*

Christopher Wren

(General Photographic Agency/Getty Images.)

■ Personal

Born October 20, 1632, in East Knoyle, Wiltshire, England; died February 25, 1723, in London, England; son of Christopher (a clergyman) and Mary (Cox) Wren; married Faith Coghill, December, 1669 (died, 1675); married Jane Fitzwilliam, 1677 (died, 1680); children: (first marriage) Gilbert (died in infancy), Christopher; (second marriage) Jane, William. *Education:* Educated at Westminster School, 1645; Wadham College Oxford, B.A., 1650; Oxford University, M.A., 1653; fellow of All Souls College, 1654; Oxford University, D.C.L., 1661.

■ Career

Architect and mathematician. Gresham College London, London, England, professor of astronomy, 1657-61; Oxford University, Oxford, England, Savilian professor of astronomy, 1661-73; surveyor-general of the King's Works, London, 1669-1718; surveyor for Greenwich Palace, 1696; commissioner for building fifty new churches, London. Member of Council, Hudson's Bay Company.

■ Member

Royal Society (president, 1681-83).

■ Awards, Honors

Knighted, 1673.

■ Writings

Wren, Stephen, compiler, *Parentalia: or, Memoirs of the Family of the Wrens. . . chiefly of Sir Christopher Wren. . . Compiled, by His Son Christopher, Now Published by His Grandson, Stephen Wren, Esq., with the Care of Joseph Ames,* T. Osborn and R. Dodsley (London, England), 1750, published as *The Life and Works of Christopher Wren,* Samuel Buckley & Company (New York, NY), 1903.

Wren's "Tracts" on Architecture and Other Writings, edited by Lydia M. Soo, Cambridge University Press (New York, NY), 1998.

The Architectural Drawings of Sir Christopher Wren at All Souls College, Oxford: A Complete Catalogue, Lund Humphries (Aldershot, England), 2008.

■ Sidelights

Christopher Wren is best known as the architect who restored most of London's churches after the Great Fire of 1666. He was also an important figure in the development of English science; he helped found the Royal Society, one of the first groups

Sir Christopher Wren designed the chapel and cloisters at Emmanuel College Cambridge in 1677. (Photograph © by Philippa Lewis; Edifice/Corbis.)

devoted to advancing scientific knowledge through research. "Wren was an outstandingly gifted individual, born at a defining moment in English history, when the intellectual world was changing with astonishing rapidity, providing a fertile environment within which his extraordinary mind burgeoned and blossomed," Lisa Jardine noted in her biography *On a Grander Scale: The Outstanding Life of Sir Christopher Wren.* Jardine added, "Wren's virtuoso mind produced innovative solutions to an extraordinary range of difficult problems—reaching far beyond architecture and design. His diverse talents were more exceptional by far than a single building, however magnificent, could convey. He was a landmark figure in a landmark age."

Wren was most influential as an architect, however, dominating English architecture for fifty years and supervising the rebuilding of St. Paul's Cathedral in London. "By using the values of 17th-century science to analyze and redefine architecture, Wren undermined the foundations of Renaissance classicism," a critic wrote in *International Dictionary of Architects and Architecture.* As a result, Wren's work "saw its ultimate consequences in the historical revivalism and new aesthetic categories of the next centuries."

Wren was born in East Knoyle, Wiltshire, England, on October 20, 1632, the only surviving son of the dean of Windsor, a clergyman who held an official appointment to the court of King Charles I. Wren's uncle, Matthew Wren, was the bishop of Ely, and young Christopher might also have been destined for a career in the Anglican Church. When civil war broke out in 1642, however, the bishop of Ely was imprisoned in the Tower of London and Dean Wren's family was forced to leave Windsor the following year. Young Christopher was attending school in London during the war; after King Charles lost the war—and his head—in 1649, it was more prudent for a young man from a Royalist family to keep close to home. Although Wren had been an outstanding student at Westminster School, excelling in math, drafting, and astronomy, he now left to study near his family for two years.

A Mind for Math

Wren had always been a sickly child, and at age fifteen he was placed in the home of a notable London physician named Charles Scarburgh. After recovering his health, Wren stayed on with Scarburgh as a pupil and assistant and he learned much about medical research and scientific method. By the time he entered Oxford University, Wren already had a reputation as a talented mathematician with a gift for drafting and inventions. According to Witold Rybczynski, writing in the *New York Times Book Review,* Wren's "scientific activities touched on so many different fields. He took part in medical experiments, performing the first successful injection of a substance into the blood-stream (of a dog). He directed his far ranging intelligence to the study of meteorology, and fabricated a 'weather clock' that recorded temperature, humidity, rainfall and barometric pressure. He was an adept builder of scientific apparatus as well as an unusually skillful draftsman. He once constructed a transparent beehive for scientific observation, and made an exquisitely detailed model of the moon."

Wren quickly earned both bachelor's and master's degrees, and at age twenty-four he was named professor of astronomy at Gresham College London. During his time there, he met frequently with like-minded men interested in science; these meetings led to the formation of the Royal Society in 1660. In 1661, the year after Charles II was restored to the throne of England, Wren was appointed Savilian professor of astronomy at Oxford.

In the seventeenth century, there was no specialized training required for architects; a gentleman needed only a certain amount of mathematic skill and interest in the subject. Occupied with mathematical theory, astronomy, medical science, and other subjects, Wren did not turn his attention to architecture until he was thirty years of age. His uncle, the restored bishop of Ely, then commissioned him to design a chapel at Pembroke College Cambridge, and Wren produced an adequate design that was simple and classical in its forms. Next, he designed the Sheldonian Theatre at Oxford, a building intended for university ceremonies. Based upon the concept of a Roman theater, Wren's ingenious interior design left a large space free of supports or columns, but for the exterior he resorted to unimaginative copying from existing architectural pattern books.

In 1665, the budding architect traveled to France for several months to study French Renaissance and baroque architecture. He toured the buildings King Louis XIV was adding to the Louvre, and he met with established architects such as the Italian sculptor Bernini. The French journey significantly influenced Wren's work and provided him with a rich source of inspiration. He would incorporate many of the Baroque characteristics he observed in France in his own future works: a broader nave (the central aisle of a church), dramatic use of light and shade, stucco or marble ornamentations, and ceiling frescoes.

Rebuilding London

A few months after Wren's return to London in early 1666, a huge fire destroyed much of the city. The Great Fire burned more than 12,000 homes and numerous public houses and churches. King Charles appointed Wren a member of the commission created to supervise the reconstruction of the city. Wren had already drawn up a visionary plan for a new London. His design was typical of seventeenth-century city planning and called for a combination of radiating and grid-plan streets accented by squares and vistas. Although his plan was not accepted, Wren was given responsibility for replacing the eighty-seven parish churches demolished by the Great Fire. Between 1670 and 1686 he designed fifty-one new churches; they constitute a major part of the vast amount of work done by him and are known as the City Churches. They are uneven in quality both in design and execution, and their varied plans and famous steeples reveal Wren's ingenuity and broad range of inspirations. The churches are essentially classical in design, although some evidence baroque variations on classical themes adapted to English taste and the requirements of Anglican worship. His work on the City Churches firmly established Wren's position as England's leading architect; he was appointed surveyor general in 1669, and was knighted in 1673.

While Wren was working on the City Churches, he undertook many other projects. One of the most important was Trinity College Library at Cambridge University (1676-1684), an elegantly severe building inspired by the late Italian Renaissance. Its classic elements, reminiscent of ancient Rome, recall the works of Italian Andrea Palladio and British architect Inigo Jones. By 1670 Wren was also at work on designs for a new St. Paul's Cathedral. St. Paul's, which took nearly thirty-five years to build, is considered Wren's masterpiece. The Great Fire had so damaged the old St. Paul's as to render it dangerous, and the authorities decided that a new cathedral was needed. In 1673 Wren presented an impressive design in the form of a large wooden model known as the Great Model. The Great Model, which still exists, shows a cathedral based on a Greek-cross plan (four arms of equal length) and dominated by a massive central dome. The exterior of the building was to have curved walls and an entrance block faced with a portico of giant Corinthian columns. The design of the Great Model is Wren's expression of baroque vitality tempered by classicism and it reveals the influence of French and Italian architecture as well as that of Inigo Jones.

The English were accustomed to cathedrals built on the medieval Latin-cross plan with a long nave; the Great Model design, which was much criticized, departed from this tradition and seemed to the Protestant English to be too continental and too Catholic. In the face of such opposition, Wren prepared a new design based on the elongated Latin cross, with a dome over the crossing and a classical portico entrance. This compromise, known as the Warrant Design, was accepted in 1675, but Wren was crafty enough to appeal to Charles II for permission to make minor adjustments without supervision, claiming that seeking approvals would slow down the project. As the building progressed,

Wren was able to make changes that reflected his increasing knowledge of French and Italian baroque architecture. The cathedral as finished in the early eighteenth century is very different from the Warrant Design; the building, a synthesis of many stylistic influences, is also Wren's uniquely organic creation. With its splendid dome, impressive scale, and dramatic grandeur, St. Paul's is fundamentally a baroque building, but it is English Protestant baroque in its restraint and disciplined gravity.

A Change in Style

After 1675 English architecture began to turn away from the sober classicism of Wren's Trinity College Library and manifest influences from continental baroque architecture. These trends are evident in St. Paul's as well as in Wren's subsequent works. English taste rejected the emotional drama and fluid design of Italian and German baroque and honed closely to the classical baroque of France. Nevertheless, during the last quarter of the seventeenth

Constructed by Wren in London between 1675 and 1708, St. Paul's Cathedral stands on the site of a Norman church.
(Photograph © by Adam Woolfitt/Corbis.)

century English architects began to conceive of buildings in baroque terms, that is, as sculptural masses on a large scale, and to introduce elements of richness, grandeur, and royal splendor that reflected the temper of the age. Important examples of Wren's design in the idiom of the English baroque are the Royal Hospital at Chelsea (1682-1689), the work done at Hampton Court Palace (1689-1696) for King William III and Queen Mary, and the Royal Naval Hospital at Greenwich (1696-1705).

Sometime after 1675, Wren began articulating a theory of architecture based on his study of various buildings throughout history, using descriptions from the Bible and the classics. These "Tracts on Architecture" were published posthumously by his grandson, in *Parentalia: or, Memoirs of the Family of the Wrens. . . chiefly of Sir Christopher Wren. . . Compiled, by His Son Christopher, Now Published by His Grandson, Stephen Wren, Esq., with the Care of Joseph Ames,.* "Because of the scientific viewpoint of his investigation," a critic noted in the *International Dictionary of Architects and Architecture,* "Wren's account constitutes the first history of architecture, expressing an understanding of each monument as the product of a particular time and place."

Wren was eighty-six years old when he finally retired from his post as surveyor-general of the King's Works. Already the English baroque style he had pioneered was falling out of favor, and Wren spent his final years on scientific concerns like the problem of determining longitude. He wondered whether he had misspent his career on architecture, when he could have had a distinguished—and more lucrative—career in science; giants of physics such as Sir Isaac Newton and Blaise Pascal had lauded his early work in mathematics.

Located in London, the Church of St. Stephen features a sanctuary designed by Wren; the altar was the work of painter Henry Moore. (Photograph © John Heseltine/Corbis.)

words of Jardine, "Wren's contributions to knowledge and to beauty are lasting and timeless," adding, "We are the lasting beneficiaries of Wren's genius. The consequences of his inspired ideas and innovative practices are all around us, as are the great buildings he built so solidly that they have—as he hoped—stood the test of time. Everything Wren undertook, he envisaged on a grander scale—bigger, better, more enduring, that what had come before. The work stands."

Wren was hailed in life as one of the greatest architects of his age; when he died in London on February 25, 1723, he was buried in St. Paul's. His tomb bears a simple inscription: "Reader, if you seek his monument, look about you."

If you enjoy the works of Christopher Wren, you may also want to check out the following:

The designs of French architect Louis le Vau, including the Collège des Quatre Nations.
The works of French architect Jules Hardouin Mansart, who helped design the St. Louis des Invalides.
The designs of Italian architect Filippo Juvarra, including the Basilica di Superga.

Nonetheless, Wren left a lasting legacy as an architect; his designs for St. Paul's dome influenced buildings as significant as the U.S. Capitol. In the

■ **Biographical and Critical Sources**

BOOKS

Dutton, Ralph, *The Age of Wren,* Batsford (New York, NY), 1951.
Hollis, Leo, *The Phoenix: St Paul's Cathedral and the Men Who Made Modern London,* Weidenfeld & Nicolson (London, England), 2008.
International Dictionary of Architects and Architecture, St. James Press (Detroit, MI), 1993.

View of the ornate mosaic ceilings of St. Paul's Cathedral, considered the high point of Wren's career. (Photograph © by Angelo Hornak/Corbis.)

Jardine, Lisa, *On a Grander Scale: The Outstanding Life of Sir Christopher Wren*, HarperCollins (New York, NY), 2002.

Sekler, Eduard F., *Wren and His Place in European Architecture*, Faber & Faber (London, England), 1956.

Summerson, John, *Sir Christopher Wren*, Collins (London, England), 1953.

Tinniswood, Adrian, *His Invention So Fertile: A Life of Christopher Wren*, Oxford University Press (New York, NY), 2001.

Whinney, Margaret, *Christopher Wren*, Praeger (New York, NY), 1971.

PERIODICALS

Architectural Review, November, 2008, Richard Reid, review of *The Architectural Drawings of Sir Christopher Wren at All Souls College, Oxford: A Complete Catalogue*, p. 95.

Contemporary Review, May, 1991, Muriel Julius, "Sir Christopher Wren—A Renaissance Man," p. 257.

Daily Mail (London, England), April 17, 2004, Moira Petty, "Genius with a Heart of Stone," p. 25; May 14, 2008, "The Big Picture," p. 22.

Economist, April 6, 1991, "Sly like a Fox," p. 89; September 1, 2001, "Monumental; Sir Christopher Wren."

History Today, November, 1997, Bruce Marsden, "From St. Paul's to Silk Stockings," p. 34.

New York Times Book Review, February 2, 2003, Witold Rybczynski, "If Anybody Calls, Say I Am Designing St. Paul's," p. 12.

Spectator, September 7, 2002, Christopher Woodward, "The Master of Reticence and Timelessness," p. 35.*

Author/Artist Index

The following index gives the number of the volume in which an author/artist's biographical sketch appears: